EVOLUTION AND
HUMAN KINSHIP

EVOLUTION AND HUMAN KINSHIP

Austin L. Hughes

New York   Oxford
OXFORD UNIVERSITY PRESS
1988

Oxford University Press

Oxford   New York   Toronto
Delhi   Bombay   Calcutta   Madras   Karachi
Petaling Jaya   Singapore   Hong Kong   Tokyo
Nairobi   Dar es Salaam   Cape Town
Melbourne   Auckland
and associated companies in
Beirut   Berlin   Ibadan   Nicosia

Library of Congress Cataloging-in-Publication Data
Hughes, Austin L., 1949–
Evolution and human kinship.
Bibliography: p.
1. Kinship.   2. Sociobiology.   3. Human behavior.   I. Title.
GN487.H84   1988   306.8′3   87-14073
ISBN 0-19-505234-X

2 4 6 8 10 9 7 5 3 1

Printed in the United States of America
on acid-free paper

For Marianne

Dim gair a ysgrifennais i, mi wn,
Yn unig; 'chynlluniais
I ddim, na chur anturiais;
Dy gariad a'm rhoddodd lais.

PREFACE

I wrote this book in Oxford while supported by a N.A.T.O. postdoctoral fellowship from the U.S. National Science Foundation. I am grateful to the N.S.F. for giving me this opportunity; to Prof. William D. Hamilton for acting as sponsor; to Dr. David McFarland of the Animal Behaviour Research Group for making facilities available to me; and to the Department of Zoology for logistical support. I have benefited greatly from discussion with many people in Oxford, particularly Drs. Hamilton and McFarland, R. Dawkins, A. Grafen, N. Hillgarth, and R. M. Fisher of the Department of Zoology; and G. A. Harrison and V. M. Reynolds of the Department of Biological Anthropology. I am grateful to Monique Borgerhoff Mulder for carefully reading the manuscript and offering many helpful suggestions. My wife, Marianne, assisted me in numerous ways. I discussed the ideas developed here in greater detail with her than with any other person. She drew the illustrations, typed the manuscript, and in general imposed organization on the chaotic task of preparing the book.

I should like to take this opportunity to comment on certain usages in this book. I have retained the use of the singular pronoun "he" in a few cases when the sex of the referent is unspecified. This used to be standard practice in American English and still is in the U.K.; I have retained this usage for the sake of brevity with no intention of any sexist implication. I have avoided the use of the term "man" to refer to the human species, as I have done in my other publications. The argument that this usage is sexist is convincing to me, since there are so many alternative expressions available, especially for a biologist.

It is a pleasure for me to acknowledge the influence of three great teachers: W. Desan, W. V. O. Quine, and M. W. Schein. In recent years I have benefited from interactions with numerous colleagues, including R. D. Alexander, L. Betzig, M. Carey, D. C. Dunning, J. M. Emlen, H. Flinn, M. Itzkowitz, P. Jameson, E. D. Ketterson, J. A. Marshall, R. J. Meier, C. E. Nelson, V. Nolan, Jr., W. J. Rowland, W. A. Searcy, P. Turke, and G. C. Williams. I owe a special debt of gratitude to B. Gilbert, who first encouraged my interest in natural history, and to W. J. Iliff, who first suggested that I study zoology.

Needless to say, the opinions expressed herein are entirely my own, and I take responsibility for any faults.

Toward the end of the last century, Thomas Hughes arrived in New York with five children and a wife pregnant with the sixth, who was to become my grandfather. According to family legend, Thomas Hughes was an engineer who was involved in the building of some famous bridge, although which bridge it was exactly (perhaps the Brooklyn Bridge?) has since been lost to memory. In any event, with the love of heroic epithets so characteristic of the Celt, he was ever after known by all his numerous kin and progeny as "Thomas Hughes that Built the Bridge." Drawing on an academic background that includes not only zoology but also philosophy and anthropology, I have hoped in writing this book to follow in the footsteps of my illustrious forebear.

Houston   A.L.H.
August, 1987

CONTENTS

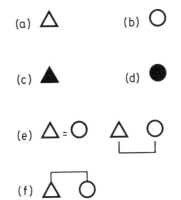

Key for genealogies: (a) living male; (b) living female; (c) deceased male; (d) deceased female; (e) mating; (f) siblings. In general, genealogies are intended to represent biological rather than merely social relationships; exceptions are noted in the text.

EVOLUTION AND
HUMAN KINSHIP

1

Philosophical Background

My view of natural science is that it is the systematic investigation of the structure of the universe as it is revealed to us through our senses. There are certain important separate branches of science, each of which deals with a certain class or kind of structures, the aim being to discover the characteristics of all structures of that kind. So atomic physics deals with the structure of atoms, chemistry with the structure of molecules, cyrstallography and colloidal chemistry with the structure of crystals and colloids, and anatomy and physiology with the structures of organisms. There is, therefore, I suggest, place for a branch of natural science which will have for its task the discovery of the general characteristics of those social structures of which the component units are human beings.

RADCLIFFE-BROWN (1940)

1.1 General Plan of the Work

In this book I present a theoretical approach to the analysis of social behavior that is rooted in evolutionary biology. The theory developed here is quite general, being applicable to any animal society. However, I apply it mainly to human societies. There are two reasons for doing so. First, there are kinds of data available concerning human societies that are rarely available as yet for nonhuman societies. Since Rivers (1900), social anthropologists have routinely gathered genealogical data, which are often accompanied by behavioral data of various sorts. For societies in which confidence of paternity is reasonably high, genealogies can provide estimates of coefficients of relatedness. As first pointed out by Hamilton (1963, 1964), coefficients of relatedness can be a basis for explicit predictions regarding social behavior, assuming that the behavior under study represents an adapted phenotype. The body of theory that I develop here draws its inspiration from Hamilton's insight, which has come to be known as the theory of kin selection (Maynard Smith, 1964).

Second, I believe that kin selection theory can make a real contribution to the anthropological study of social behavior. In recent decades social anthropology has encountered theoretical problems that have impeded its progress to a considerable extent. Although some anthropologists have strongly resisted the application of kin selection theory to humans, I will argue that this theory can

3

in fact resolve some theoretical problems that have plagued social anthropology and thus can revitalize the entire field. The mathematical techniques I present here facilitate the application of kin selection theory to questions of interest to social anthropologists, since they extend the insights of kin selection theory to complex interactions involving a number of different individuals.

I hope that this book will be of interest to individuals working in at least two different areas. I hope it will be of some use to biologists, in particular to behavioral ecologists working with nonhuman species, who may be able to adapt some of the techniques presented here to the animal societies that interest them. In addition, I hope that anthropologists will find it worthwhile to overcome any initial aversion they might feel toward "sociobiology" and give the theory presented here an open-minded examination. Since I address a dual audience, I will initially have to clarify, for the benefit of half of the audience, some matters that may seem obvious to the other half. I can only ask that my readers bear with me.

This introductory chapter is devoted to conceptual clarifications and historical background. First I address some philosophical issues surrounding the application of evolutionary theory to human social behavior. The point of view I adopt is similar to that of Alexander (1977, 1979), to whose works I refer the reader for a more detailed discussion of these issues than is possible here. Second, for those unfamiliar with it, I introduce the field of social anthropology, sketch its history, and suggest ways that an evolutionary approach can resolve some of its historic dilemmas.

I should like to remark at the outset that the theory I present in this book represents a scientific hypothesis, not any sort of dogma. It is unfortunate that, perhaps as a result of their enthusiasm for a Darwinist approach to human behavior, some sociobiologists have sounded more like polemicists or evangelists than scientists. Although I share their enthusiasm, I hope to avoid the rhetoric of a "true believer." Indeed, I wish to emphasize the hypothetical nature of my work and further note that, although I present here some preliminary tests of this theory, the process of testing and refining a biological theory of social behavior will take a long time and involve many individuals using many different approaches. Beyond the specific theory developed here, the idea that evolutionary theory has anything important to tell us about human behavior is itself a hypothesis that requires testing; that is, it is in need of attempts at falsification (cf. Popper, 1934). Finally, at a still deeper level, the theory of organic evolution remains a hypothesis. Virtually all biologists and anthropologists currently accept the hypothesis of evolution by natural selection, but at the same time all are involved in testing its adequacy and generality by a wide variety of methods.

In a critique of sociobiology Kitcher (1985) stated, "The dispute about human sociobiology is a dispute about evidence." I agree. Unfortunately, as Betzig (1986a) pointed out, Kitcher himself cites little in the way of evidence in his discussion of human sociobiology. His approach consists largely of a philosophical analysis of statements in Wilson (1975) and other early sociobiological works. Kitcher scores some telling points, but I feel that little progress can come from such an abstract, backward-looking approach. Rather, progress in science is made by refining theory to yield clear-cut testable predictions and by testing these against data.

1.2 Adaptive Phenotypes and Human Behavior

The concept of adaptation has been central to biology ever since the work of Darwin; despite recent criticisms (e.g., Gould and Lewontin, 1979), it is likely to remain so (Mayr, 1983). Prior to Darwin, any observation of a good fit between the traits of an animal and the demands of its environment was likely to be explained (if it was explained at all) by the theological platitude of divine providence (Mayr, 1982). Darwin saw adaptation as the result of natural selection acting on the traits of animals. An adaptive trait is one that enhances the individual's inclusive fitness in the environment faced by the individual relative to the inclusive fitness of individuals possessing alternative traits. Inclusive fitness (see Section 2.3 below) refers to the reproduction of the individual's genes either through his own direct descendants or through reproduction of closely related individuals sharing genes with him.

It is worth noting that adaptation is, strictly speaking, a property of the phenotype. It really makes no sense to speak of adapted genes. Obviously, an adapted phenotype will not develop in every case where the genes that ordinarily underlie this phenotype are present. The phenotype may not develop as usual if something is amiss in the environment in which it develops, for example, if a teratogenic agent is present. Furthermore, it may be that the "instructions" given by the genes to the developing organism allow for alternatives. We can envision how this would work by imagining a set of "instructions" which "read" as follows: given environment A, develop phenotype X; given environment B, develop phenotype Y. [The inducible enzyme systems in the genomes of bacteria (e.g., Levine, 1973) represent a simple mechanism that produces a set of "instructions" of this sort. The mechanisms of gene expression in animals are yet to be fully elucidated but they are doubtless capable of producing the same sort of switching mechanism.] Development will then be, as biologists say, phenotypically plastic. Yet such phenotypic plasticity is itself a result of natural selection, and each of the resulting phenotypes can be said to be adaptive under the circumstances that trigger its development.

There are examples from the animal kingdom of phenotypic differences within species that are nongenetic and yet are apparently adaptive. In the mosquitofish *Gambusia affinis,* males born early in the breeding season mature rapidly at small body sizes; those born later in the year delay maturation and achieve, on the average, much larger sizes. The size difference between early and late summer males (which is accompanied by behavioral differences) is clearly not genetic; rather, it seems to be a phenotypically plastic response on the part of late summer males to the presence of already mature males (Hughes, 1985a). Yet there is good evidence that it is adaptive for a male to be small in early summer and midsummer and large in late summer and autumn (Hughes, 1985b).

From a philosophical point of view, human culture is in no essential respect different from any other phenotypically plastic response. Like many animals, humans have the capacity to adjust their behavior phenotypes to suit environmental conditions. To be sure, behavioral plasticity seems more far-reaching in humans than in any other animal. On the other hand, our species is capable of whole categories of behavior—symbolic, artistic, religious, political—which have only the faintest analogies in other animal species. We may sometimes imagine that we are capable of greater behavioral plasticity than is in fact the case, simply because there are so many spheres of activity in which our plasticity expresses itself. In any event, if we accept that the human species as we find it is the product of evolution, it is a reasonable hypothesis that behavioral phenotypes that are of widespread occurrence in human populations are, in the main, adaptive, even though behavioral differences among human cultures are not likely to be based on genetic differences.

I hypothesize that humans are genetically so constituted that each individual's behavior has the function of maximizing (insofar as possible under the circumstances) that individual's inclusive fitness. The fact that human behavior has this function means that it appears (when observed, so to speak, "from the outside") to be directed toward the "goal" of inclusive fitness maximization. However, the apparent goal of human behavior viewed from the outside is generally different from the conscious goals of the human actors themselves. Further, I hypothesize that humans are capable of observational learning regarding the consequences of a given behavior pattern in terms of the actor's inclusive fitness. Thus individuals will tend to imitate behavioral tactics that enhance inclusive fitness and avoid behavioral tactics that decrease inclusive fitness. Because of oral (and, in some societies, written) tradition, an individual may have access to the results of more such observations than he can have personally accumulated in his own lifetime. Similarly, the accumulated wisdom within a society on the fitness consequences of various courses of action can be continually tested against experience and refined in the course of its passage from generation to generation. The body of information we call "culture" enables individuals to choose courses of action that will be adaptive under the circumstances which they face.

Popular writers (e.g., Kitcher, 1985) often lead us to believe that the major questions of interest to sociobiologists are whether and to what extent human behavior is "genetically determined." On the viewpoint taken here, the answer to such questions depends on the level of analysis at which we are looking. For example, suppose we are interested in a specific behavioral tendency, such as the tendency to marry polygynously. In this case, I would predict that, either within a particular society or across the human species as a whole, only the minutest fraction of observable variation in the tendency to marry polygynously is likely to be heritable, that is, due to additive genetic factors. Any allele that somehow increased a man's tendency to marry polygynously might be favored under certain environmental circumstances but not others; even in societies in which polygyny is commonly practiced, some individuals will face circumstances (such as poverty) in which polygyny is ill-advised. On the other hand, suppose we consider a more generalized behavioral tendency, such as the tendency to adopt behavioral tactics that maximize one's inclusive fitness under whatever circumstances one happens to face. Selection is likely to act strongly on any genes that have a nonspecific effect on this tendency. Although the particular environmental circumstances faced by individuals are likely to vary from generation to generation and from individual to individual within a generation, it is likely that the additive genetic portion of the variance in a generalized tendency to maximize one's inclusive fitness should remain high. Of course the existence of such an innate tendency need not mean that individual humans ever or very frequently are conscious that their behavior exhibits this tendency.

On the hypothesis that humans adopt adaptive behaviors on the basis of both observational learning and traditional lore, we can make certain predictions about variation among human cultures. For example, one would expect the role of traditional lore in inculcating adaptive behaviors to be more pronounced in societies that have been exposed to little environmental, technological, or social change for a long period of time. In societies such as our own, in which technological and social changes occur so rapidly that each generation is likely to face a world very different from that faced by its parents, one would expect there to be a greater reliance on personal observational learning and on the ability to modify one's behavioral tactics frequently throughout life. As a consequence, one should see a greater rigidity of behavioral tactics and a closer adherence to norms in societies that have been little exposed to change, in comparison with those in which change is frequent. A corollary is that one should see more behavior that is maladaptive—more failed attempts to achieve an adaptive strategy—in societies undergoing rapid change than in stable societies. In general, it is my impression that these predictions are borne out by the ethnographic record. Finally, if the hypothesis developed here is true, one should not be surprised to see from time to time, in bodies of traditional lore regarding "wise" or "correct" behavior, more or less explicit reference to the fitness consequences of behavioral acts. One example, from ancient Hebrew "wisdom" literature, will suffice here: "A good man leaveth an inheritance to his children; and the wealth of the sinner is laid up for the just" (Proverbs 13:22).

As should be obvious from the foregoing discussion, the "adaptationist" approach to human social behaviors does not presuppose that all human behavior is adaptive, any more than all behavioral or other traits of other animals are adaptive. It does predict that widespread, frequently adopted behaviors will be inclusive fitness-maximizing ones. In the zoological literature, the most dramatic reports of maladaptive behavior generally involve responses by animals to human alterations of their environment for which the animals' genetic makeup has left them totally unprepared. For example, certain species of dragonfly, which ordinarily lay their eggs in water, have begun to lay eggs on shiny automobile hoods, where they are doomed to perish (Evans, 1968). Similarly, some of the most dramatic examples of maladaptive human behavior have occurred in times of rapid environmental change. For example, the behavior of the Sioux during the "ghost dance" fervor of 1890 contained obviously maladaptive elements, such as the belief that "ghost shirts" could not be penetrated by the bullets of white soldiers. However, the general pattern of behavior exhibited by the ghost-dancers—the type of response to foreign domination or the threat of extinction which Wallace (1956) has called a "revitalization" movement—is one that has occurred repeatedly in human history and has often been successful in repelling invaders. The tragedy of the 1890 Sioux outbreak was that a revitalization movement could not succeed against overwhelmingly unfavorable odds of numbers and firepower.

Some authors have suggested that sociobiological approaches to human behavior are inadequate because they fail to take into account the role of culture (e.g., Sahlins, 1976). Others have suggested that we need a theory of cultural evolution analogous to the Neo-Darwinist theory of genetic evolution (e.g., Plotkin and Odling-Smee, 1981). I believe, on the other hand, that we already have a perfectly good theory of cultural evolution. Cultural anthropologists since the time of Boas have described and analyzed the various processes by which cultural traits appear, are modified over time, and spread geographically. Although there are serious flaws in the theoretical perspective of the Boasian school of "cultural anthropology" (see Alexander, 1981, and Section 1.4 below), anthropologists of this school have provided a perfectly adequate theory of cultural evolution; their theories have not been formulated quantitatively, but a quantitative framework is easily imposed if needed (e.g., Cavalli-Sforza and Feldman, 1981). Further, I would argue that the extent to which we need to take cultural differences into account in our explanations of human behavior depends on the type of questions we are asking. In fact, there are important questions regarding the adaptive significance of human social behaviors that can be answered without reference to cultural evolution. The fact that Boasian cultural anthropology did provide an adequate theory of cultural evolution and yet was woefully inadequate as a general theory of social behavior should suggest how little insight into social behavior a consideration of culture alone can provide.

1.3 Functional and Comparative Questions

Questions regarding human social behavior can be classified in two categories: *functional* questions (which can be either *specific* or *general*) and *comparative* questions. The same classification can be applied not only to the questions social scientists ask but also to the hypotheses that are formulated as answers to these questions. In posing a functional question, we ask how a given behavior pattern functions in terms of the hypothesized overall function of human behavior, that is, inclusive fitness maximization. In posing a specific functional question, we isolate a specific element of social behavior in a particular society (e.g., Omaha marriage rules, the mother's brother–sister's son relationship in the Trobriand Islands, Iroquois matrilineal clans) and seek its function within the social context in which it is found. Posing general functional questions is a more difficult enterprise. Here we seek a more general explanation for a more general category of social behavior (e.g., lineage exogamy, the avunculate, matrilineal clans) that will explain its function in all or most societies where it is found. The danger in posing general functional questions is "typological thinking": the assumption that all behaviors which we can group together in a given category are necessarily alike in function.

Comparative questions, on the other hand, are explicitly historical. In posing comparative questions, we ask how a given behavior pattern in one society has come to differ from behavior in another society or societies. Perhaps an example will help to clarify this distinction.

The Crow and Omaha were two peoples of the North American Plains. Both spoke languages belonging to the Siouan family; thus, at least to some extent, the two peoples shared a cultural heritage. When encountered by Europeans, both Crow and Omaha had adopted the horse, and equestrian bison hunting played a major role in their economies. In spite of these similarities, the Crow and Omaha differed markedly in social organization, so much so that each people has become for anthropologists proverbial as an example of a contrasting type of social organization. The Crow provide a classic example of matrilineal social organization, whereas the Omaha provide a classic example of patrilineal social organization. In asking functional questions, we need not concern ourselves with the historical processes by which Crow and Omaha came to differ so markedly in social organization. Instead, we isolate a specific element of social behavior or organization within one of these societies and seek its function within that society. Comparative and historical data are not necessary in order to do this, since our only interest in the social institution in question is its function in the ethnographic context (which may be the actual present time in some investigations or a historical "ethnographic present" in others). In posing a functional question, we seek to ascertain the inclusive-fitness consequences of the behavior in the environment in which it occurs—where the term "environment" encompasses not only the physical environment but also the technological, economic, and social context.

Functional questions in social anthropology bear a close analogy to functional questions in the biological sciences. Evolutionary biologists frequently seek to answer questions about function; for example, function of an organ or of a behavior pattern. Evolutionary theory predicts that the functions of both organs and behavior patterns lie in their contribution to the inclusive fitness of the individual. When physiologists study the function of an internal organ, they often see it in terms of homeostasis, that is, the maintenance of a constant internal environment in the face of perturbations originating in the external environment. However, homeostasis is not an end in itself for any organisms; the ultimate value of homeostasis lies in its contribution to the inclusive fitness of the individual. This point is not always appreciated by all biologists. Similarly, some anthropologists who have attempted to borrow functional ideas from biology have created a false analogy between social behavior and physiological function. Radcliffe-Brown, for example, often used physiological analogies to explain what he meant by the concept of "function" in social anthropology; he seems frequently to have seen the function of social behaviors to lie in some sort of "social homeostasis." But homeostasis is not necessarily desirable from the point of view of individual actors; indeed, it is not desirable unless it maximizes inclusive fitness.

Like social anthropologists, evolutionary biologists may pose either specific or general functional questions. In biology a specific functional question asks the function of a set of homologous structures or behavior patterns within any mon- ophyletic taxonomic unit at any level (a population, species, genus, family, etc.). Examples of specific functional questions include "What is the function of the insect Malpighian tubule?" "What is the function of lekking behavior in sage grouse?" General functional questions in biology seek generalizations to explain the occurrence throughout the organic world of a set of analogous structures or behaviors; for example, "What is the function of uric acid excretion by terrestrial organisms?" "What is the function of lekking behavior in general?" Again, for biologists, general functional questions pose the danger of typological thinking. Biologists have learned to avoid this pitfall by and large and have learned to live with the fact that almost no general functional hypothesis will fit all cases with- out exception (cf. Mayr, 1982).

Both specific and general functional questions are answered by what Mayr (1982) has called *teleonomic* thinking. To answer a functional question about any system we must have some idea of the end—the telos (τέλος) in Greek— toward which the system is geared. In the case of living systems, the telos is the function for which the structure or behavior under analysis has evolved, that is, the contribution it makes to inclusive fitness maximization. It is the error of *teleological* thinking to suppose that the telos need be someone's conscious pur- pose: the "divine plan" of the natural theologians (Mayr, 1982). Of course, for man-made machines, the telos is the conscious goal of the manufacturer; thus the functioning of some part of an automobile lies in making the automobile go, and so on. But no conscious plan provides the telos for a scientific understanding of the biotic world. The hypothesis developed in this book is that inclusive fit- ness maximization is the appropriate telos for analyzing not only the structures and behaviors of animals but human social behavior and organization as well.

To answer a comparative question, the social anthropologist must bring to bear data from a wide variety of sources. For example, suppose we are interested in explaining why, given their linguistic affinity, the Crow and Omaha came to differ to such an extent in their kinship terminologies and clan systems. In attempting to answer this question, we must examine any archeological or his- torical evidence that has a bearing on the origin of these peoples and the migra- tions that brought them to the regions which they occupied at the time of Euro- pean contact. We must consider differences between the environments to which the two peoples had adapted, differences between the two with respect to pro- ductive technologies, and the varying influences from other peoples to which the two might have been exposed. It should be obvious that such a study would by no means be easy in the case of the Crow and Omaha. For example, it seems unlikely that we can find a straightforward correlation between economic activ- ities and social organization in this case, since Crow and Omaha had similar bison-hunting economies at the time of European contact. It may be that the Crow and Omaha had adopted their respective forms of social organization in response to conditions prevailing before the arrival of the horse in the region. For example, the Omaha may have originally led a life similar to that of the Northern Woodland peoples, such as the Fox, in which cooperative hunting among related males was important (cf. Fletcher and LaFlesche, 1911). The Crow, on the other hand, may have led a life similar to matrilocal Plains peoples such as the Pawnee, to whom cooperative agricultural labor by related women was important (cf. Holder, 1970). In any event, this example should make clear some of the difficulties facing those who would answer comparative questions in social anthropology. In many cases, as perhaps in our example, comparative questions are likely to remain unsolved.

Again there is a close analogy with established procedure in the biological sciences. Frequently biologists have been interested in comparative questions. For example, biologists have wondered why a frog's heart has only a partial septum in the ventricles, whereas the ventricular septum in the human heart is complete. To answer this question fully, we must trace the evolutionary history of frog and human back to a common ancestor and ascertain how the structure of the heart diverged from the amphibian condition in the line leading through reptiles to modern mammals. Since there are no fossils of heart tissue, the reconstruction of this history involves examination of living forms that are believed to have diverged little from ancestral morphological patterns. In the comparison between frog and human, there is good evidence regarding the traditional steps from partial to complete separation of the ventricles. However, with some other groups of animals or with other characters (such as innate behavior patterns), comparative questions are not so easily answered since one often lacks a firm basis for deducing intermediate forms.

Incidentally, currently accepted evolutionary theory demands that we draw no conclusions about "progress" from a comparative investigation in biology (Ruse, 1986; Williams, 1966). Unfortunately, biologists still sometimes err in this respect. Comparative anatomy instructors can rarely resist giving their students the impression that the human heart is somehow "better" than the frog's heart. In Darwin's own generation and the generation immediately following, confusion on this point was widespread among biologists. Most biological teaching and writing at the time conveyed a clear message that evolutionary change is equivalent to progress. Thus a school of social anthropologists arose who described themselves as "evolutionists" and who saw their task to be the reconstruction of a historical sequence by which "primitive" forms of social life gradually gave rise to more "advanced" forms (the epitome of which, as far as the anthropologists were concerned, could be found in northwestern Europe and in the parts of North America settled by colonists from northwestern Europe). Twentieth-century social anthropology began with a revolt against the "evolutionary" school (Radcliffe-Brown, 1941). Evolutionary theory itself has advanced far beyond the naive idea that evolution implies progress. But it may be that some of the distrust anthropologists feel today toward biological explanations of social behavior is a legacy of their predecessors' rejection of a mistaken conception of "evolution."

1.4 Social Anthropology as Sociobiology (and Vice Versa)

Modern scientific anthropology began in the second half of the nineteenth century with the work of the "evolutionary" school. Some members of this school were theorists only, who attempted to synthesize the large body of data that had recently become available both concerning the customs of ancient European societies and concerning the customs of non-European peoples. Others, notably L. H. Morgan and W. H. R. Rivers, made important advances in the methodology of collecting field data on social organization of nonliterate peoples. The assumptions of the "evolutionary" school fell into disrepute for two reasons: the implication of "progress" culminating in Western society was seen as unjustified and ethnocentric; and reconstructions of "evolutionary" schemes were questioned on epistemological grounds as inevitably subjective and, as we should say today, untestable. New approaches arose to replace the "evolutionary" school. By and large, these can be assigned to one or the other of two broad traditions which have remained more or less separate throughout the twentieth century. The school of "cultural" anthropology, in which the seminal influence was Franz Boas, has been dominant in the United States. The school of "social" anthropology, in which the seminal influence was A. R. Radcliffe-Brown, has been dominant in Britain and other nations of the British Commonwealth. The French anthropologist Claude Lèvi-Strauss had an independent influence, most pronounced in the 1960s; his work draws on both traditions. Some British anthropologists, such as Edmund Leach (1982) and E. E. Evans-Pritchard in his later work (e.g., 1950), have come to adopt a philosophical viewpoint closer to the Boasian school. Likewise, in America there have been occasional workers whose approach has (consciously or unconsciously) been close to that of the British "structural–functional" school.

I next attempt to characterize briefly these two dominant trends in twentieth-century anthropology, drawing attention to what I consider the strengths and weaknesses of each approach, noting that I find myself in much greater sympathy with the approach identified with British social anthropology than with that associated with American cultural anthropology. In spite of some very serious errors, the social anthropologists have had a goal which is consistent with the goals of modern behavior biology: the development of a scientific understanding of social behavior. Radcliffe-Brown and his school endeavored to apply the scientific method to understanding human social behavior. Many of the failings later critics noted in their work derived from a rather imperfect understanding of the scientific method—an imperfect understanding that was not unique to them but common to many contemporaneous philosophers of science and indeed many contemporaneous natural scientists.

In recent years, cultural anthropologists have sometimes explicitly expressed interest in a very different goal. This goal is to interpret "cultures" as systems of "symbols" rather in the way that certain schools of literary criticism expound the symbolic systems of particular works of literature. I see nothing particularly reprehensible in pursuing this goal, although I do have problems with the implicit assumption that any "culture" is necessarily a unified and coherent system of symbols. I also see pitfalls in the methods of data gathering generally used in such studies. Many "cultural anthropologists" appear to believe that the fact that they are studying cultural symbols frees them from the ordinary rules of data gathering and hypothesis testing. I should prefer to see hypotheses about culture tested by adequate sampling on the population studied rather than merely asserted, as is done, apparently on the basis of intuition, by authors such as Schneider (1968). Nonetheless, I do not question that the study of cultural symbols can produce works of a high order; for example, Witherspoon's (1977) *Language and Art in the Navajo Universe*. Another notable contribution of cultural anthropology, alluded to in the last section, has been the study of the processes of cultural diffusion and cultural change.

Throughout the history of American cultural anthropology, however, there has been a disturbing tendency to try to apply the conceptual framework of cultural anthropology to the study of social behavior. Rather than concentrating on the study of symbols alone, anthropologists of the Boasian tradition have repeatedly appealed to "culture" as a factor that can be used to explain behavior. The results have been disastrous. Indeed, this sort of cultural anthropology represents a revival in a new guise of the discredited philosophical position known as idealism. Idealism asserts that mental events or ideas are primary, that events in the physical world, including behavior, merely reflect or act out ideas. Scientific materialism, on the other hand, asserts that events in the physical world are primary and that ideas (including cultural symbols) reflect events in the physical world. Cultural anthropologists have tended to take an idealist approach to comparative questions (as defined in the last section) regarding social behavior. To explain differences in social behavior between two or more societies (as in our Crow–Omaha example), cultural anthropologists sometimes write as if the societies differ *because* their cultures differ. Thus they view culture as a *cause* of behavior. Now it is of course true in one sense that a human individual may behave in a given way because he has been taught by his "culture" to behave so; that is, he may engage in behavior which he learned from his parents or other society members through the medium of their culture. But this explanation of the individual's behavior is valid only at the proximal level. At a more ultimate level, surely we are entitled to ask why the culture itself has taken the form it has. An answer to this question qualifies as a more fundamental explanation of the individual's behavior than merely to repeat the truism that the individual's behavior is a result of his "culture." Indeed, we may ask in general why certain types of behavior are inculcated by some "cultures" and not by others. It is questions of this sort that a science of social behavior should attempt to answer, and an appeal to "culture" as a terminus of explanation is of no help at all. A scientific approach to social behavior should be materialist in the sense that all science is materialist. It seeks explanations in terms of factors that are material—including the genetic constitution of the individuals involved and the evolutionary history that shaped it—and the physical, biotic, and social environments. Scientific materialism need not be accompanied, it seems to me, by an ontological commitment to the belief that only material entities exist or can be objects of reference; but it appeals only to material entities and processes as termini of explanation.

In fact, whenever cultural anthropologists have advanced idealist hypotheses to account for human social behavior, if the matter has been examined more closely, the idealist hypothesis has been falsified. For example, it has been said that individuals in certain East African pastoral societies will struggle to keep alive ailing cattle because their culture places a high value on cattle ownership (e.g., Herskovits, 1926). The rather patronizing implication is that these people are so infatuated with cattle that they will even behave maladaptively, damaging their own long-term interests, to hold on to useless herd members. However, more detailed economic analyses have shown that cattle are important exchange items for East African pastoralists and have been so for many centuries (H. K. Schneider, 1979). Cattle are "money" for East African pastoralists (Einzig, 1966), and even a sick cow may yield a return if exchanged shrewdly. Freeman's (1983) falsification of Mead's idealist hypotheses about Samoan adolescence is another example.

A familiar expression of the idealist approach to social behavior is Benedict's *Patterns of Culture* (1934). This book has probably influenced a great many people's idea of what anthropology is all about, at least in the United States, because it is widely read by undergraduates. In it, Benedict "explains" a whole suite of behavioral traits of a number of peoples as resulting from differences in culture, with no examination of environmental factors to which the cultures in question were presumably adapted. As an explanation, the appeal to culture is hardly adequate; yet one can almost forgive Benedict when one understands her reasons for adopting this position. As she herself makes plain, she is writing to oppose the racist nonsense then widespread (e.g., Gobineau, 1915; Grant, 1921; Huntington, 1924), which "explained" behavioral differences among societies as being caused by genetic differences among "races." The argument developed here should make it plain that I do not see "sociobiological" explanations as a way of resurrecting this sort of discredited racism. I believe that Benedict, Boas, and Mead were right to oppose the racist paradigm; I do not believe, however, that the paradigm they attempted to erect in its stead goes far to account for the varieties of human social behavior in a testable, materialist fashion.

In addition to their tendency toward idealist explanations of social behavior, cultural anthropologists have sometimes impeded progress in the study of human social behavior by advocating an extreme form of cultural relativism. Sometimes cultural anthropologists write as if the theoretical framework of Western science were merely an aspect of our own culture lacking any cross-cultural validity. Thus to try to formulate a theory to account for the behavior of people belonging to any other culture is "ethnocentric." The implication is that the behavior of individuals can be explained only within the framework of their own culture. This view is surely unnecessarily pessimistic. The aim of science, since the time of the Ionian philosophers, has always been to formulate theories that are universal in the sense of transcending the immediate cultural context of the scientist. Although it is true that this goal is not always met in practice, the natural sciences over the past 500 years or so have provided ample evidence that it is not an unrealistic hope. The social sciences have not as yet been so successful in producing a body of theory that transcends the cultural context of the scientist. However, the enterprise of anthropology has always been to provide such a theory. Anthropologists, in urging a cross-cultural perspective, have traditionally sought a science of humanity that transcends ethnocentric concerns in a way that neither sociology nor psychology has ever done. It is indeed ironic that today anthropologists question the goal which traditionally set their science apart from others.

A particularly egregious example of cultural relativism is provided by the writings of David Schneider on kinship (e.g., 1968, 1972). Schneider considers the concept that kinship is based on some "shared biogenetic substance" to be part of the "American kinship system." He apparently arrived at this conclusion by a process of induction based on numerous interviews of "Americans"—an apparently nonrandom sample of residents of the United States belonging to a variety of ethnic groups. Like Schneider's other conclusions about "American culture," it is presented without quantitative supporting data. Be that as it may, I will dispute neither the conclusion that a belief that kinship is based on a "shared biogenetic substance" is widespread in America nor the implication that analogous beliefs need not exist in other cultures. However, Schneider seems to want to go further and suggest that our scientific view of genetic relatedness (based on the sharing of gene copies that are identical by virtue of descent from a common ancestor) is itself merely a part of our cultural worldview and lacks universal validity. Biologists know, on the contrary, that the facts of genetics are applicable not only to humans of all cultures but to all organisms (most of which lack any cultural notions whatsoever). Studying differences between cultures in beliefs about kinship is an important and worthwhile pursuit. But this pursuit will be greatly enriched if we can compare people's beliefs about kinship with the actual biological facts about genetic relatedness obtaining in their societies. For further discussion of this point, see Hughes (1986a).

In fairness to Schneider and his followers, it is worth remarking that his viewpoint represents an understandable reaction to mistaken notions of "biology" which were held by some social anthropologists. Frequently in discussions of kinship, social anthropologists of the British school were fond of asserting that human kinship systems are ultimately based on biological "universals"—"the irreducible facts of parenthood, siblingship, and marriage" (Fortes, 1959). However, as recent research has clarified, even within our own species, the biological facts of reproductive behavior are not universal (or "irreducible") but vary from society to society. Several factors can influence biological relatedness among "kin" in human social groups, and they vary from society to society. These include the mating system (monogamy, polygyny, polyandry, or some mixture of these); the relatedness of parents to each other and thus the degree of inbreeding of their offspring; confidence of paternity (Alexander, 1974, 1977, 1979), that is, the degree to which the legal father ("pater") and the biological father ("genitor") are one and the same individual in a particular society.

The last-mentioned factor has caused more confusion among anthropologists than any other. Since humans are mammals and fertilization is internal, no male is 100% certain that he is actually the father of his putative offspring. If anthropologists are concerned with ascertaining the facts about biological relatedness within some human social group, how can they ever obtain reliable data on actual relatedness since pater and genitor need not be the same person? The response of early social anthropologists to this problem was to attempt to obtain information about true paternity by careful questioning of informants. W. H. R. Rivers (1900), who first proposed the use of a "genealogical method" for gathering ethnographic data, reports (p. 75): "The term which was open to the most serious liability to error was that of father, but I was able to make the natives understand very thoroughly that I wanted the 'proper father.'" Schneider (1972) ridicules the complacency of Rivers's assumption that the "proper father" can indeed be ascertained by questioning. Schneider's concern is valid; but his reaction—a kind of antiscientific despair—is unacceptable to anyone who hopes to progress in the study of social behavior. Since we can never know the facts of paternity, Schneider argues, we must conclude that kinship as a social and cultural phenomenon has nothing to do with biology. We can talk about what people believe about "kinship" but cannot relate this to biological facts. The widespread acceptance of Schneider's defeatism by American cultural anthropologists (and even to some extent by British social anthropologists) has emasculated the entire field within the past decade, giving an increasingly subjective and idealist quality to anthropological writings.

In fact, even when informants do not know the facts about paternity, actual paternities can often be ascertained by the use of genetic markers. In the relatively small and isolated social groups that are usually studied by anthropologists, the chance of identifying an individual's actual father by genetic markers is good. Even in much more populous societies (such as our own) genetic markers frequently make it possible to exclude certain individuals as fathers. Under certain circumstances, DNA fingerprinting can be used to determine paternity even when the putative father is unavailable for testing (e.g., Jeffreys, Brookfield, and Semeonoff, 1985). Of course, genetic markers cannot be used to check a genealogy involving individuals which are all dead at the time the genealogy is collected; but if, in a given society, one finds that confidence of paternity is low among the living, it may be reasonable to extrapolate backward and conclude that confidence of paternity has also been low in previous generations. Such a conclusion would lead one to question any estimates of relatedness in the male line that one could derive from a putative genealogy. However, even if one lacks any reliable information on relatedness through males, one can still test hypotheses regarding the relationship between biological relatedness and a variety of social behaviors. In studies of nonhuman primates, field workers generally have no knowledge of paternity. This is particularly true for species which form multimale troops such as the macaques *(Macaca)* and baboons *(Papio).* In the future, studies using genetic markers may provide some of the missing information (as has already been done with captive troops; e.g., Smith, 1982). However, even in the absence of any information regarding relatedness through males, information regarding relatedness through females permits one to test numerous hypotheses concerning kin-directed social behavior, as, for example, Kurland (1977) has done in his study of the Japanese macaque.

On the other hand, there are human societies in which confidence of paternity, although never perfect, is quite high. Sometimes behavioral evidence suggests that confidence of paternity is high. For example, when males practice claustration of females or similar strategies that ensure fidelity (e.g., Dickemann, 1981) one can be fairly confident that such measures are in general successful. Ideally, of course, this expectation should be checked with genetic markers whenever possible. But even in the absence of genetic information, when males devote considerable time and energy to practices designed to ensure fidelity, one should feel fairly confident in assuming that pater and genitor are the same (except in cases of levirate marriage and so forth, which informants will generally point out). Further, in some societies in which the position of women is much less constrained and divorce rates are high, marriages may tend to be monogamous while they last and confidence of paternity fairly good (for an apparent example, see Goody, 1962).

It is true that whether they have simply an orally collected genealogy to work with, written birth records, or a mass of genetic information, investigators can ultimately produce no more than an estimate of the biological relatedness of any one individual to another. This estimate is only the best possible estimate under the circumstances and can never be considered perfect. However, all science deals with estimates of quantities, none of which is immune from error. This is a point that nonscientists, and those whose understanding of the natural sciences is limited, often fail to appreciate. Even in the physical sciences, investigations are unable to do any more than provide estimates of such quantities as the speed of light, the atomic weight of a particular element, the length or mass of a given object, and so on. Often the amount of error in estimates made by physical scientists is much less than in those made by behavioral biologists (such as coefficients of relatedness between two individuals) or by social scientists (such as the prevalence of a given type of marriage in a given society). But estimation is a routine activity of all scientists. Anthropologists should not be led to accept Schneider's defeatist approach to kinship studies merely because they are able to provide only "estimates" of relatedness rather than "facts." The search for indisputable "facts" is indeed a hopeless quest in any earthly endeavor.

In contrast to the idealism and skepticism characteristic of cultural anthropologists, social anthropologists of the British school have been characterized by a pragmatic, positivistic approach toward their data and a confidence in their ability to construct a science of mankind. Perhaps because they were often themselves the product of a society in which kinship still mattered, they were quick to perceive the importance kinship holds for most nonliterate peoples and did not doubt that real biological kinship is what human kinship systems are fundamentally all about. The native North American societies studied by American cultural anthropologists have typically been defeated and dependent, wholly stripped of their traditional means of livelihood, by the time they have become subjects of anthropological study. It is hardly surprising that anthropologists studying such peopled were able to see "culture" as a factor largely independent of social behavior and environmental conditions, since the peoples as they found them were endeavoring to salvage or remember as much as possible of their ancient culture under vastly altered environmental circumstances. British social anthropologists, on the other hand, tended to study societies, particularly in Africa, that were still vigorous and fully functional, although undergoing acculturation to varying degrees. Social anthropologists thus placed a wholesome emphasis on the correlation between social organization and the physical, biotic, and economic environment (e.g., Forde, 1934) and on the close relationship between cultural categories and actual social behavior. In the rest of this chapter, I consider in detail some of the weaknesses as well as the strengths of social anthropology and suggest how an evolutionary approach to human social behavior is in remarkable continuity with this field's major goals.

The school of social anthropology founded by Radcliffe-Brown has frequently been called the "structural–functional" school of social anthropology. Radcliffe-Brown, in breaking with the "evolutionary" concerns of his mentor W. H. R. Rivers, sought to analyze contemporaneous societies as he found them rather than reconstruct an unrecoverable past. He sought first to identify social "structures," that is, what we would today call emergent features of social behavior or complex patterns of social behavior existing at a level above that of the individual. Next he sought functional explanations for these structural elements and for other widely occurring social behaviors. From the point of view adopted here, Radcliffe-Brown and his followers were more successful in the former task than in the latter. They were unable to answer functional questions about human society adequately for lack of the appropriate telos.

As mentioned, social anthropologists of the structural–functional school assumed that the appropriate telos for social behavior must be the harmony and continuity of the society as a whole. Radcliffe-Brown thus writes (1935, p. 396):

> The *function* of any recurrent activity, such as the punishment of a crime, or a funeral ceremony, is the part it plays in the social life as a whole and therefore the contribution it makes to the maintenance of structural continuity.

Radcliffe-Brown seems to have adopted this viewpoint as a result of a misapplied biological analogy. Alexander (1979) effectively criticized the tendency of anthropologists to see the telos of social behavior in terms of the good of the society as a whole. His argument stems from the work of Williams (1966), who criticized biologists for making the assumption that traits of organisms might frequently be explained as adaptations having as a telos the good of a social group or the good of the species as a whole (i.e., might be explained by "group selection"). Williams pointed out that natural selection, as we understand it, is most unlikely to produce any adaptation having as its telos the good of a social group or species. Rather, the appropriate telos is the inclusive fitness of the individual. If it is correct that widespread human social behaviors represent adapted phenotypes, then Williams's strictures apply to such behaviors as well. By providing the appropriate telos, evolutionary biology can thus contribute to a revival of functionalist social anthropology.

Confusion regarding the appropriate telos is understandable when one is dealing with truly emergent properties of social systems—systems of descent, patterns of marital exchange, and so forth—that appear to transcend the individual. If the evolutionist sees the inclusive fitness of the individual as the appropriate telos, how can he come to terms with the emergent properties of social systems? One alternative is to treat emergent properties as mere epiphenomena that cannot be studied at all. Murdock (1972) tended toward this view, which I feel is overly pessimistic. I believe that emergent properties can be subjects for scientific study and that it is important for an evolutionary theory of human behavior not to shy away from them. Sociobiologists have been criticized (e.g., Hendrichs, 1983) for failing to come to terms with the emergent properties of social systems. Furthermore, the mistaken notion that such complex properties require some sort of "group selection" mechanism in order to account for their occurrence has become widespread (e.g., Fox, 1979).

Interestingly, Radcliffe-Brown in certain passages provides indications of the way out of this dilemma. He writes, for example (1940, p. 9):

A social relation exists between two or more individual organisms when there is some adjustment of their respective interests, by convergence of interest, or by limitation of conflicts that might arise from divergence of interests.

Complex patterns of social behavior can be seen as the result of each individual's effort to maximize his or her inclusive fitness, subject to the constraint that compromise with others will be necessary. Compromise among antagonistic self-interests is surely fundamental to social life in all animals. Radcliffe-Brown's realization of this fact is surprisingly modern and in marked contrast to his bland reliance, in other passages, on the good of the society as a whole as a telos for social behavior. If individual social actors can compromise their self-interests and join together in a united action, then a behavior pattern transcending the individual can result. Any such compromise will not permit each individual to realize perfectly his self-interest (i.e., his inclusive fitness). But it may often be in each individual's self-interest to compromise in the first place, for example, if no one individual is able to impose his will on others and if the cost of conflict is prohibitive. Given the need for compromise, each individual will strive to maximize his self-interest insofar as possible under the circumstances. Thus behavior patterns that result from a compromise among individuals can be explained in terms of individual inclusive fitness and do not require group advantage as an explanatory telos.

In Radcliffe-Brown's time, the two dominant fields of biology were physiology and systematics. We have seen how he borrowed from the former his unfortunate notion of social homeostasis. From the latter, Radcliffe-Brown borrowed the notion that classification and nomenclature are important aspects of any science. Indeed he sometimes (e.g., 1957) writes as if classification were the most important task of a scientist. Today, practicing biologists tend to have a much less exalted view of the importance of biological classification than they did in Radcliffe-Brown's day. Classification is seen as an indispensable prelude to scientific work in biology but not as an end in itself. In general, the view seems to be widespread among scientists that an obsession with classification and naming of the phenomena under study is characteristic of an early stage in the development of any science. Radcliffe-Brown and his school have been criticized for an excessive interest in classification and naming of social phenomena. The criticism may be justified; but when one considers that they were indeed pioneers in a new field of endeavor, a certain amount of concern with classification was to be expected.

Schneider (1965) rightly castigated social anthropologists of Radcliffe-Brown's era for confounding the distinction between "culture" (which exists at the level of rules, beliefs, and symbols) and "society" (which exists at the level of actual behavior). This confusion appears to have resulted from a methodological shortcut employed by these anthropologists in their work. In using the genealogical method to obtain data regarding kinship systems, field anthropologists frequently would question an informant regarding appropriate behavior on his part toward individuals standing in a particular relationship toward him. From the informant's statements about how kin "typically" act or "should" act, the anthropologists tended to make inferences about actual behavior. Today, however, most social anthropologists are aware that one cannot infer actual behavior from stated "rules." As one social anthropologist recently expressed it, people are likely to "state a convention as if it were a fixed rule only to interpret it to meet a specific contingency" (Lawrence, 1984). In recent years, social anthropologists have placed an increasing emphasis on the reporting of actual behavior. A particularly positive tendency has been the adoption of quantitative observational techniques from ethology and behavioral ecology (e.g., Borgerhoff Mulder and Caro, 1985; Hames, 1978).

In conclusion, I find that many of my interests as a "sociobiologist" are in a direct line of descent from the interests of Radcliffe-Brown and the other founders of British social anthropology. I view the theory developed here as a continuation of their work. I share their confidence that the material world is knowable and that a science of society is possible. Indeed, in the future, the appearance of human sociobiology may be seen primarily as a revival and theoretical strengthening of social anthropology. Adoption of the sociobiological viewpoint will enable social anthropology to throw off the shackles of Boasian idealism and Schneiderian skepticism and reclaim its heritage as a "natural science of society." Although the conceptual roots of sociobiology are in the behavioral ecology of animals (as is my own academic background), it is interesting to note that the founders of modern behavioral ecology have occasionally acknowledged an intellectual debt to British social anthropology (e.g., Eisenberg, 1981). The continuity between social anthropology and sociobiology is illustrated most tellingly by the career of Robin Fox, who followed contributions to social anthropology (1967a, 1967b) by pioneer work in human sociobiology (e.g., 1967c, 1975), later to return to a classic anthropological study of social structure, *The Tory Island-*

ers (1978). In a marvellous passage in the introduction to that book, Fox revels in the irony of his situation (page xv):

> And, finally, I cannot resist a word to those of my colleagues who, knowing that my interests over the last ten years (or more) have been in the evolution of behaviour, ethology, sociobiology, etc., express surprise that I should be writing this at all, and not a piece on "primatology." To those innocents I can only reply that this *is* a piece on primatology, and that if they would only grasp that, then a lot would become clear and much nonsense avoided.

The point I hope I have made in this introductory chapter is that if the science of human social behavior envisaged by Radcliffe-Brown is ever to mature, it will have to be grounded in evolutionary biology and to share a great deal of its theory and its methods with behavioral ecology. Succeeding chapters represent a contribution to the development of a theory of social behavior that is at once "structural–functionalist" and evolutionary.

The ensuing chapters first develop a theory, based on evolutionary biology, which makes predictions regarding complex human social behaviors. The theory (Chapters 2 and 3) is necessarily mathematical, especially in Chapter 3; the appendices provide a brief summary of specific mathematical concepts (matrix algebra and graph theory) which may not be familiar to the reader. Chapter 4 considers practical methods of analysis, which are perhaps more intuitively straightforward than the models in Chapters 2 and 3. Chapters 5, 6, and 7 consider applications of the theory to some questions of interest to social anthropologists, while Chapter 8 discusses some applications and implications of a biologically based social anthropology.

2

The Theory of Kin Selection

Modern science defines the method, not the aim of its work. It is based upon numbering and calculating—in short, upon mathematical processes; and the progress of science depends as much upon introducing mathematical notions into subjects which are apparently not mathematical as upon the extention of mathematical methods and conceptions themselves.

MERZ (1896)

μηδὲ κασιγνήτῳ ἶσον ποιεῖσθαι ἑταῖρον
"Don't set a stranger equal to a kinsman."

HESIOD, Works and Days

2.1 The Concept of Kin Selection

Mathematical modeling is an important tool in any science. Models vary in complexity, but in general it seems that the most influential models are those that reduce the complexity of some aspect of nature to a relatively simple mathematical formulation. Hamilton's model of kin selection (1963, 1964) is such a model, and it played a seminal role in the development of sociobiology. The question Hamilton posed is one that had vexed evolutionary biologists since Darwin: how can natural selection account for the evolution of "altruistic" behaviors? An "altruistic" behavior is one that enhances the fitness of a beneficiary at the expense of the fitness of the actor. An apparent example is the behavior of sterile workers in the social insects, which do not reproduce but work to raise offspring belonging to the queen (who is typically their mother).

Hamilton proposed that such altruistic behavior will be favored by natural selection when

$$\frac{b}{c} > \frac{1}{r} \tag{2.1}$$

where c is the cost to the altruist, b is the benefit to the recipient, and r is the coefficient of relatedness of recipient to altruist. The cost c is the reduction to the altruist's individual fitness as a result of his altruism, while the benefit b represents the corresponding increase to the beneficiary's individual fitness. The coefficient of relatedness measures the probability that, at a given locus, a gene in the beneficiary is identical by descent with the homologous gene in the altruist.

A great many different "coefficients of relatedness" have been proposed. For reviews of these see Michod and Anderson (1979) and Pamilo and Crozier (1982); these authors also review the complex and contradictory notation associated with the various measures of relatedness. Michod and Hamilton (1980) show that the following formulation is most appropriate for calculating r in (2.1) and in other sociobiological models derived therefrom:

$$r_{ij} = \frac{2f_{ij}}{1 + F_i} \tag{2.2}$$

In (2.2) r_{ij} is the regression coefficient of individual j to individual i; f_{ij} is the coefficient of consanguinity between individuals i and j; and F_i is the inbreeding coefficient of individual i. Since the measure given by (2.2) is technically speaking a regression coefficient, it is sometimes denoted b_{ij}, in order to maintain consistency with the usage of statisticians for regression coefficients. I feel, however, that it is worthwhile to retain the use of the letter r, since (2.1), widely known as Hamilton's rule, has gained such currency in the behavioral literature.

The coefficient of consanguinity between two individuals f_{ij} represents the probability that two alleles at a given locus, one drawn at random from i and the other drawn at random from j, are identical by descent. It can be calculated from an analysis of their pedigree. Standard population genetics texts provide the following formula for the case where one can trace the descent of individuals i and j back to c common ancestors:

$$f_{ij} = \sum_{k=1}^{c} \left(\frac{1}{2}\right)^{n_{ik}+n_{jk}+1} (1 + F_k) \tag{2.3}$$

For each common ancestor k, we calculate n_{ik} = the number of steps from the common ancestor to individual i and n_{jk} = the number of steps from the common ancestor to individual j. (If the pedigree is regarded as a digraph, n_{ik} has a precisely defined meaning, as the distance from i to k. See Appendix B.) F_k represents the inbreeding coefficient of the common ancestor.

All genealogies have a finite depth. Thus F_k is usually unknown. When one is working with a small population, however, it is reasonable to assume that some inbreeding has taken place in the past and that apical ancestors themselves may have been somewhat inbred. One can at least approximate the effect of inbreeding resulting from small population size by adding a correction factor to the estimate of f_{ij}. Suppose we call $f_{ij}(0)$ our first estimate of f_{ij}, assuming $F_k = 0$ for all k; we can estimate the actual or "total" coefficient of consanguinity $f_{ij}(T)$ as follows:

$$f_{ij}(T) = f_{ij}(0) + [1 - f_{ij}(0)] \alpha \tag{2.4}$$

where α represents the probability that two alleles at the same locus from any member of the population taken at random are identical by descent. With effective population size N_e and g generations of isolation, one can estimate α by the formula

$$\alpha = 1 - \left(1 + \frac{1}{2N_e}\right) e^{-g/2N_e} \tag{2.5}$$

A number of factors contribute to N_e, including variance among individuals in numbers of offspring that survive to reproduce. An approximate formula that takes these factors into account in stable populations is given by Hill (1979):

$$N_e \sim \frac{8N}{V_m + V_f + 4} \tag{2.6}$$

where N is the number of breeding individuals; V_m is the variance in number of surviving offspring sired per male; and V_f is the variance in number of surviving offspring per female. Substitution of trial values shows that α is likely to be negligible for N_e greater than about 1000, except after unreasonably long periods of isolation. Population effective sizes of at least 1000 can probably be assumed for most human societies, except a few true isolates.

The inbreeding coefficient of individual i, F_i, represents the probability that, at a given locus in the same individual, both alleles are identical by descent. The inbreeding coefficient of an individual is equal to the coefficient of consanguinity between his parents. The effect of F_i in (2.2) is to decrease the value of r_{ij} if i is inbred. If individual i is not inbred, r_{ij} is simply twice f_{ij} and is easily calculated from (2.3). Discussion of the coefficients of consanguinity and inbreeding can be found in standard texts of population genetics (e.g., Cavalli-Sforza and Bodmer, 1971; Crow and Kimura, 1970; Jacquard, 1974; Spiess, 1977; Wright, 1969).

Another measure of relatedness which has frequently been used in sociobiological contexts is the *correlation* coefficient of relatedness (Wright, 1922). Unlike the regression coefficient given by (2.2), this coefficient is invariably symmetric. For two individuals x and y, this coefficient is given by

$$r_{xy} = \frac{2f_{xy}}{[(1 + F_x)(1 + F_y)]^{1/2}} \tag{2.7}$$

When neither x nor y is inbred, the regression and correlation coefficients of relatedness are identical.

The logic behind Hamilton's rule is straightforward. Suppose there is a rare gene predisposing an individual to behave altruistically. It will increase in the population even if the bearer's own fitness is decreased whenever the harm to the altruist is more than compensated by benefit to a related individual. Because the beneficiary is related to the donor, he has some probability of bearing the gene for altruism as well. If so, the gene itself will spread as a result of the donor's act of altruism. Thus in considering whether a gene for a particular behavior will spread, we need to consider not only the behavior's effect on the fitness of an individual actually exhibiting it but also its effect on the fitness of potential carriers, who may or may not themselves actually exhibit the behavior. Thus any individual's behavior may affect not only his individual fitness (via his direct descendents) but his inclusive fitness (via the offspring of his close relatives, whose fitness his behavior affects).

Some population geneticists have preferred to model kin selection differently. Rather than focusing on a dyadic interaction of beneficiary and donor, they have considered a population subdivided into a number of families (Wade, 1978). These models show that a gene for altruism might spread by a process of interfamily selection. The theoretical importance of "family-structured" models is that they are expressed only in terms of classical population genetics theory. They do not appeal to the newly developed notion of inclusive fitness. Thus they represent an example of scientific reductionism, whereby the statements of one theory are derived in terms of another theory. (The classic example is the reduction of the gas laws of statistical mechanics.) Family-structured models "reduce" inclusive fitness theory to classical population genetics and, in so doing, yield predictions similar to Hamilton's rule (Abugov and Michod, 1981; Michod, 1982).

In actual empirical testing of theory, there may be situations where the family-structured approach may have advantages and situations in which it is more fruitful to concentrate on dyadic interactions. Clearly, the empirical difficulty facing any direct test of (2.1) is the difficulty in measuring costs and benefits. There may be situations in which it is easier to measure fitness differences between and among groups, as required by family-structured models. However, this may require population-level data, which again are difficult to gather.

2.2 A Quantitative Genetic Model of Kin Selection

Hamilton (1964) proposed that reasoning similar to that expressed in (2.1) would apply to "altrusim" if it were a polygenic trait. It is obvious that when there is a heritable component to complex behaviors, it is likely to be the result of genes acting at many different loci. For this reason, many animal behaviorists and social scientists have been suspicious of reasoning based on single-locus models. Thus it is surprising that for a long time after Hamilton's seminal papers, no polygenic models of kin selection appeared in the literature. This deficit has been overcome in recent years; and a number of authors have modeled the evolution of "altruism" as a quantitative trait controlled by additive effects of numerous loci (e.g., Aoki, 1982; Cheverud, 1985; Engels, 1983; Yokoyama and Felsenstein, 1978).

Here I present a simple model of kin selection for a polygenic quantitative trait. I develop this model in some detail because in doing so I am able to introduce the standard concepts of quantitative genetics, which will be useful in succeeding chapters. The general approach used is identical to that of Cheverud (1985), although I consider the mode of selection in considerably greater detail than he does. This is a "family-structured" model, and it illustrates both the strengths and the weaknesses of the family-structured approach. Since the process modeled here is somewhat different from that usually considered, the model presented here yields a prediction not exactly identical to (2.1). But there is broad agreement between my model and the rest of kin selection theory in that it predicts that kin selection will be enhanced by high r and a high benefit/cost ratio.

The process I consider involves selection for a trait ("benevolence") which has positive effects on the fitness of family members but which can be detrimental to an individual's own fitness (i.e., becomes "altruism") when the individual is significantly more benevolent than most other family members. The model is based on the mathematical treatment of family-level selection developed in the literature of quantitative genetics, with applications to animal breeding (e.g., Falconer, 1981; Lerner, 1950; Lush, 1947). Animal breeding programs frequently made use of the genetic covariance among relatives, even long before any knowledge of genetics was available. For example, whenever a cock was chosen for breeding because his mother or sisters had high levels of egg production, the breeder made use of the fact that there is a genetic correlation among relatives even when they differ phenotypically due to lack of expression of a particular trait in certain individuals. This fact is, of course, fundamental to Hamilton's concept of inclusive fitness as well.

I suppose that there is some trait P, which I call benevolence, that can be measured on a continuous scale; let it be scaled in such a way that the population mean is zero and the variance σ_P^2. This trait can be seen as consisting of a number of independent components, the phenotypic value for individual i, (P_i) being the sum of the components,

$$P_i = A_i + D_i + I_i + E_i \qquad (2.8)$$

where A_i is the additive genetic component, D_i is the component due to dominance, I_i is the component due to epistatic interactions among loci, and E_i is the component due to the environment. I assume that there is no gene–environment interaction. Within the population, the phenotypic variance with respect to this trait can be similarly partitioned:

$$\sigma_P^2 = \sigma_A^2 + \sigma_D^2 + \sigma_I^2 + \sigma_E^2 \qquad (2.9)$$

The heritability of the trait is defined as follows:

$$h^2 = \frac{\sigma_A^2}{\sigma_P^2} \qquad (2.10)$$

Consider a diploid population which is subdivided at some stage of its life history into families, each of size n. These families need not actually live in groups but they must interact at some stage of their life history. One can partition P_i in another way under these circumstances (Lush, 1947). For individual i belonging to group j

$$P_i = A_i + C_j + S_i \qquad (2.11)$$

where A_i is as previously defined; C_j represents the effect of any factor other than A_i that affects P_i in the same way for all members of the jth family but may differ from one family to another; and S_i represents all factors, except A_i, which affect P_i but are no more alike for members of the same family than for individuals of different families. The C_j are specific to each family, whereas the S_i are random with respect to family membership. For the jth family, the mean value of P_i can be expressed as Y_j.

I suppose that there are two levels of selection in operation, one at the level of the individual and another at the level of the family. For ease of presentation I initially model both of these as processes of truncation selection; I show later how this assumption can be relaxed. I assume that members of all families for which Y_j falls below a certain value will experience reproductive failure; thus there is positive truncation selection on P at the family level. On the other hand, I assume that any individual with $P_i - Y_j$ above a threshold value also experiences reproductive failure; thus there is negative selection at the individual level. If an individual is excessively benevolent, beyond the average level of benevolence found in his family, that individual is a complete altruist with no individual fitness.

The expected response to selection is given by

$$R = I_p \sigma_P h^2 \tag{2.12}$$

where I_P is the standardized selection differential for P, that is, the mean value of individuals selected as parents (which we may denote $\bar{P}_S$) minus the mean value for the population prior to selection (which is here defined to be zero), divided by σ_P. In this model R is the result of two independent components, selection on Y and selection on $P - Y$. Thus

$$R = I_{P-Y} \sigma_{P-Y} h^2_{P-Y} + I_Y \sigma_Y h^2_Y \tag{2.13}$$

where I_{P-Y} is the standardized selection differential for $P - Y$; σ_{P-Y} is the population standard deviation for $P - Y$; and h^2_{P-Y} is the heritability of $P - Y$. Likewise, I_Y is the standardized selection differential for Y; σ_Y is the population standard deviation for Y (the standard deviation of family means); and h^2_Y is the heritability of Y (the heritability of family means). I assume $\sigma^2_P > 0$, $\sigma^2_{P-Y} > 0$, $\sigma^2_Y > 0$, $h^2_P > 0$, $h^2_{P-Y} > 0$, and $h^2_Y > 0$. Given our assumptions about the process of selection against altruism, we expect $I_Y > 0$ and $I_{P-Y} < 0$.

Formulas are available that make it possible to express the variance and heritabilities of $P - Y$ and Y in terms of the variance and heritability of P (Falconer, 1981). To present these formulas, we need expressions for the additive genetic and phenotypic correlations among family members. The additive genetic correlation among family members is denoted by r. When each family member is related to each other in exactly the same way (e.g., all are full sibs), the coefficient of relatedness [given by (2.2) or (2.7)] can be used for r. When group members are not all related to each other in the same way (e.g., in multisired families), methods such as those of Pamilo and Crozier (1982) can be used to estimate r. Alternatively, one may use $\bar{r}$, the average coefficient of relatedness [as given by (2.7)] to estimate r (Cheverud, 1985). Let t represent the phenotypic correlation among family members. The following formula may be used to compute t:

$$t = \frac{\sigma_B^2}{\sigma_P^2} \tag{2.14}$$

where σ_B^2 is the between-group component of the phenotypic variance σ_P^2. Another useful relationship is the following:

$$t = \frac{r\,\sigma_A^2 + \sigma_C^2}{\sigma_P^2} \tag{2.15}$$

High h^2 and σ_C^2 (relative to σ_A^2 and σ_S^2) will make t large relative to r, whereas low h^2 and low σ_C^2 will make t small relative to r. In this section, I assume $r < 1$ and $t < 1$.

For a family of finite size, the additive genetic variance of family means Y is

$$\frac{1 + (n - 1)r}{n}\,\sigma_A^2$$

and the phenotypic variance of family means is given by

$$\frac{1 + (n - 1)t}{n}\,\sigma_P^2$$

See Falconer (1981). Thus

$$h_Y^2 = \frac{1 + (n - 1)r}{1 + (n - 1)t}\,h^2 \tag{2.16}$$

The additive genetic variance of individual deviations from the family mean ($P - Y$) is given by

$$\frac{(n - 1)\,(1 - r)}{n}\,\sigma_A^2$$

and the phenotypic variance of individual deviations from the family mean is

$$\frac{(n - 1)\,(1 - t)}{n}\,\sigma_P^2$$

Thus

$$h_{P-Y}^2 = \frac{1 - r}{1 - t}\,h^2 \tag{2.17}$$

See Falconer (1981).

Substituting these values in (2.13), we can see that there will be a positive response to selection on P when

$$I_Y\left(1 + \frac{nr}{1 - r}\right) > I_{P-Y}\sqrt{(n - 1)\left(1 + \frac{nt}{1 - t}\right)} \tag{2.18}$$

Inequality (2.18), given the preceding assumptions, expresses the conditions for an increase in the mean level of benevolence ($\bar{P}$) in the population given the two-edged process of selection here envisaged, that is, positive selection on family mean value and negative selection on individual deviations from the family mean.

Inequality (2.18) may superficially appear to have little resemblance to (2.1); this is not entirely surprising since (2.1) and (2.18) model different processes. The two do yield similar predictions. Factors that will facilitate an increase in $\bar{P}$ according to (2.18) include high r, high I_Y, and low $|I_{P-Y}|$. These are analogous to the prediction by (2.1) that a gene for altruism will increase in a population when r is high, b is high, and c is low.

Matessi and Karlin (1986) propose the term "Hamilton property" for the property possessed by models of kin selection which show that altruism is more likely to evolve when r is high even if the exact conditions of the Hamilton rule (2.1) are not met. In this sense, inequality (2.18) has the Hamilton property.

One interesting prediction of (2.18) is that an increase in $\bar{P}$ will be most likely when t is low relative to r. Thus for a given value of r, the lower the phenotypic correlation within families, the greater the likelihood that evolution will produce an increase in $\bar{P}$. This somewhat paradoxical conclusion makes good biological sense. If the phenotypic correlation within families is low relative to r, there may be some individuals with high $P - Y$ (including some altruists) which raise Y for the family; but altruists will not be very numerous in comparison to nonaltruists within a given family. By (2.14), we would expect t to be low relative to r when σ_C^2 is low. One way this might happen is if the parent manipulates the behavior of family members such that $P - Y$ scores are positively skewed, thus including some scores higher than the family mean along with a substantial majority of lower scores (below the threshold for altruism).

It may be objeced that truncation selection is unlikely to occur in nature, although selection at the level of the individual against complete reproductive altruism does represent an example of truncation selection. However, altruism is not always complete. In any event, it may be more reasonable to suppose that fitness is some continuous function of phenotypic value. If so, we can express selection differentials in terms of the weighted average of P_i, where the weights w_i represent fitness of individuals. Since $\bar{P} = 0$, $I_P = \bar{P}_S/\sigma_P$, where $\bar{P}_S$ is the weighted average of P for individuals selected as parents. Let w_i be the fitness of an individual with phenotypic value P_i and group mean Y_j. This fitness will be the product of two components, one due to selection on $P_i - Y_j$ and the other due to selection on Y_j:

$$w_i = w_{P-Y}w_Y \qquad (2.19)$$

where w_{P-Y} is a function of $P - Y$ and w_y is a function of Y.

In this case,

$$\bar{P}_S = \frac{1}{\Sigma w_i} [\Sigma w_{P-Y}w_Y (P_i)] \qquad (2.20)$$

and

$$\bar{P}_S = \frac{1}{\Sigma w_i} [\Sigma w_{P-Y}w_Y (P_i - Y_j)] + \frac{1}{\Sigma w_i} [\Sigma w_{P-Y}w_Y (Y_j)] \qquad (2.21)$$

The two terms of (2.21), when divided by σ_P, can then be substituted for I_{P-Y} and I_Y in (2.18), yielding a generalized expression. Truncation selection as just considered represents a special case, where for $P - Y$ above the threshold value $w_{P-Y} = 0$ and for all other $P - Y$, $w_{P-Y} = 1$; and where for Y below the threshold $w_Y = 0$ and for all other Y, $w_Y = 1$.

Since $\overline{P} = \overline{Y} = 0$, it is also true (cf. Price, 1972) for the above that

$$\overline{P}_S = \frac{\text{cov}(w_i, P_i - Y_j)}{\overline{w}_i} + \frac{\text{cov}(w_i, Y_j)}{\overline{w}_i} \qquad (2.22)$$

This formulation is analogous to that of Wade (1985) for family-level selection in the single-locus case.

The model presented here may be unrealistic in some features. Like that of Yokoyama and Felsenstein (1978) and other family-structured models, it makes the generally rather unrealistic assumption that the population is subdivided into families each of size n. Nonetheless, models such as this may have value if they shed light on the process by which social behaviors evolve. The model presented here is particularly useful in highlighting the role that can be played by factors in addition to additive genetic effects in lowering t relative to r and thus facilitating kin selection. One such factor is parental manipulation of the behavior of offspring; this parental behavior might itself be innate (but independent of the "benevolent" behavior itself) or might, at least in humans, be merely cultural. Further, the model may have applicability to actual behavioral traits (e.g., food sharing, labor sharing) that can be measured on a quantitative scale and can be assumed to be "benevolent." In such cases, it may actually be reasonable to assume that an altruist is an individual who performs the behavior in question to a greater extent than other group members do, that is, one who puts in more than he gets out of an otherwise mutualistic system.

2.3 Inclusive Fitness and Polygenic Models

The concept of inclusive fitness has a relatively straightforward meaning in a single-locus model; in this case, inclusive fitness is a property of the genotype at the locus in question (Michod, 1982). In a polygenic model, the term must have a somewhat different meaning. When a large number of loci are involved in coding for a quantitative trait, the genotype of each individual in a population may be unique or nearly so. Thus in a polygenic case it may be more useful to speak of the inclusive fitness of an individual. I propose that the inclusive fitness of an individual i, symbolized g_i, can be defined by

$$g_i = \frac{\mathbf{r}_i'\mathbf{b}_i}{\Sigma b_{ij}} \qquad (2.23)$$

where $\mathbf{r}_i$ is a vector of the coefficients of relatedness of each of n individuals (including individual i) to individual i; $\mathbf{b}_i$ is a vector of fitness increments to which i's action contributes, whose elements are b_{ij}. (For a brief summary of the principles of matrix algebra see Appendix A.) The n individuals are all those possibly affected by i's action. In referring to an action to which i contributes, I mean to include not only an individual action of i but any concerted action involving other individuals along with i. Further, I specify that the action in question is such that the tendency to perform it is heritable; that is, some portion of the variance in the population with respect to the tendency to perform this action is additive genetic.

For example, in the family-structured model developed earlier for the evolution of benevolence, the inclusive fitness of any individual i in family j, all of whom are related to one another by r, is

$$w_i + r \sum_{k \neq i} w_k$$

which equals

$$w_{Yj} \left(w_{Pi-Yj} + r \sum_{k \neq i} w_{Pk-Yj} \right)$$

Behavioral biologists frequently assume that natural selection will favor a behavioral strategy that maximizes inclusive fitness. Given this polygenic definition of inclusive fitness, it is easy to see that this should indeed be so.

Imagine that the tendency to maximize inclusive fitness is a threshold character. In other words, there exists some underlying continuous variable P, which is unobservable. P is assumed to be constituted as in (2.8), and σ_P^2 can be partitioned as in (2.9). I assume no dominance or epistasis. Further, let the units be standardized such that $\sigma_P^2 = 1$. In the case of a threshold character, all that we actually observe is some discrete variable X, which takes the value of 0 or 1. When P is greater than or equal to some threshold value P', then the behavior in question (here, maximization of one's inclusive fitness) is observed and $X = 1$; when $P < P'$, the behavior is not observed and $X = 0$. If the mean of P is zero (before selection begins), let the mean of all individuals with $P \geq P'$ be μ_1; the mean of all individuals with $P < P'$ will then be $-\mu_1$. The mean additive genetic value A for all individuals with $P \geq P'$ is μ_A, while the mean of all individuals with $P < P'$ is $-\mu_A$.

The regression coefficient of relatedness defined in (2.2) can be expressed as follows:

$$r_{ij} = \frac{\text{cov}_A(i, j)}{\sigma_A^2(i)} \tag{2.24}$$

where $\text{cov}_A(i, j)$ is the additive genetic covariance between individual i and individual j; that is, the covariance between the additive genetic values of these two individuals at all loci contributing to the trait in question. Similarly, $\sigma_A^2(i)$ is the variance within individual i with respect to additive genetic values at these loci (Michod and Anderson, 1979). The equivalence of (2.24) and (2.2) is apparent from the fact that

$$\sigma_A^2(i) = (1 + F_i) \sigma_A^2 \tag{2.25}$$

and

$$\text{cov}_A (i, j) = 2f_{ij}\sigma_A^2 \tag{2.26}$$

See Crow and Kimura (1970). Given (2.24), r_{ij} represents the regression of the additive genetic values of individual j on those of individual i.

I further suppose that there is a population divided into m identically constituted groups. In each group there is one individual i in which $P \geq P'$. In each group, all other group members' relatedness to i is described by an identical vector $\mathbf{r}_i$. An individual with $P \geq P'$ will maximize his inclusive fitness. This means that the mean A for the offspring (which we may call A') of the population, on the assumption that mating is random with respect to A, will be given by

$$A' = \frac{1}{2} \mu_A \left(\frac{\mathbf{r}_i'\mathbf{b}_i}{\Sigma b_{ij}} \right)$$

The term in parentheses is assumed to be at a maximum. Suppose there is some other threshold trait, say Q, uncorrelated with P, with additive genetic component A_q, such that individuals with $Q \geq Q'$ pursue some strategy with regard to inclusive fitness other than to maximize it. If the units are standardized such that $\sigma_Q^2 = 1$ and prob $(P \geq P') = $ prob $(Q \geq Q')$, then the mean of individuals with $Q \geq Q'$ will be μ_A. Suppose that we have a second population divided into identically constituted subgroups and that $Q > Q'$ in one individual per group. Since inclusive fitness in (2.27) is at a maximum, $A' > A_q'$. Thus the mean A will increase more rapidly in the former population than will the mean of A_q in the latter.

In this rather artificial model, it is merely assumed that inclusive fitness is maximized. How exactly that maximum is reached depends on what sort of constraint limits the values of the b_{ij}. In the next chapter, I consider a plausible limit on the b_{ij} which makes it possible to estimate optimal "strategies" of inclusive fitness maximization.

Grafen (1982, 1984) has criticized behavioral biologists' use of definitions of inclusive fitness which, while generally expressed verbally rather than mathematically, are equivalent, or approximately equivalent, to (2.23). His major basis for complaint is that (2.23) and formulations like it do not correspond to the notion of "inclusive fitness" as originally defined by Hamilton (1964). He is correct about this; but it is my feeling that the concept of inclusive fitness, as originally defined, is not exactly what is needed for a robust theory of behavioral interactions among kin. For one thing, as originally defined, inclusive fitness is extremely difficult, if not impossible, to measure empirically.

Hamilton (1964, p. 8) writes:

> Inclusive fitness may be imagined as the personal fitness which an individual actually expresses in its production of adult offspring as it becomes after it has been first stripped and then augmented in a certain way. It is stripped of all components which can be considered as due to the individual's social environment, leaving the fitness which he would express if not exposed to any of the

harms or benefits of that environment. This quantity is then augmented by certain factors of the quantities of harm and benefit which the individual himself causes to the fitnesses of his neighbours.

There is no doubt that this definition of inclusive fitness is necessary for Hamilton's original model and for his appealing formulation of a rule (2.1) for the spread of a gene for altruism. But in empirical cases, the quantity described is virtually unmeasurable, depending as it does on a contrary-to-fact condition.

Of course, empirical measurement of a quantity like (2.23) is itself no mean feat. But the utility of the formulation, in context of the models developed here and in Chapter 3, is that it provides a criterion which we can expect natural selection to maximize, subject to the constraints imposed by the environment. In his original paper Hamilton (1964, p. 18) acknowledges the utility of a "more comprehensive mathematical argument with inclusive fitness more widely defined" for generalizing kin selection theory. Here and in Chapter 3, I develop at least the rudiments of one such more generalized theory, which of necessity entails some modifications to the concepts of inclusive fitness. The references cited by Grafen (1982, 1984) give me confidence that the definition I employ is close to the working definition already in use by most behavioral biologists.

Grafen (1982, 1984) makes an additional point: often in empirical cases, the best way to study empirical fitness effects is to measure individual fitness. This point has in effect been made previously by those who take a family-level approach to kin selection (e.g., Wade, 1978). For example, in bird species in which young adults help rear their younger siblings by sharing in parental duties, one can test for the beneficial effects of "helping" by comparing reproductive output of pairs with helpers to that of pairs without helpers. In this point, I wholly agree with Grafen and employ such methods later (especially in Chapter 6). Also, in modeling mutualistic interactions, I show how the assumption that (2.23) is maximized can along with certain other assumptions lead to predictions of *individual* fitness of a number of related individuals living in a social group (Sections 3.5 to 3.7).

3

Cooperation and Sharing among Kin

If there were many present, the mother would be apt to say, "Eat, do not wait." After that, anyone who had been served would be at liberty to partake of the food. Each person was served separately except in the case of infants or very young children. When the meal was at an end the dishes were handed back to the mother. In returning his dish, each person gave thanks by mentioning a term of relationship.

FLETCHER AND LA FLESCHE (1911)
The Omaha Tribe

3.1 Inclusive Fitness: Beyond Altruism

In addition to specifying the conditions under which altruistic behavior might have evolved, the theory of kin selection has implications for interactions among kin in present-day societies. A great deal of theoretical effort has been devoted to examining the conditions for the evolution of altruism under a variety of assumptions (see Chapter 2 above). But relatively few models have used kin selection theory to derive explicit predictions about the inner dynamics of social groups.

There is a real need for such models, because the literature is full of confusion regarding the empirical consequences of kin selection theory. Both proponents and opponents of sociobiology seem to have the impression that kin selection theory predicts that individuals will be nice to their kin and not so nice to non-kin. But this expectation is seldom expressed in quantitative terms, and the nature of the amicable interactions expected to occur among kin is rarely specified. Formal models have seldom addressed the question whether cooperation will be greater among kin than among non-kin. Cases of "altruistic" behavior may be rare in nature, outside of the social insects, but few researchers have considered whether the logic of kin selection can also be applied to mutually beneficial behaviors. In addition, theoreticians have not clarified whether there are conditions under which interactions among kin are predicted to be hostile rather than amicable.

Such confusions have given opponents of kin selection theory the impression that it is easily falsified. For example, Sahlins (1976) argued that kin selection theory is falsified by the observation that humans are "closer" to affines among whom they live than to consanguines with whom they do not live. He might, of course, have cited even more flagrant examples of human behavior contrary to the naive expectation that interactions among kin will always be friendly. Both historical and ethnographic literature are full of cases of intense competition among close kin. Among early Medieval Celtic nobility, there was no custom of primogeniture. An estate was divided among the male heirs, but very frequently the result was a fratricidal conflict by which one brother eventually supplanted the others (Davies, 1982; Smith, 1986). Indeed, primogeniture itself, since the parents favor one offspring over others equally related to them, may seem contradictory to kin selection theory (cf. Sahlins, 1976).

In this chapter I present a body of theory that makes explicit predictions regarding cooperation and sharing among kin. These models confirm that the basic logic of kin selection can be extended to mutually beneficial interactions. The models are based on kin selection theory and also incorporate assumptions about the nature of the resources to be shared by cooperating individuals. Indeed, the models show that the nature of the resources to be shared is a crucial factor in predicting whether, and to what extent, kin will share or will compete. In this introductory section, I discuss a few simple models of sharing among kin that have appeared in previous literature. In the next section I discuss a game theory model, which confirms predictions of earlier models but also suggests that surprising complexities may arise even in the simplest social groups. Finally, in the remainder of the chapter I develop an approach based on inclusive fitness maximization.

Trivers (1971) in his discussion of "reciprocal altruism" predicts a "lowered demand for reciprocity from kin" in comparison to non-kin. It may be worthwhile to make this prediction more explicit mathematically by means of a simple model of reciprocal exchanges among kin. This simple model will show that we should indeed expect kinship to affect reciprocal or cooperative interactions.

Suppose that we are concerned with a type of reciprocity that involves the exchange of resources which are crucial to fitness; that is, resources which are necessary for reproduction or for the survival of offspring. If two individuals have equal shares of such a resource at the same time and simply exchange them, there is no net effect on either individual's fitness and nothing happens that is of evolutionary (or even of economic) interest. But suppose that there is a certain maximum amount of the resource in question that any individual can use at a given time; further, suppose that the resource cannot be stored for the future. Many foods meet these criteria for human societies which lack refrigeration; for example, a large animal carcass. For individual x a certain proportion of his resources at a given time represents a surplus beyond what he can use. Suppose that at the same time individual y lacks sufficient resources; thus the surplus possessed by x would be useful to y. One possibility is that x will share his surplus with y on the condition that y make repayment at some future date when y has a surplus and x is in need. This type of reciprocity should be advantageous to x if y is likely to make repayment and/or is related to x. Let b_1 be the gain in individual fitness to x from the portion of his resources that is immediately useful to him, and b_2 the value in fitness units of the surplus. If x does not exchange, his gain will be simply b_1. If x exchanges with y, his gain in inclusive fitness will be

$$g_x = b_1 + p_y b_2 + (1 - p_y)\, r_{xy}\, b_2 \tag{3.1}$$

where p_y is the probability that y reciprocates. If $p_y = 0$ but $r_{xy} > 0$, then x will benefit from his surplus only indirectly through the fitness increase of y. If x has the choice of initiating an exchange with either of two individuals y and z, it will be to his advantage to choose y over z when

$$p_y b_2 + (1 - p_y)\, r_{xy}\, b_2 > p_z b_2 + (1 - p_z)\, r_{xz}\, b_2 \tag{3.2}$$

If $r_{xy} > r_{xz}$, inequality (3.2) can still hold even if $p_z > p_y$.

This simple model then supports the statement of Trivers that relatedness lowers the threshold (here measured by p) for initiating a reciprocal exchange. The type of behavior modeled here might not strictly be considered altruistic, in that the resources x gives represent a surplus. But individuals are hypothesized to behave altruistically toward kin in the sense that they are more willing to forgive the debts of kin.

Another important conclusion from this model is that one must make certain assumptions before one can make predictions about reciprocity between kin. Here I have assumed that individuals control private shares of the resource in question, that the resource may be temporarily scarce for one individual while another has a surplus, and that an individual for whom a resource is scarce at one time may expect abundance in the future. If any of these assumptions is violated, the model is no longer applicable. Even in such a simple model, in order to make predictions about cooperation between kin, we must pay attention to the nature of the resource involved.

Wrangham (1982) in modeling cooperative interactions among kin makes a crucial distinction. He defines "noninterference" mutualism as resource sharing by two or more individuals which in no way decreases the resource shares of any third party. In "interference" mutualism, on the other hand, two or more individuals share in such a way as to exclude or reduce the resource shares of one or more others. He predicts that in noninterference mutualism, kinship will not make a difference, whereas in cases of interference mutualism more closely related individuals will exclude less closely related individuals. Since, as Malthus first pointed out, resources are always likely to be in limited supply relative to the capacity of organisms to reproduce, interference mutualism is much more likely to occur in nature than is noninterference mutualism. In the rest of this chapter I will model strategies of mutualism among kin when resources are in limited supply.

3.2 "Odd Man Out": A Game Theory Approach

Hamilton (1975) was apparently the first to suggest that the evolution of social interactions, in particular the formation of coalitions, might be modeled as an

n-person game. Here I present a model of a three-person game of coalition formation and show how patterns of relatedness affect the outcome of the game (Hughes, 1986b). The same approach might be extended to games involving larger numbers of players, although the analytical complexity of the game is sufficiently great when there are only three players to make anyone hesitate before tackling larger games.

I first briefly outline the way in which these games are ordinarily set up, with kinship among the players not considered. Then I extend these ideas to an evolutionary game with payoffs ultimately expressed in terms of inclusive fitness. Suppose there is some resource which is to be shared in some way by three individuals. Each individual's share is correlated with his individual fitness. The total value of the resource, in some arbitrarily chosen units, is 1. The shares obtained by each of the three players are elements (b_i) of a 3×1 payoff vector **b**. Any two players are presumed able to form a coalition and overpower the third, thus dictating the payoffs to their own advantage. A payoff vector $\mathbf{b}_w$ is said to "dominate" another $\mathbf{b}_z$ if two or more individuals receive higher payoffs under $\mathbf{b}_w$ than under $\mathbf{b}_z$; that is, for at least two individuals i and j, $b_{wi} > b_{zi}$ and $b_{wj} > b_{zj}$.

The solution set to this game can be expressed as a set of payoff vectors having the following properties:

1. None of the payoff vectors in the set of solutions dominates any other vector in the set.
2. Every payoff vector not in the set is dominated by one in the set.

The solution set to this game is infinite, unless we add some further assumptions. One way to make it finite is to restrict the possible individual payoffs to the values 0, ½, x, and y where x is some fraction such that $0 < x < ½$ and $y = 1 - x$ (thus $½ < y < 1$). For an elementary discussion of games of this type see Harary, Norman, and Cartwright (1965) and Luce and Raiffa (1957).

To consider games of this sort in an evolutionary context, we need to add some further detail not considered in a general treatment of the game. First, I assume the b_i are measured in units of individual fitness. However, if individuals behave so as to maximize inclusive fitness, it is not the elements of **b** that ultimately matter but the elements of some payoff vector **g** in inclusive fitness units. The relationship between **g** and **b** is

$$\mathbf{g} = \mathbf{Rb} \qquad (3.3)$$

where **R** is the matrix (3×3 in this case) of coefficients of relatedness r_{ij} (the relatedness of individual j to individual i) (Hughes, 1983). (See Appendix A for a brief summary of matrix algebra.) Note that if all off-diagonal elements of **R** are identical ($r_{ij} = r_{ji} = r$ for all i and j), then $\mathbf{g} = c\mathbf{b}$ where c is a scalar constant (equal in our three-person case to $1 + 2r$). In general, when considering this game in an evolutionary context, we must look for a solution set by comparing values of **g** not of **b**; however, since **g** is a fixed linear function of **b** for a given group, we can express the solution set for a given group (with a given **R**) in terms of **b**. And when all off-diagonal elements of **R** are the same, we need not consider the g_i at all, since these are directly proportional to the b_i.

A second factor that needs to be considered is the relationship between the concept of the solution set, as defined for our game, and the concept of an "evolutionarily stable strategy" (ESS) (Maynard Smith, 1982). An ESS is a strategy which, when it is widespread in a population, will defeat any "mutant" strategy that might invade. The members of the solution set as defined above fit this definition in that at least one vector in the solution set dominates any vector outside the set; thus two out of three individuals will do better by pursuing a strategy described by a member of the solution set than by pursuing any other strategy.

A straightforward way to represent solutions to this sort of game is by a digraph with the points or vertices representing possible **b** vectors (of which there are nine, given our restrictions on the values of the b_i). An arrow from point i to point j indicates that the vector represented by point i dominates the vector represented by point j. Thus the solution set will be a 1-basis for the digraph, that is, a set of points such that

> 1. Every point of the digraph is reachable (by movement only in the direction in which the arrows point) in no more than one step from at least one point in the set.
>
> 2. No point within the set is reachable from any other point in the set in only one step.

See Harary et al. (1965) for further details.

When our three-person game is considered without reference to inclusive fitness (with reference to **b** only), the solution set is as shown in Figure 3.1. The solution set consists of all cases in which two individuals split the resource equally between themselves and exclude the third. The solution set will be the same even if "dominance" relations among vectors are decided on the basis of **g** rather than **b** whenever either (1) the three individuals are unrelated (**R** = **I**, an identity matrix), or (2) the off-diagonal elements of **R** are all equal. In either of these cases, considering inclusive rather than individual fitness has no effect on the solution set.

On the other hand, relatedness does affect the solution set when the off-diagonal elements of **R** are not all equal. Consider the example of three non-inbred diploid players related in the following way: two are full sibs to each other ($r = 0.5$), while the third is a half-sib to the other two ($r = 0.25$). Again, the b_i must be only 0, ½, x, or y. But let us consider "dominance" of one vector over another in terms of inclusive fitness **g** rather than individual fitness **b**. For **b** vectors including x and y, I interpret dominance at the level of **g** as follows. If vector $\mathbf{b}_w$ includes x and y but $\mathbf{b}_z$ does not, $\mathbf{b}_w$ will be said to dominate $\mathbf{b}_z$ when there are values of x and y which, when appropriately substituted into $\mathbf{b}_w$ cause, for at least two individuals i and j, $g_{wi} > g_{zi}$ and $g_{wj} > g_{zj}$. If both $\mathbf{b}_w$ and $\mathbf{b}_z$ include x and y, $\mathbf{b}_w$ will be said to dominate $\mathbf{b}_z$ whenever there exist values of x and y such that, if these values are appropriately substituted into $\mathbf{b}_w$, then for at least two

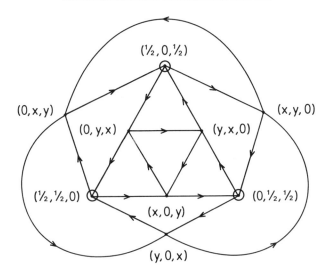

FIGURE 3.1. Digraph showing the relationship among payoff vectors in a three-person game of "odd man out" when scoring is based on individual fitness payoffs (the elements of the payoff vectors) or all individuals are equally related to one another. One payoff vector dominates another if an arrow is drawn from the point corresponding to the former to the point corresponding to the latter. The solution set consists of the vectors corresponding to the circled points. (From Hughes, 1986b.)

individuals i and j, $g_{wi} > g_{zi}$ and $g_{wj} > g_{zj}$ for *all* values of x and y that might be substituted into $\mathbf{b}_z$.

Now the solution set is as in Figure 3.2. (This figure is incorrectly drawn in Hughes, 1986b.) It contains three elements. These are the three vectors in which the two full sibs split the resources either equally or unequally and nothing is given to their half-sib. The same solution set will obtain if we change $\mathbf{R}$ such that there are two sibs and a third individual who is a first cousin ($r = 0.125$) to them or if we change $\mathbf{R}$ such that there are two sibs and a third individual who is unrelated to them.

To those familiar with previous applications of game theory to behavioral strategies (Maynard Smith, 1982), the concept of a solution set rather than a single ESS may be first seem difficult to interpret. However, I believe there are some commonsense ways of interpreting a solution set that shed considerable light on the evolution of behavior. We might say, for instance, that the solution set indicates a domain within which observed behavior is predicted to fall if the assumptions of the game are met. Which actual vector from the solution set will be observed in any particular case will be decided by factors extrinsic to the game itself.

For example, it is predicted that when all individuals are either unrelated or equally related, the solution set will consist of all three possible two-member coalitions. If we imagine a situation where all individuals are equal in competitive ability (and thus no coalition is inherently more powerful than any other)

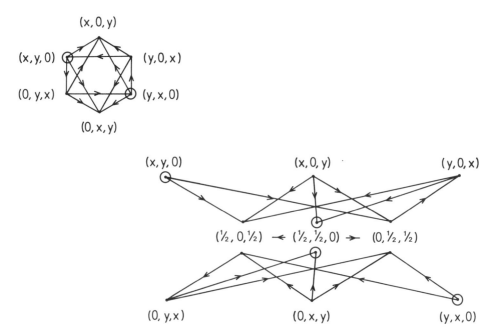

FIGURE 3.2. Digraph showing the relationship among payoff vectors in a game of "odd man out" played by two full sibs and a half-sib. The payoff vectors are expressed in units of individual fitness, but scoring is based on inclusive fitness. Though two separate figures are drawn for ease of presentation, these represent a single digraph. The solution set consists of the vectors corresponding to the circled points. (Redrawn from Hughes, 1986b.)

and the game is replayed many times, we might expect the net payoff after numerous iterations to yield an equal share to each player. That is, the net payoff might be expected to be the mean of the three vectors in the solution set. It is important to emphasize that this expectation is in no sense a mathematical solution to the game but simply a prediction regarding what might actually happen in an empirical context where such a game is repeatedly played. On the other hand, if one individual is inferior to the other two in competitive ability, we might expect to see the payoff vector which excludes the weaker individual to occur every time the game is repeated.

In cases where two individuals are more closely related to each other than either is to a third, we should expect the individual that is least related to the others to be excluded in every case. Which of the three vectors in the solution set would be observed in practice would again depend on factors extrinsic to the game. Consider the case where the players are two full sibs and one half-sib. If the two full sibs are equal in competitive ability and the game is repeated many times, we might expect that on the average their net gain will be about equal; that is, the vector of relative net gains will be the mean of the three vectors in the solution set. But if there is a difference between the two in competitive ability, we might expect the larger share y to go consistently to the stronger of the two siblings.

This very simple model of a three-person game supports the prediction that kinship will affect resource sharing in a system of interference mutualism (Wrangham, 1982). It predicts that, when resources are in limited supply, close kin will form coalitions and exclude less closely related individuals.

Yet even in such a simple model there is surprising indeterminacy. Exact predictions of individual shares cannot be made, but only a rather broad set of solutions can be constructed. The next section introduces a more flexible model that makes explicit predictions regarding resource-share vectors and shows how these depend on the relationship between an individual's resource share and fitness.

3.3 Inclusive Fitness Maximization

In this section I model resource sharing among kin on the assumption that resources are in limited supply. The model is expressed in terms of a generalization of kin selection theory using matrix algebra (Hughes, 1983, 1984). (See Appendix A for a brief summary of the principles of matrix algebra.) Given specific assumptions regarding limits on resources, I show how it is possible to predict optimal strategies of resource sharing. In Section 3.8 I consider some ways in which this model can be related to classical theory of quantitative genetics.

Let there be a group of n interrelated individuals. These individuals may or may not reside together, and the group may or may not contain all individuals residing in any given area. All that is important is that they constitute a distinct "group" for some purpose or from some point of view. As in the last section, $\mathbf{R}$ is defined as the $n \times n$ matrix of coefficients of relatedness, r_{ij} [equation (2.2)] among the n individuals. When there is no inbreeding and individuals are diploid, $\mathbf{R}$ will be a symmetric matrix: $r_{ij} = r_{ji}$ for all $i \neq j$. When males are haploid and females are diploid (as in the Hymenoptera and a few other insects), $\mathbf{R}$ will not in general be symmetric. In diploid species, like humans, inbreeding will also render $\mathbf{R}$ asymmetric.

It might be useful at this point to define a similar matrix $\mathbf{R}_w$, the matrix of Wright's correlation coefficients of relatedness [as defined by (2.7)]. For diploids with no inbreeding $\mathbf{R} = \mathbf{R}_w$. If there is inbreeding, $\mathbf{R}_w$ will be symmetric even when $\mathbf{R}$ is not.

Let $\mathbf{a}$ be a vector $(n \times 1)$ of shares in some resource correlated with fitness apportioned to group members as a result of some behavioral act or interaction taking place within the group. A typical element of this vector, denoted a_i, represents the share of this resource obtained by the ith individual. I assume that the resource is in limited supply. Thus, in whatever units the resource is measured, the units can be reexpressed such that

$$\sum_{i=1}^{n} a_i = 1 \tag{3.4}$$

I define a second vector $\mathbf{b}$ $(n \times 1)$ of benefits in units of potential individual fitness. Each element of $\mathbf{b}$, b_i, represents the potential increase in individual fitness that can accrue to individual i as a result of the resource share a_i. I further assume that a particular relationship holds between a_i and b_i:

$$b_i = a_i^{1/2} \tag{3.5}$$

Thus

$$\Sigma b_i^2 = 1 \tag{3.6}$$

or, in matrix terminology

$$\mathbf{b'b} = 1 \tag{3.7}$$

Thus assumption (3.4) and (3.5) are equivalent to the assumption that $\mathbf{b}$ is a vector of unit length. For further discussion of these assumptions, see Section 3.4 below.

The units in which the b_i are expressed are said to be units of potential individual fitness. By this I mean that a given resource share a_i is assumed to be capable of causing a given increase in individual fitness b_i whenever the individual recipient is maximally able to actualize this potential increase in individual fitness. In fact, not all individuals are maximally able to translate potential fitness into actual fitness. To take an obvious example, a postreproductive human female is not able to translate any resource given her into any further reproductive output. In an outbred population, a given individual's 80-year-old grandmother and 18-year-old niece are equally related to him ($r = 0.25$), but if he wants to dispense resources to one or the other in such a way as to increase his inclusive fitness (by production of offspring sharing genes with him), he would do better to give the resources to his niece than to his grandmother.

Differences in the ability of individuals to realize potential individual fitness can be expressed quantitatively. Let $\mathbf{V}$ be a diagonal matrix (one whose entries are all zero, except for those on the diagonal) of dimensions $n \times n$. A typical diagonal entry of $\mathbf{V}$, v_j, represents the reproductive potential of the jth individual. Reproductive potential ($0 \le v_j \le 1$) is a measure of the individual's ability to convert the potential individual fitness represented by b_j into actual individual fitness (i.e., actual offspring). In a long-lived species like humans, age will be the major factor affecting v_j; for example, for females past reproductive age, $v_j = 0$.

As in (3.3) above, let $\mathbf{g}$ represent a vector of changes in inclusive fitness due to the resource apportionment described by $\mathbf{a}$. Taking $\mathbf{V}$ into account,

$$\mathbf{g} = \mathbf{RVb} \tag{3.8}$$

If all individuals in the group are of equal reproductive potential, (3.8) reduces to (3.3) since $\mathbf{V} = \mathbf{I}$ (an identity matrix). For purposes of exposition, it is convenient to assume that $\mathbf{V} = \mathbf{I}$; I will make this assumption henceforth in this chapter. In empirical cases, it may sometimes be reasonable to assume that $\mathbf{V} \approx \mathbf{I}$. Consider, for example, the following situations. (1) The individuals in the group described by $\mathbf{R}$ may all be of roughly equal age, for example, if they are all of the same generation. (2) The vectors $\mathbf{a}$ and $\mathbf{b}$ may not describe a single act of apportionment of benefits but the net result of a number of acts of apportionment of benefits over the lives of all n individuals; thus all individuals will have passed through all stages of reproductive potential in the life cycle. (3) The resources described by **a** may be such that they continue to yield benefits over the entire reproductive life, for example, if the benefits represent shares of land in a peasant economy.

Whenever, in an empirical case, one requires an estimate of **V**, it may be obtained by means of standard tables or curves of reproductive value (e.g., Keyfitz, 1968). Reproductive value is sex-specific, so there are separate curves for each sex. Reproductive value for a given age class of a given sex (or a sex–age class) represents the expected future contribution of offspring to the population by an individual of that age class and sex. If reproductive values are scaled such that the highest reproductive value is 1, then reproductive value can be used as a first approximation for the reproductive potential v_j. When appropriately scaled, the reproductive value is the mean reproductive potential of all individuals of a given sex–age class. The reproductive potential, on the other hand, is the property of an individual, not a sex–age class. If we have some information suggesting that a particular individual is likely to deviate from the mean of his or her sex–age class, we may be able to incorporate that information in an estimate of the individual's reproductive potential. For example, if we know that a given individual is sterile, we know that $v_j = 0$ even if the individual is of reproductive age.

Given assumptions (3.4) and (3.5), one can ask what apportionment of benefits among group members will maximize the inclusive fitness of a particular individual i. In other words, what is the optimal strategy of nepotism given these assumptions? When $\mathbf{V} = \mathbf{I}$, the solution vector $\mathbf{b}_{si}$ will be found by solving the matrix equation

$$(\mathbf{r}_i \mathbf{r}_i' = \lambda \mathbf{I})\mathbf{b}_{si} = 0 \tag{3.9}$$

subject to the constraint $\mathbf{b}_{si}'\, \mathbf{b}_{si} = 1$. In (3.9) $\mathbf{r}_i$ is the vector of relatedness r_{ij} of all n group members to individual i; that is, $\mathbf{r}_i$ is the ith column vector of $\mathbf{R}'$. From $\mathbf{b}_{si}$, the corresponding vector of actual resource shares $\mathbf{a}_{si}$ is readily computed. If $\mathbf{V} \neq \mathbf{I}$, we need instead to solve

$$[(\mathbf{V}\mathbf{r}_i)\,(\mathbf{V}\mathbf{r}_i)' - \lambda \mathbf{I}]\, \mathbf{b}_{si} = 0 \tag{3.10}$$

subject to the same constrain as above.

When $\mathbf{V} = \mathbf{I}$, the elements of $\mathbf{b}_{si}$, the b_{sji}, are proportional to the corresponding elements of $\mathbf{r}_i$. Each element can be computed by the formula

$$b_{sji} = r_{ij} \sqrt{\frac{1}{\sum_{i=1}^{n} r_{ij}^2}} \tag{3.11}$$

The proof of (3.11) is straightforward. Equation (3.9) can be rewritten as a series of n equations, with the rows and columns arranged such that $i = 1$, as follows:

$$b_{s11} (1 - \lambda) + b_{s12}r_{12} + b_{s13}r_{13} + \cdots + b_{s1n}r_{1n} = 0$$
$$b_{s11}r_{12} + b_{s12} (r_{12}^2 - \lambda) + b_{s13}r_{12}r_{13} + \cdots + b_{s1n}r_{12}r_{1n} = 0 \tag{3.12}$$
$$b_{s1n}r_{1n} + b_{s12}r_{12}r_{1n} + b_{s13}r_{13}r_{1n} + \cdots + b_{s1n} (r_{1n}^2 - \lambda) = 0$$

Take any equation from this series other than the first; say we choose the kth equation. Then multiply the first equation by r_{1k} and subtract the kth equation from the first. The result is

$$b_{s1k} = r_{1k}b_{s11} \qquad (3.13)$$

If this is true for all $k \neq 1$, and $\mathbf{b}_{si}'\mathbf{b}_{si} = 1$, then

$$b_{s11}^2 (1 + r_{12}^2 + r_{13}^2 + \cdots + r_{1n}^2) = 1 \qquad (3.14)$$

which is easily rearranged to form (3.11). Henceforth, when I wish to refer to the constant of proportionality in (3.11) which relates b_{sji} to r_{ij}, I shall call it k_i. That is,

$$b_{sji} = k_i r_{ij} \qquad (3.15)$$

Thus $\mathbf{b}_{si}$ represents $\mathbf{r}_i$ standardized to unit length and k_i is the constant of proportionality.

3.4 Individual Fitness and Resource Share

Assumptions (3.4) and (3.5) have convenient mathematical properties. They also may be at least approximately valid in certain real cases; furthermore, they illustrate a theoretical point of general interest. Assumption (3.5) implies that the potential fitness increment b_i accruing to an individual as a result of obtaining a particular resource share a_i is an increasing function of the quantity of resources obtained but that fitness increment increases with resource share at a less than linear rate. The relationship assumed to hold between resource share and fitness increment is thus what is called (somewhat misleadingly) a negatively allometric relationship, that is, an exponential relationship where the exponent is less than 1, in this case being equal to ½ (Figure 3.3).

The predicted optimal strategy for an allometric exponent not equal to ½ but greater than 0 and less than 1 is closely analogous to the solution to (3.9). In general, if we suppose

$$b_i = a_i^{1/x} \qquad (x > 1) \qquad (3.16)$$

and (3.4) holds, then

$$\Sigma b_i^x = 1 \qquad (3.17)$$

By reasoning like that of (3.11) to (3.15), a typical element of $\mathbf{b}_{si}$ will be given by

$$b_{sji} = (r_{ij})^{1/x-1} \sqrt[x]{\frac{1}{\Sigma r_{ij}^{x/(x-1)}}} \qquad (3.18)$$

This is the general solution for any negatively allometric relationship; (3.11) is a special case of (3.18). Note that as $1/x$ becomes smaller, the shares given to kin become relatively larger. This is intuitively reasonable because, the smaller $1/x$ is, the less individual fitness increases as a function of resource share (by 3.16). Conversely, for $j \neq i$

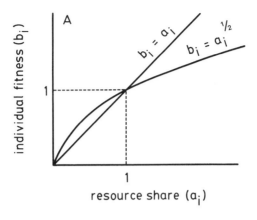

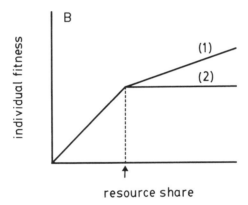

FIGURE 3.3. (A) Hypothetical relationship between individual fitness (b_i) and an individual's resource share (a_i), $b_i = a_i^{1/2}$. The line $b_i = a_i$ is added for comparison. (B) Plausible relationships between individual fitness and resource shares which are approximately negatively allometric. Increase is at a linear rate up to some maximum usable share (arrow). Thereafter, increase is at a lower rate (1) or is not possible (2). (From Hughes, 1986b.)

$$\lim_{x \to 1} (b_{sji}) = 0 \qquad (3.19)$$

In many real cases, it is plausible to suppose that the relationship between resource share and fitness is at least approximately a negatively allometric one. In some cases, up to a certain point fitness increases with resource share at a roughly linear rate. Beyond this point, either (1) the slope of the line relating fitness to resource share drops sharply; or (2) no further increases in fitness are possible no matter how much the individual's resource share increases. These two possibilities are illustrated in Figure 3.3. As an example, consider the utilization of a large animal carcass by members of a human society lacking refrigeration or other means of preserving meat. It is reasonable to assume that meat consumed contributes to one's fitness, but no single individual can consume all of the meat on a large carcass before it decomposes. Thus any surplus beyond what a single individual can consume will be wasted if it is not shared. In other cases, certain costs associated with reproduction may increase at a positively allometric rate with the number of offspring produced, that is, at a greater than linear rate. For example, in many animal species giving parental care and probably in many human societies, the costs of obtaining resources for a brood or family of young may be a positively allometric function of the number of young. Even if an individual parent obtains an increment in one resource that would permit an increased reproductive output, the parent may be unable to obtain any increase in numbers of offspring actually raised (i.e., actual fitness) because costs of obtaining some other needed resource escalate (see Figure 3.4). Again, the result would be a negatively allometric relationship between an individual's share in the former resource and the number of offspring actually reared (see Figure 3.4).

Such considerations suggest that the assumption of a negatively allometric relationship between individual fitness and resource share may be reasonable in some cases. Further, when $\mathbf{V} = \mathbf{I}$, the model developed in the last section predicts that it will never be advantageous for an individual to share resources correlated with fitness even with close kin unless this relationship is negatively allometric. If $v_j = 1$ and the relationship between b_i and a_i is either linear or

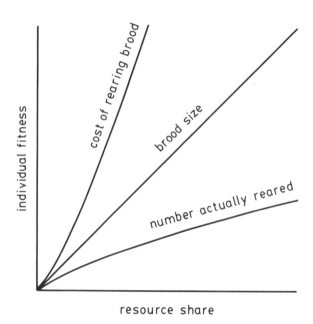

FIGURE 3.4. Hypothetical relationship between individual resource share and brood size and the cost of rearing a brood (in the same units). With escalating costs, as illustrated, and a linear relationship between resource share and brood size, the net result can be a negatively allometric relationship between resource share and the number of young actually reared. (From Hughes, 1986b.)

positively allometric, individual j will maximize his inclusive fitness by keeping all of the resource for himself and not sharing it. Note that when $\Sigma b_i = 1$, the relationship between a_i and b_i is linear (by 3.4). Thus, although it may seem intuitively sensible to assume $\Sigma b_i = 1$, in fact when this is true *no sharing of resources with kin is predicted* (assuming $\mathbf{V} = \mathbf{I}$). Together (3.16) and (3.19) constitute a statement of the conditions for nepotistic sharing which may prove of heuristic value in the study of the evolution of nepotistic behavior equal to the value of Hamilton's rule (2.1) in the study of the evolution of altruism.

One way to interpret $\mathbf{b}_{si}$ is to say that $\mathbf{b}_{si}$ represents an axis of nepotistic bias in n-dimensional space. That is, as a surplus of resources becomes available to i beyond what he can himself use he will give to the other individual j with the highest r_{ij}, then to the individual with the next highest r_{ij}, and so on. The relative magnitude of the elements corresponding to each of the n individuals thus represents the relative magnitude of i's bias toward each individual and the extent to which i will channel surplus resources toward each individual.

When $\mathbf{V} \neq \mathbf{I}$, sharing of resources with kin may occur even when the relationship between a_i and b_i is linear or positively allometric. For example, when $v_i = 0$, individual i is predicted to share with kin even when the relationship between a_i and b_i is linear or positively allometric. However, under these circumstances, i should give all resources to the individual with the highest $r_{ij}v_j$. On the other hand, the type of social group characteristic of humans and some other mammals—a social group involving several reproductive individuals ($\mathbf{V} \approx \mathbf{I}$) which assist each other in various ways—should not be found unless the relationship between resource share and individual fitness is negatively allometric.

There are certain mammalian social groups in which only one dominant pair breed, but other adults assist them as nonbreeding "helpers" (e.g., Cebul and Epple, 1984; Kleiman, 1977; Rood, 1978). A helper is often close kin to the breeding pair, such as a sibling of one pair member or an older offspring; but far from helping their kin to breed, the dominants actively prevent breeding attempts by subordinate helpers. In terms of the model presented here, the role of breeding adult in such a social group can be viewed as a "resource." Perhaps the territory in which the group lives can support only as many offspring as a single female can produce. For a discussion of this possibility and some evidence, see Kleiman (1977). If this assumption is true, the relationship between individual fitness and share of the resource (i.e., the position of dominant) is linear. Thus no sharing with kin is predicted.

Examples of fratricidal conflict among humans (see Section 3.1 above) may result from analogous situations, in that the resources over which conflict occurs bear a similar relation to fitness. In humans, of course, dominant individuals lack the pheromonal means of suppressing reproduction in subordinate siblings which are believed to occur in other mammalian species (e.g., Cebul and Epple, 1984). However, there are interesting parallels. In Medieval European society, for instance, the institutions of primogeniture and a celibate priesthood (the destiny of many a younger son) seem to have become established around the same time (Goody, 1983).

3.5 An Optimal Compromise

In this section I consider the following problem. Resources are limited in the way described by (3.4) and (3.5). In a group of n individuals, each has his preferred distribution of resources, summarized by $\mathbf{a}_{si}$ and $\mathbf{b}_{si}$, which will maximize his inclusive fitness. Assume, however, that (1) no individual is able to impose his preferred resource distribution on the other, and (2) the cost of continued fighting among group members is prohibitive for all. The group then is ready for some sort of compromise. How can we predict the compromise distribution of resources that will occur under these circumstances?

I consider one plausible candidate for a compromise resource distribution. Call the compromise vector of resource shares $\mathbf{a}_m$ and the corresponding vector of fitness increments $\mathbf{b}_m$, with respective typical elements a_{mi} and b_{mi}. Let $\mathbf{b}_m$ be the vector of appropriate length that is as close as possible to all the $\mathbf{b}_{si}$; that is, choose $\mathbf{b}_m$ such that the sum of squared distances from $\mathbf{b}_m$ to all n $\mathbf{b}_{si}$ is minimized. For any given individual i, the squared distance is

$$k_i^2 \sum_{j=1}^{n} (r_{ij}^2 - \overline{r_{.j}^2})^2 - \left[\sum_{j=1}^{n} b_{mj} (r_{ij} - \overline{r_{.j}}) \right]^2$$

where $\overline{r_{.j}^2}$ is the mean of the r_{ij}^2; $\overline{r_{.j}}$ is the mean of the r_{ij}; b_{mj} is the payoff under $\mathbf{b}_m$ to individual j; and k_i is as in (3.15). To minimize the sum of n terms of the preceding form, we must maximize

$$\sum_{i=1}^{n} \sum_{j=1}^{n} b_{mj}^2 r_{ij}^2$$

which will be maximized if $\mathbf{b}_m$ is chosen to be the solution to the matrix equation

$$(\mathbf{R}'\mathbf{R} - \lambda\mathbf{I}) \, \mathbf{b}_m = 0 \tag{3.20}$$

subject to the constraint that $\mathbf{b}_m$ is of unit length. Thus $\mathbf{b}_m$ will be the eigenvector corresponding to the largest eigenvalue of $\mathbf{R}'\mathbf{R}$. This eigenvector may also be termed the first characteristic vector of $\mathbf{R}'\mathbf{R}$ or the first principal component of $\mathbf{R}'\mathbf{R}$ (or PC1 of $\mathbf{R}'\mathbf{R}$). When $\mathbf{R}$ is a symmetric matrix (i.e., when $r_{ij} = r_{ji}$ for all $i \neq j$), the eigenvector corresponding to the largest eigenvalue of $\mathbf{R}'\mathbf{R}$ will be equivalent to the eigenvector corresponding to the largest eigenvalue of $\mathbf{R}$ (PC1 of $\mathbf{R}$).

One might also derive $\mathbf{b}_m$ in the following alternative way. The vector of inclusive fitnesses of all group members, $\mathbf{g}_m$, represents a point in n-dimensional space. Let us choose $\mathbf{b}_m$ in such a way as to maximize the distance of $\mathbf{g}_m$ from the origin. This distance is given by $\mathbf{g}_m'\mathbf{g}_m$ or $(\mathbf{R}\mathbf{b}_m)'(\mathbf{R}\mathbf{b}_m)$. The value of $\mathbf{b}_m$ which maximizes this distance is given by the solution to (3.20).

When $\mathbf{V} \neq \mathbf{I}$, the optimal compromise strategy may be derived in parallel fashion to the solution to the matrix equation

$$[(\mathbf{RV})'(\mathbf{RV}) - \lambda\mathbf{I}] \, \mathbf{b}_m = 0 \tag{3.21}$$

That is, $\mathbf{b}_m$ is the eigenvector corresponding to the largest eigenvalue of $(\mathbf{RV})'$ $(\mathbf{RV})$.

3.6 Concentration of Relatedness

Patterns of relatedness within a group of interrelated individuals may take a number of forms. All may be equally related to one another (e.g., when all are full sibs); for such groups, all off-diagonal values of $\mathbf{R}$ will be equal. On the other hand, in other groups, all off-diagonal values of $\mathbf{R}$ may not be equal. The eigenvalues of $\mathbf{R}$ provide a way of quantifying the degree to which its off-diagonal values are unequal, that is, the degree to which relatedness is concentrated on one or more members of the group. Consider first the case where $\mathbf{R}$ is a symmetric matrix, as it will be when all individuals are diploid and non-inbred. Define

$$r^* = \frac{\lambda_1 - 1}{n - 1} \tag{3.22}$$

where λ_1 is the largest eigenvalue of $\mathbf{R}$. The quantity r^* ranges from 0 to 1, as does r. Let $\bar{r}$ be defined as the mean of the $n(n - 1)$ off-diagonal values of $\mathbf{R}$, that is, the average relatedness within the group. When $r^* = \bar{r}$, all individuals will be equally related to one another and all off-diagonal values of $\mathbf{R}$ will be equal (Hughes, 1984). When $r^* > \bar{r}$, relatedness is concentrated on one or more individuals. The magnitude of r^* relative to $\bar{r}$ indicates the degree to which relatedness is concentrated; in other words, this indicates the degree to which the off-diagonal values of $\mathbf{R}$ depart from uniformity.

The relative magnitude of elements of PC1 of $\mathbf{R}$ provide additional information about the concentration of relatedness. If the element of PC1 of $\mathbf{R}$ corresponding to some individual i is larger than the elements corresponding to other individuals, then relatedness within the group is concentrated on individual i. In other words, $\bar{r}_{i\cdot}$ (the average relatedness of all individuals to i) and $\bar{r}_{\cdot i}$ (the average relatedness of i to all individuals) are higher for i than for the average group member. Thus the elements of PC1 of $\mathbf{R}$ will be closely correlated with those of $\bar{r}_{i\cdot}$ (the vector of row means of $\mathbf{R}$).

Since algorithms for computing eigenvalues of nonsymmetric matrices are seldom available, it is worthwhile to have a formula for computing r^* in the general case, whether or not $\mathbf{R}$ is symmetric. In general,

$$r^* = \frac{\sqrt{\lambda_1'} - 1}{n - 1} \tag{3.23}$$

where λ_1' is the largest eigenvalue of $\mathbf{R}'\mathbf{R}$. Note that $\mathbf{R}'\mathbf{R}$ will be symmetric even when $\mathbf{R}$ is not. When $\mathbf{R}$ is symmetric, (3.23) is equivalent to (3.22). In the general case, the relative magnitude of the elements of PC1 of $\mathbf{R}'\mathbf{R}$ indicate the degree to which relatedness is concentrated on particular individuals. Again when $\mathbf{R}$ is symmetric, the elements of PC1 of $\mathbf{R}'\mathbf{R}$ will be identical to those of $\mathbf{R}$; all other eigenvectors of $\mathbf{R}$ and $\mathbf{R}'\mathbf{R}$ will also be identical when $\mathbf{R}$ is symmetric.

When $\mathbf{V} \neq \mathbf{I}$, it may similarly be useful to measure the degree to which the off-diagonal elements of $(\mathbf{RV})'(\mathbf{RV})$ are unequal. To do this, one can compute

$$r_v^* = \frac{\sqrt{\lambda_{v1}'} - 1}{n - 1} \tag{3.24}$$

where λ'_{v1} is the largest eigenvalue of $(\mathbf{RV})'(\mathbf{RV})$. This quantity can be compared with $\bar{r}_v$, the mean of the off-diagonal values of $\mathbf{RV}$.

Some simple examples will illustrate what r^* and the elements of PC1 of $\mathbf{R'R}$ can tell us about concentration of relatedness. First consider the hypothetical group where genealogical connections are illustrated as in Figure 3.5. Anthropologists may recognize a certain similarity between this hypothetical group and the celebrated "kinship atom" of Lévi-Strauss (1963). With individuals listed in the order M1, F2, M3, M4, F5, for this group

$$\mathbf{R} = \begin{bmatrix} 1 & 0.5 & 0 & 0.25 & 0.25 \\ 0.5 & 1 & 0 & 0.5 & 0.5 \\ 0 & 0 & 1 & 0.5 & 0.5 \\ 0.25 & 0.5 & 0.5 & 1 & 0.5 \\ 0.25 & 0.5 & 0.5 & 0.5 & 1 \end{bmatrix} \qquad (3.25)$$

Here $\bar{r} = 0.35$ and $r^* = 0.365$; thus relatedness is concentrated only slightly ($r^*/\bar{r} = 1.04$). Since $\mathbf{R}$ is symmetric, we can compute eigenvectors or PCs from $\mathbf{R}$ itself. Here PC1 of $\mathbf{R}$ is (0.339, 0.471, 0.355, 0.518, 0.518) and $\bar{r}_{.1}$ is (0.4, 0.5, 0.4, 0.55, 0.55). Relatedness is concentrated on M4 and F5 and, to a slightly lesser extent, on their mother F2. This makes intuitive sense, since all group members are related to M4 and F5, and since F2 provides the link connecting them all to her children.

Figure 3.6 illustrates a similar hypothetical group. However, in this case, M1 and F2 are only half-siblings, as are M4 and F5. The genealogy in Figure 3.6 shows what might happen to Lévi-Strauss's "kinship atom" in a society in which confidence of paternity is low or the rate of divorce is high. With individuals listed in the same order as in (3.25), we now have

$$\mathbf{R} = \begin{bmatrix} 1 & 0.25 & 0 & 0.125 & 0.125 \\ 0.25 & 1 & 0 & 0.5 & 0.5 \\ 0 & 0 & 1 & 0 & 0.5 \\ 0.125 & 0.5 & 0 & 1 & 0.25 \\ 0.125 & 0.5 & 0.5 & 0.25 & 1 \end{bmatrix} \qquad (3.26)$$

So much for the supposed universality of the "kinship atom"! (Lévi-Strauss might counter that he never was talking about any real set of people but about

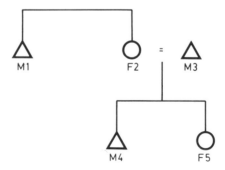

FIGURE 3.5. Example of a group of interrelated individuals.

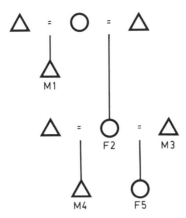

FIGURE 3.6. A group of individuals with similar social relationships to those in Figure 3.5 but with different biological relationships because of polyandry or low paternity confidence.

some sort of Platonic essence of kinship. If so, we can part company with him, for such essences have no role in science. The groups discussed in this section are intended to be *simulations* of real groups, not any sort of essence or abstractions.) Now average relatedness is much lower, $\bar{r} = 0.225$; but the concentration of relatedness is higher, with $r^* = 0.253$ and $r^*/\bar{r} = 1.12$. Relatedness is concentrated on F2 and, to a slightly lesser degree, F5; PC1 of $\mathbf{R}$ is (0.267, 0.570, 0.279, 0.454, 0.565). Now F5 is the only individual to whom all are related, but some of these ties are more distant than ties to F2. The fact that there is a greater variance in the elements of PC1 of $\mathbf{R}$ from Figure 3.6 than in the elements of PC1 of $\mathbf{R}$ from Figure 3.5 is another indicator of greater concentration of relatedness in the former group.

Patterns of concentration of relatedness have a particular relevance to the model of optimal compromise developed in the previous section. When $\mathbf{V} = \mathbf{I}$, the model predicts that the optimal compromise described by $\mathbf{a}_m$ and $\mathbf{b}_m$ will allocate resources according to the relative magnitude of the elements (or "weights" as they are sometimes called) of PC1 of $\mathbf{R}'\mathbf{R}$. Thus if $r^* = \bar{r}$, the optimal compromise will result in an egalitarian distribution of resources; that is, the b_{mi} and a_{mi} will be identical for all i. But if $r^* > \bar{r}$, the optimal compromise will result in a nonegalitarian distribution of resources. Resources will be given disproportionately to individuals on whom relatedness is concentrated.

This prediction is broadly consistent with the results of the game theory model developed in Section 3.2. In that model, when all three individuals playing the game are equally related to one another (and thus $r^* = \bar{r}$), the solution set is identical to that found when all three players are unrelated ($\mathbf{R} = \mathbf{I}$). In these cases, the solution set shows no bias against any particular individual. However, when two individuals are more closely related to each other than to the third, relatedness is concentrated on these two. In this case, the solution set excludes the less related individual. Similarly, in the model of Section 3.5, the optimal compromise leads to reduced resource shares for individuals less closely related to other group members because more closely related individuals have a larger overlap in common interest in terms of inclusive fitness.

3.7 Differences in Competitive Ability

The optimal compromise modeled in Section 3.5 is based on the assumption that no individual is able to impose his will on the others; that is, no individual i is able to bias the distribution of resources away from $\mathbf{a}_m$ toward $\mathbf{a}_{si}$. All individuals are thus assumed to be equal with respect to competitive ability. In reality, this is seldom likely to be the case. Individuals can be expected to differ with respect to competitive ability. Furthermore, a group of kin may be divisible into two or more subgroups such that relatedness within these subgroups is higher than relatedness between them. Jockeying for power among such subgroups may lead to a resource distribution that is biased away from $\mathbf{a}_m$ toward the advantage of the more powerful subgroup.

Here I consider a simple way of incorporating individual differences in competitive ability into the model of Section 3.5. Let $\mathbf{T}$ be an $n \times n$ transformation matrix such that all column sums of $\mathbf{T}$ be equal to 1. Its elements, the t_{ij}, measure coercion of j by i; t_{ij} represents the portion of a_{mj} (j's ideal share) which actually goes to i as a result of coercion. The actual payoff vector in resource units is given by

$$\mathbf{a}_t = \mathbf{T}\mathbf{a}_m \tag{3.27}$$

In individual fitness units, the actual payoff vector is

$$\mathbf{b}_t = \mathbf{T}^{1/2}\mathbf{b}_m \tag{3.28}$$

Let f_i be the ith individual's competitive ability. I assume that for $i \neq j$,

$$t_{ij} = \phi(f_i - f_j) \tag{3.29}$$

That is, t_{ij} is a function of the difference between the two individuals in competitive ability. When $r^* > \bar{r}$, var($\mathbf{a}_t$), the variance in the elements of $\mathbf{a}_t$, will have two components. Define $\mathbf{X} = \mathbf{I} - \mathbf{T}$. Then

$$\text{var}(\mathbf{a}_t) = \text{var}(\mathbf{a}_m) - \text{var}(\mathbf{X}\mathbf{a}_m) \tag{3.30}$$

The vector $-\mathbf{X}\mathbf{a}_m$ represents each individual's losses or gains in comparison to $\mathbf{a}_m$ due to differences in competitive ability. When competitive abilities are all equal, the right-hand term in (3.30) will be zero. On the other hand, when $r^* = \bar{r}$, the left-hand term in (3.30) will be zero. Thus when $r^* = \bar{r}$, all variance in the predicted payoff vector $\mathbf{a}_t$ will be due to differences in competitive ability; but when $r^* > \bar{r}$, there will be a component in the variance of $\mathbf{a}_t$ due to differences in degree of relatedness.

In practice, one might estimate the deviations from $\mathbf{a}_m$ due to differences in competitive ability by a multiple regression approach in which data on resource shares are obtained for a number of replicate groups all with the same **R** and fitted to the model

$$a_{ti} = \beta_0 + \beta_1 (a_{mi}) + \beta_2 (f_i - \bar{f}.) + \epsilon \qquad (3.31)$$

where $\bar{f}.$ is the within-replicate mean of the f_i. In the f_i some independent estimate of competitive ability should be used. Alternatively, one might substitute for f_i the weight i receives on additional principal components of **R** (or **R′R**), that is, PC2–PCn. Such components will partition the group into subgroups (see Section 4.1 below). They may thus indicate the tendency of members of subgroups to form coalitions against other subgroups (cf. Hughes, 1984).

3.8 Genetic Models

In this section, I relate the models of Section 3.3 and 3.5 to some concepts of quantitative genetics. Given resources such that assumptions (3.4) and (3.5) hold, let the distribution of resources correlated with fitness by an individual member of a group of n interrelated individuals be described by a continuous variable P_s. I define P_s to be proportional to the linear correlation between the resource distribution that individual i actually makes ($\mathbf{b}_i$) and $\mathbf{b}_{si}$ as derived from (3.9). P_s has a range from -1 to $+1$ and

$$\begin{aligned} P_{si} &= \text{corr}(\mathbf{b}_{si}, \mathbf{b}_i) - \text{mean}[\text{corr}(\mathbf{b}_{si}, \mathbf{b}_i)] \\ &= \text{corr}(\mathbf{r}_i, \mathbf{b}_i) - \text{mean}[\text{corr}(\mathbf{r}_i, \mathbf{b}_i)] \end{aligned} \qquad (3.32)$$

Thus at each generation the mean of P_s, $\bar{P}_i$, is reset to equal zero. P_s consists of the usual additive components, defined as in (2.8), and $h^2 > 0$. I assume that the mean of the additive component of P_s, $\bar{A}_s$, is also equal to zero and that environmental effects are random with respect to group membership.

Let the population contain m groups (numbered $k = 1, 2, \ldots, m$). Each group contains exactly n individuals. Not all population members need be contained within these groups. For example, the groups might contain males only, and females might not be group members (or vice versa). All that is required is that the interactions with which we are concerned take place within groups. Furthermore, all m groups are assumed to be identical in terms of their internal relatedness structure; that is, in each group, the n individuals are interrelated in exactly the same way. The matrix of coefficients of relatedness for the kth group, $\mathbf{R}_k$, equals that for any other group, say the jth, $\mathbf{R}_j$. Thus the members of each group are ordered in such a way that there is a structural role, corresponding to a given row or column of $\mathbf{R}_k$, which is filled by a given individual in each group. For simplicity (but with no loss of generality) I assume that the trait P_s is expressed in only one individual (i) per group; the fitnesses resulting from this resource distribution are given by $\mathbf{b}_{ik}$. However, the particular individual is randomly chosen with respect to his structural position in $\mathbf{R}_k$. I assume that mating in the population takes place at random with respect to group membership and P_s.

The mean additive genetic value will be greater for the offspring than for the parental generation (whose mean is zero) when

$$\frac{h^2}{2} \sum_{k=1}^{m} \frac{\text{corr}(\mathbf{r}_{ik}, \mathbf{b}_{ik}) \, \mathbf{r}'_{ik}\mathbf{b}_{ik}}{\sum_{j=1}^{n} b_{jik}} > 0 \qquad (3.33)$$

I assume that $\mathbf{b}'_{ik}\mathbf{b}_{ik} = 1$ for all k. When $\text{corr}(\mathbf{r}_{ik}, \mathbf{b}_{ik}) = 1$, $\mathbf{r}'_{ik}\mathbf{b}_{ik}$ will be at a maximum. On the other hand, when $\text{corr}(\mathbf{r}_{ik}, \mathbf{b}_{ik})$ is low or negative, $\mathbf{r}'_{ik}\mathbf{b}_{ik}$ will be much lower. Thus (3.33) will hold, and the population will evolve in the direction of increased $\overline{A}_s$ and $\overline{P}_s$.

Suppose that individuals of a population, structured as in the preceding discussion, encounter conditions favoring a compromise distribution of resources (and corresponding fitnesses) as discussed in Section 3.5. Under these conditions, I define $\mathbf{p}_{mk}$ to be a vector variable each of whose elements, the P_{mi}, is proportional to the correlation between $\mathbf{b}_m$ and the fitness distribution to group members preferred by individual i, $(\mathbf{b}_i).P_{mi} = \text{corr}(\mathbf{b}_i, \mathbf{b}_m) - \text{mean }[\text{corr}(\mathbf{b}_i, \mathbf{b}_m)]$. Again the P_{mi} are assumed to be constituted of the usual additive components and $h^2 > 0$. The actual compromise vector that occurs, $\mathbf{b}_k$, will bear the same relationship to the $\mathbf{b}_i$ as $\mathbf{b}_m$ bears to the $\mathbf{b}_{si}$ (see Section 3.5); that is, $\mathbf{b}_k$ will be chosen such that the sum of the squared distances from the $\mathbf{b}_i$ to $\mathbf{b}_k$ is at a minimum.

In (3.33) as in (2.27), the regression coefficient of relatedness (2.2) is used to estimate the additive genetic value of one individual from that of a related one. The latter additive genetic value is estimated as a portion h^2 of the individual's phenotypic value; and only that individual's phenotypic value is known, since the trait is expressed in only one individual. Here, the P_{mi} for n individuals are assumed to be known; their values are the elements of the vector $\mathbf{p}_{mk}$. If we consider that P_{mi} is composed of the sum of a number of atomlike constituents, the probability that any given one of these constituents is an additive genetic contribution is h^2. Given that a particular gene contributing to A_m occurs in the ith individual, the probability that it also occurs in the jth individual is r_{ij}. Thus we can estimate the vector of additive genetic values for the kth group by

$$h^2\mathbf{D}\mathbf{R}'\mathbf{p}_{mk}$$

where $\mathbf{D}$ is a diagonal matrix whose ith nonzero element is

$$\frac{1}{\sum_{i=1}^{n} r_{ij}}$$

Thus the additive genetic value of each individual i is estimated as the weighted average of the $h^2 P_{mj}$; the weights are the r_{ij}. For a given individual i, this weighted average is

$$h^2 \frac{\mathbf{r}'_i \, \mathbf{p}_{mk}}{\sum_{i=1}^{n} r_{ij}} = h^2 \left[\text{mean}(\mathbf{p}_{mk}) + \text{cov}(\mathbf{r}_i, \mathbf{p}_{mk}) \right] \qquad (3.34)$$

When there is a positive covariance between $\mathbf{r}_i$ and $\mathbf{p}_{mk}$, this information increases the estimate of A_{mi}. But when the covariance is negative, this fact decreases the estimate of A_{mi}, since it is assumed that variance not correlated with the pattern of relatedness must be of environmental origin.

There will be an increase in the mean additive genetic value of offspring over parents when

$$\frac{h^2}{2} \sum_{k=1}^{m} \frac{\mathbf{p}_{mk}'\mathbf{DRb}_k}{\sum_{i=1}^{n} b_{ki}} \tag{3.35}$$

I assume $\mathbf{b}_k'\mathbf{b}_k = 1$ for all k. Again (3.35) will hold for $h^2 > 0$ since when all elements of $\mathbf{p}_{mk}$ are equal to 1, $\mathbf{b}_k = \mathbf{b}_m$ and $\mathbf{Rb_k}$ *is maximal*.

It is of interest to consider one genetic consequence of the model of Section 3.5 given some simplifying assumptions. As above, I assume the population contains m identically structured groups of size n. I assume mating does not take place within any of the m groups; that all group members are outbred; and that fitnesses within all groups are assigned by $\mathbf{b}_m$ as defined in (3.20). Consider any polygenic trait P such that mating is random with respect to P; P is again assumed to be constituted of the usual additive genetic components. The mean additive genetic value of the offspring of the members of the kth group for such a trait will be given by

$$\overline{A}_k = \frac{\mathbf{X}_k'\mathbf{b}_m}{\Sigma b_{mi}} \tag{3.36}$$

where $\mathbf{X}_k$ is the vector of additive genetic values for the n members of the kth group. If additive genetic values are scaled such that $\sigma_A^2 = 1$, then

$$\mathrm{var}(\mathbf{X}_k) = \mathbf{R} \tag{3.37}$$

That is, $\mathbf{R}$ is the variance–covariance matrix of the vector variable $\mathbf{X}_k$. Thus

$$\mathrm{var}(\overline{A}_k) = \left(\frac{1}{\Sigma b_{mi}}\right)^2 \mathbf{b}_m'\mathbf{Rb}_m \tag{3.38}$$

Since $\mathbf{b}_m$ is the eigenvector corresponding to the largest eigenvalue of $\mathbf{R}$ ($\mathbf{R}$ being assumed to be symmetric), the quantity $\mathrm{var}(\overline{A}_k)$ will be at a maximum when the fitnesses of all group members are assigned according to $\mathbf{b}_m$. For any heritable trait, then, the strategy described by $\mathbf{b}_m$ will maximize the variance among the mean additive genetic values of the offspring of the different groups. Although the assumptions made here are unrealistic, the result suggests an important conclusion. The optimal compromise strategy, $\mathbf{b}_m$, has a disruptive effect on additive genetic variance among offspring of different groups. Mutualism within kin groups leads to genetic divergence among them. When a population is divided into groups within which relatedness is concentrated, the theory predicts mutualism within these groups. If such groups diverge genetically from each other, one result should be friction and conflict among them. Thus one might expect feuding to be particularly common in such populations.

It is interesting that anthropologists have recognized a type of society known as a "feuding society" (e.g., Black-Michaud, 1975; Brown, 1986; Campbell, 1964; Hasluck, 1954). Such societies appear to be characterized by a concentration of relatedness which parallels a concentration of wealth. Typically there is no strong central government that might mediate or suppress conflicts among powerful nobles or chieftains. The feuding chief himself derives his position from the support of an army of retainers, consisting of a kin network supplemented in some cases by feudal retainers.

4

The Structure of Relatedness

> The kind of mathematics which will be required ultimately for a full development of the science of society will not be metrical, but will be that hitherto comparatively neglected branch of mathematics, the calculus of relations, which, I think, is on the whole more fundamental than quantitative mathematics.
>
> RADCLIFFE-BROWN (1957)

4.1 The Relatedness Matrix

Relatedness within any group can be summarized by $\mathbf{R}$. However, especially when the group under consideration is large, it may be difficult to detect patterns in $\mathbf{R}$ by inspection. In this chapter I discuss ways of detecting patterns within $\mathbf{R}$. These methods make it possible to identify subgroupings within $\mathbf{R}$ and to quantify the relative importance of any such subgrouping, in terms of its contribution to the overall variation in relatedness within the group. Also, these methods make it possible to summarize most of the information in $\mathbf{R}$ in terms of a smaller matrix of derived quantities. These quantities in turn can be used in testing hypotheses regarding the relationship between biological relatedness and some behavioral variable. Finally, I present some alternative methods that do not depend on estimating $\mathbf{R}$ but can be used in much the same way.

Consider $\mathbf{R}_w$, the matrix of correlation coefficients of relatedness (2.7), equivalent to $\mathbf{R}$ when the latter is symmetric. The elements of $\mathbf{R}_w$ represent correlations among the additive genetic values A_i of all n individuals for any phenotypic trait P. These additive genetic values represent the contribution of some number p of loci; p is unknown but can be assumed to be several thousand in the case of most quantitative traits. Each individual in a group of n individuals corresponds to an axis in n-dimensional space. The additive genetic values for all n individuals at a given locus constitute a vector ($n \times 1$) or a point in this n-dimensional space. There are p such vectors or points. The eigenvector corresponding to the largest eigenvalue of $\mathbf{R}_w$, which is also called the first principal component (PC1) of $\mathbf{R}_w$, defines an axis in n-dimensional space along which most of the variance among these p points lies. Equivalently, we can say that PC1 of $\mathbf{R}_w$ is the axis to which the sum of the squared distances of all p points is at a minimum. There are consequences of the fact that $\mathbf{R}_w$ is a correlation matrix; that is, $\mathbf{R}_w$ is a covariance matrix among variables whose values are standardized to a mean of zero and unit variance. For proofs of these properties of principal components of a covariance matrix, see any text in multivariate statistics (e.g., Morrison, 1976).

On this interpretation, the elements (also called "weights") of PC1 of $\mathbf{R}_w$ can be interpreted as measures of the relatedness of each individual to the group as a whole. When $r^* > \bar{r}$, high weights correspond to individuals on whom relatedness is concentrated. If $r^* = \bar{r}$, all weights of PC1 of $\mathbf{R}_w$ will be equal. Let $\bar{r}_i$ represent the average relatedness of all group members of i; elements of PC1 of $\mathbf{R}_w$ are closely correlated with the corresponding $\bar{r}_i$.

Note that $\mathbf{R}_w$ (or $\mathbf{R}$ or $\mathbf{R'R}$) can be considered as describing a network (see Appendix B) or "valued graph." Each element r_{ij} measures the strength of the tie (of relatedness) between individuals i and j. Network theorists have proposed indices for measuring "prestige" within networks. An index of prestige for individual i is chosen to measure (1) the number and strength of ties i has with other individuals; and (2) the prestige of the other individuals with which i has ties. Assume that we are dealing with a symmetric matrix, say, $\mathbf{R}_w$. For the n individuals in a group, let $\mathbf{p}$ be a vector of prestige scores, p_i. In each case, p_i might be defined as

$$p_i = c(\mathbf{r}_i'\mathbf{p}) \tag{4.1}$$

where $\mathbf{r}_i'$ is the row vector of $\mathbf{R}_w$ corresponding to individual i and c is a constant of proportionality. If so, $\mathbf{p}$ is the solution to the matrix equation

$$\left(\mathbf{R}_w - \frac{1}{c}\mathbf{I} \right) \mathbf{p} = \mathbf{O} \tag{4.2}$$

If we choose c such that all p_i are nonnegative, $1/c$ will be the largest eigenvalue of $\mathbf{R}_w$ and $\mathbf{p}$ will be the first eigenvector, or PC1, of $\mathbf{R}_w$. For a discussion of similar prestige indices in other contexts, see Knoke and Kuklinski (1982). The elements of PC1 of $\mathbf{R}_w$ can be interpreted as prestige scores for a relatedness network in close analogy with prestige indices for other networks studied by social scientists.

If one has access to a computer program that can extract eigenvectors from a nonsymmetric matrix, one can construct a similar index from $\mathbf{R}$ even when inbreeding renders $\mathbf{R}$ asymmetric. However, most readily available programs for extracting eigenvectors require a symmetric matrix. If using such a program when $\mathbf{R}$ is asymmetric, one can extract eigenvectors from $\mathbf{R}_w$ or from $\mathbf{R'R}$, both of which will be symmetric in any case.

Other eigenvectors or principal components of $\mathbf{R}_w$ (or other PCs) can be interpreted in a fashion similar to the first. PC2 of $\mathbf{R}_w$, the eigenvector corresponding to the second largest eigenvalue λ_2, represents an axis orthogonal to PC1 such that, after PC1, the next greatest proportion of the variance in $\mathbf{R}_w$ lies along PC2. Subsequent components PC3, PC4, . . . , PCn (which correspond to eigenvalues $\lambda_3, \lambda_4, . . . , \lambda_n$) are axes orthogonal to all other PCs which account for decreasing proportions of overall variance of $\mathbf{R}_w$. For each PC, the proportion of the variance accounted for is given by λ/n. If $\mathbf{R}_w$ is interpreted as a covariance matrix among standardized variables, the overall variance is given by the trace of $\mathbf{R}_w$ (or the sum of all diagonal elements). The trace is equal to n, since $\mathbf{R}_w$ is a correlation matrix.

PCs of $\mathbf{R}_w$ (or of $\mathbf{R}$ or $\mathbf{R'R}$) other than the first are likely to take the form of "contrasts." In a PC that sets up a contrast, some elements are negative and some positive; some elements may also be zero or close to zero. Such a PC thus contrasts one subgroup of the n individuals with another subgroup. These PCs are useful for identifying subgroups in a group of individuals which are inter-related in complex ways. At a behavioral level, such contrasts indicate "stress lines" or "planes of cleavage" within the group. They suggest ways in which a group is likely to fission if fissioning occurs or the lines along which sides are likely to be chosen if conflict arises within the group (see Chapter 5). The relative magnitude of the eigenvalue corresponding to a given contrast gives us an idea of the relative importance of different "planes of cleavage."

The usefulness of PCs for analysis of the structure of a matrix of coefficients of relatedness can be made clear by a simple example. Figure 4.1 is a genealogy (from Karp, 1978) showing the relationships among seven adult males of the Iteso people of East Africa. For this group, $\mathbf{R}_w = \mathbf{R}$, and

$$\mathbf{R} = \begin{bmatrix} M1 & M2 & M3 & M4 & M5 & M6 & M7 \\ 1 & 0.5 & 0.5 & 0.5 & 0.25 & 0 & 0 \\ 0.5 & 1 & 0.5 & 0.5 & 0.25 & 0 & 0 \\ 0.5 & 0.5 & 1 & 0.5 & 0.25 & 0 & 0 \\ 0.5 & 0.5 & 0.5 & 1 & 0.25 & 0 & 0 \\ 0.25 & 0.25 & 0.25 & 0.25 & 1 & 0.25 & 0.25 \\ 0 & 0 & 0 & 0 & 0.25 & 1 & 0.5 \\ 0 & 0 & 0 & 0 & 0.25 & 0.5 & 1 \end{bmatrix} \qquad (4.3)$$

The first three principal components of $\mathbf{R}$ are given in Table 4.1. Together, these three PCs account for just over 70% of the variance in $\mathbf{R}$. The elements of PC1 indicate that relatedness is concentrated on the sibship containing M1, M2, M3, and M4. PC2 contrasts this sibship with the offspring of FC; that is, M5, M6, and M7. PC3 isolates M5, the only individual related to all other group members, but also the only individual with no full sibs. Since PC2 accounts for a substantial proportion of the variance in $\mathbf{R}$, one might predict that the "plane of cleavage" revealed by PC2 would be observable behaviorally. In fact, Karp (1978, p. 133) reports "considerable tension" between the two sibships contrasted by PC2.

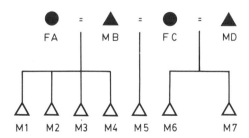

FIGURE 4.1. Genealogy of seven adult male Iteso. (Data from Karp, 1978.)

TABLE 4.1.   The First Three Principal Components of **R**
(PC1 − PC3) for the Group Illustrated in Figure 4.1

Individual	PC1	PC2	PC3
M1	0.474	−0.101	0.123
M2	0.474	−0.101	0.123
M3	0.474	−0.101	0.123
M4	0.474	−0.101	0.123
M5	0.305	0.350	−0.886
M6	0.066	0.647	0.278
M7	0.066	0.647	0.278
Eigenvalue	2.66	1.64	0.70
Percent trace	38.0	22.4	10.1

The type of analysis considered in this example corresponds to one of the major functions of principal components analysis in statistics. In statistics, principal components analysis can be used to pick up patterns of interrelation among a set of variables which are related to one another in complex ways. In this case, the variables are replaced by individuals; the goal of the analysis is the same. A second major function of principal components analysis in statistics is data reduction. A data set with information on n variables consists of a set of points in n-dimensional space. Principal components analysis can be used to derive a set of m variables (where $m < n$) which will explain a substantial proportion of the variation within the original data. This smaller set of variables can then be used in place of the original n variables in a further statistical analysis. It is worth mentioning that principal components of $\mathbf{R}_w$ or $\mathbf{R}$ can serve a similar function. Principal components of $\mathbf{R}$ or $\mathbf{R}_w$ can be used as predictor variables in statistical techniques such as multiple regression or discriminant analysis. Dependent variables in such applications would be behavioral variables of interest. The hypothesis being tested would be that the behavorial variables is a function of some aspect of the structure of biological relatedness; for examples, see Hughes (1984, 1986a) and Chapters 5 and 6 below.

4.2 Reachability from a Common Ancestor

In this and the next section, I introduce some alternative approaches to the extraction of principal components from $\mathbf{R}_w$ or $\mathbf{R}$. These approaches can be used analogously both for pattern detection and for data reduction. They have the advantage of being computationally much simpler than extraction of principal components. Although computer programs for principal components analysis are readily available, there is still the problem of the matrix of coefficients of relatedness itself. Computation of this matrix is not a trivial task when n is large. The alternative methods presented here do not depend on computing coefficients of relatedness. Another advantage they have over principal components is that they are a priori methods; that is, they depend on an a priori hypothesis about what aspects of the relatedness structure are likely to be behaviorally important. Thus they can be used readily in testing hypotheses about how biological relatedness affects behavior.

When one examines principal components of $\mathbf{R}_w$ which set up contrasts, one notes that individuals often are grouped together on the basis of shared ancestry. The example in Figure 4.1 and Table 4.1 can serve as an illustration. Here, PC2 contrasts sons of FA with sons of FC; PC3 contrasts the son of MB and FC with all individuals sharing one but not both of these parents. In general, of course, individuals who share an ancestor will tend to share genes with one another which are not shared with individuals not descended from that ancestor. This suggests one shortcut way of subdividing a group on the basis of relatedness; rather than actually computing coefficients of relatedness, we can simply classify individuals on the basis of descent from a common ancestor.

To do this, we construct for our group of interest a genealogy in digraph form (see Appendix B). Each individual in our group is represented by a vertex, or point in the digraph. Additional points are included for all individuals that are not themselves members of the group but are necessary to account for all genealogical connections among group members, for example, deceased ancestors or ancestors who are living but for some reason excluded from our group of interest. Then a directed line is drawn from each parent to each of its offspring. (This is not the only way of expressing a genealogy as a digraph; for another see Cannings and Thompson, 1981). In Figure 4.2 the genealogy of Figure 4.1 is expressed in digraph form. In a digraph, individual x is said to be *adjacent* to individual y if there is a directed line leading from x to y. In general, when x is adjacent to y, y may or may not be adjacent to x; and in the digraph form of a genealogy, y will never be adjacent to x when x is adjacent to y (and vice versa). In the digraph form of a genealogy, an *apical ancestor* can be defined as an individual represented by a point to which no member of the group of interest is adjacent but which is adjacent to at least one member of the group of interest. Thus in Figure 4.2, FA, MB, FC, and MD are all apical ancestors, whereas their offspring are not. Apical ancestors in a genealogical digraph may or (as in Figure 4.2) may not be members of the group of interest. The concept of an apical ancestor has a straightforward genetic interpretation. If any two individuals are

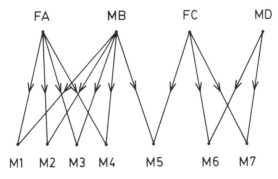

FIGURE 4.2. Genealogy of Figure 4.1 expressed as a digraph.

descended from the apical ancestor—that is, if in the digraph they are both reachable from the apical ancestor—there is a nonzero probability that both have genes identical by descent which are descended from genes in the apical ancestor.

For each apical ancestor j, define a variable X (called an apical ancestor variable) such that each individual j in the group of interest is assigned a value of the variable x_{ij}. If i is reachable from j, $x_{ij} = 1$. If i is not reachable from j, $x_{ij} = 0$. Note that by definition, any point is reachable from itself. We can construct a matrix X of the x_{ij}; X is $n \times k$, where k is the number of apical ancestors from the digraph. In the example of Figure 4.1,

$$
X = \begin{array}{c} \\ \\ \\ \\ \\ \\ \\ \end{array}
\begin{array}{c}
\text{FA MB FC MD0} \\
\left[\begin{array}{cccc}
\text{M1} & 1 & 1 & 0 & 0 \\
\text{M2} & 1 & 1 & 0 & 0 \\
\text{M3} & 1 & 1 & 0 & 0 \\
\text{M4} & 1 & 1 & 0 & 0 \\
\text{M5} & 0 & 1 & 1 & 0 \\
\text{M6} & 0 & 0 & 1 & 1 \\
\text{M7} & 0 & 0 & 1 & 1
\end{array}\right]
\end{array}
\qquad (4.4)
$$

The columns of X are labeled to indicate the corresponding apical ancestors and the rows to indicate the individual group members. In this example, it should be immediately apparent that the apical ancestor variables set up the same contrasts as the principal components of R (Table 4.1). The contrast set up by PC2 is reflected in the apical ancestor variables corresponding to FA and FC. Likewise, the apical ancestor variables corresponding to MB and MC taken together isolate M5 from other group members, as does PC3.

In some cases, two apical ancestors are ancestors to the same individuals and neither has any descendants in the group which are not shared with the other. Such apical ancestors may be called redundant. For example, in Figure 4.3, there is a group of four individuals (M1, M2, F3, and M4), two of which are full siblings (M1 and M2), both offspring of FB and MA. In this case, FB and MA are redundant apical ancestors; both have identical descendants. In constructing X, one need only define a single apical ancestor variable for the pair of redundant source ancestors.

Anthropologists have long been familiar with groups having a segmentary lineage structure. This type of structure is found in societies having unilineal descent systems. In a unilineal descent system, descent is traced in a single-sex line (male or female) from a common ancestor, either actually remembered as an individual or merely hypothesized. Lineages are groups of individuals descended unilineally from a known common ancestor. Frequently such lineages split in a segmentary fashion, giving rise to sublineages which may be identified linguistically and/or may be behaviorally distinct. The simplest application of the apical ancestor model is to such descent groups.

The example in Figure 4.4 is from a matrilineal Indian society (Kutty, 1972). In this society, the matrilineage (called a Taravad) is subdivided into property-holding groups, which may themselves be further subdivided into domestic

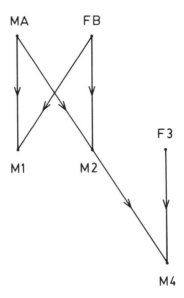

FIGURE 4.3. Hypothetical genealogy. In this case, MA and FB are redundant apical ancestors of M1 and M2.

groups that share a household. Since this is a matrilineal descent group, men married to women in the group are not group members, but only individuals descended in the female line from the apical ancestress. In fact, men often do not live with their wives but remain with their sisters, thus residing in their own natal Taravad. It seems quite possible, given that in this society husband and wife often do not share a residence, that a woman's husband is not always the father of her children; that is, confidence of paternity may tend to be low (see Alexander, 1974, 1977, 1979). I have drawn a single male as the father of each female's offspring (as did Kutty), except when the female was known to have had two husbands (e.g., F3 in Figure 4.4). Obviously, within a particular woman's family, the pattern of paternity will make a difference to the pattern of relatedness. But since fathers are not group members, knowing their exact number is not always necessary for describing patterns at the level of the entire Taravad. For example, the two property groups in Figure 4.4 are distinguished by descent from F2 and F3; the number of men by whom these women had children will not affect definition of the property groups. On the other hand, the two household groups within the property group descended from F3 are defined on the basis of descent from two different males; ME and MG respectively are the apical ancestors for these groups. Even so, the exact number of males does not entirely matter. For example, if one of the two offspring assigned in Figure 4.4 to MG were actually sired by yet a third male, these offspring would still be grouped together as not having been sired by ME (and thus not reachable from the point corresponding to ME in the digraph version of the genealogy).

One attraction, then, of the apical ancestor method for explaining the struc-

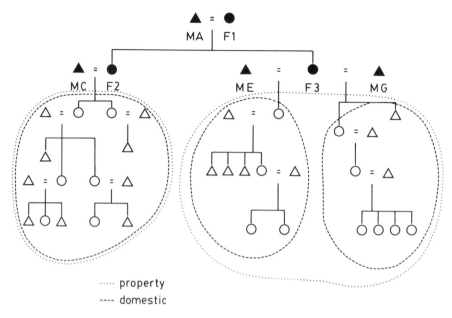

····· property
---- domestic

FIGURE 4.4. Genealogy of a South Indian Taravad or matrilineage (from Kutty, 1972), showing the subdivision of the Taravad into property groups and domestic groups.

ture of relatedness is that it does not depend on estimating **R**. When we have reason to doubt that **R** can be estimated accurately, this alternative method can be used to identify major subgroupings in a way rather similar to the examination of principal components of **R**. An additional attraction of defining dummy variables based on descent from a common ancestor is that the exact connections with the ancestor need not be traceable by informants for the values of the variables to be assigned. For example, anthropologists define a clan as a group of individuals all of whom are believed to be descended unilineally from a distant common ancestor to whom exact links are not traceable. A clan is thus distinguished from a lineage by the fact that in a lineage all ties to the apical ancestor are traceable. If one is interested in a group whose members belong to several clans—for example, an entire village or hamlet—one may add variables to define descent from the hypothetical clan ancestor.

The logic behind apical ancestor variables can also help dispose of one supposed problem for a biological approach to human kinship. Witherspoon (1975), in the apparent belief that he is presenting data truly devastating to a biological account of human kinship, mentions that the Navajo consider themselves to be descended from "the earth." He argues that they view the earth itself as "kin." Accepting his argument, we can define an apical ancestor variable corresponding to the earth; but, since for all individuals the variable will have a value of 1, including this variable adds nothing to our understanding of the relatedness structure of any Navajo group. Thus even if we are to admit such extraneous "kin," doing so will yield no falsifiable predictions about group dynamics or behavior. If the Navajo hold a theory of kinship that posits the earth as an ancestor, this element of their theory is without practical consequences; as Quine (1969) would say, their theory is underdetermined by observations.

4.3 Relatedness to Offspring

As discussed further in Chapter 5, individuals may be grouped together behaviorally and/or linguistically on principles other than descent from a common ancestor. One such factor is relatedness to dependent offspring, that is, relatedness to descendants rather than ancestors. The simplest example is the kind of group known in our own society as a "nuclear family," which consists of a husband, wife, and one or more dependent offspring. The husband and wife are typically unrelated to each other but share the property of both being related to the children. In our society, the individuals outside the nuclear family most likely to be included in a household are one or more of the spouses' parents or siblings (e.g., Young and Wilmot, 1957); these again share the property of being related to the children. More complex patterns of relationship to dependent offspring may form the basis of groupings in other societies.

To test the hypothesis that relationships to descendants are important for some aspects of social behavior, one can define *terminal descendant* variables by analogy with apical ancestor variables. When a genealogy is in digraph form, a terminal descendant is an individual represented by a point to which one or more others is adjacent but which is not itself adjacent to any other point. For each individual i in the group of interest and each terminal descendant j, let z_{ij} take the value of 1 when there exists any point such that the points corresponding to i and j are both reachable from it; let z_{ij} take the value of 0 when there exists no such point. The values of the z_{ij} can be placed in a matrix $\mathbf{Z}$. If some terminal descendants are redundant with each other (as full siblings will always be), one can eliminate redundant columns from $\mathbf{Z}$.

In some cases, it may be necessary to make finer distinctions than merely to record the fact of relatedness to a given terminal descendant. For example, in the genealogy of Figure 4.4, all members of the matrilineages (although not their spouses) are related to any set of terminal descendants. However, they are not equally related to all terminal descendants. We can replace z_{ij} with r_{ij} and each column of $\mathbf{Z}$ will be a matrix of coefficients of relatedness of each terminal descendant to each individual. Alternatively, one can choose an arbitrary cutoff value of r_{ij}, which we should call r_{min}. If $r_{ij} \geq r_{min}$, then let $z_{ij} = 1$. If $r_{ij} < r_{min}$, let $z_{ij} = 0$. This approach is particularly useful in cases where low paternity confidence makes estimates of r_{ij} uncertain. In such cases, one can make a minimum estimate of r_{ij}; for instance, one can estimate r_{ij} on the basis of the extreme assumption that any two offspring of a woman have different and unrelated fathers.

In the example of Figure 4.4, the two property groups can be separated on the basis of how closely related their members are to the youngest offspring in the group. Within the property group containing two domestic groups, the two domestic groups can also be discriminated on the basis of closeness of relatedness to terminal offspring. Thus in this example, the subdivision of the Taravad into subgroups by descent (i.e., by apical ancestors) and by proximity of relatedness to dependent offspring results in identical groupings. As will be seen in Chapter 5, this is by no means always the case.

4.4 Working with Flawed Data: Robustness of the Methods

In empirical cases to be handled by the methods described here, the aim of the research is to test hypotheses about the relationship between the relatedness structure of a group and some internal structuring of the group which results from behavioral interactions. The overall hypothesis, based on evolutionary biology and kin selection theory, is that behavioral structuring of groups of interrelated individuals will be influenced by and thus predictable from patterns of biological relatedness. In some cases, reliable estimates of biological relatedness may be difficult to come by. Section 1.4 addressed the question of paternity and how the uncertainty of paternity has led "cultural" anthropologists to reject the utility of biological approaches to kinship. Even when confidence of paternity is high, it may be difficult to estimate from genealogical data if the data are fragmentary or contradictory. A further problem arises in even the best genealogies, given that all are of finite depth; we do not know the inbreeding coefficients of apical ancestors, needed for a truly precise estimate of **R**.

On the other hand, it is my feeling that in general even anthropologists sympathetic to sociobiology have made too much of the difficulties of estimating coefficients of relatedness. Chagnon (1975), for example, attempts to evade the issue of biological kinship and replace estimates of biological kinship with estimates of genealogical connectedness as reported by informants. It is perhaps a fine philosophical nuance, but I feel it would be preferable for him to say that he is *estimating* biological relatedness on the basis of genealogical information. For if one merely tests people's behavior against their *ideas* about kinship, one is in danger of falling into the same idealist trap as the cultural anthropologists (see Section 1.4).

In the current state of sociobiology as a science, estimates of biological relatedness derived from genealogical data frequently are adequate for hypothesis testing. We have simply not yet reached a level of sophistication in formulation and testing of hypotheses where really fine discrimination of relatedness is required (cf. Hamilton, 1987). Many hypotheses regarding human social behavior can be tested given genealogical data obtained by competent ethnographic fieldwork and sufficient information regarding the level of confidence of paternity in the society under study to enable us to interpret the genealogical record sensibly. In this section, I use methods presented in this chapter to assay the robustness of inferences about the structure of biological relatedness in cases where genealogical data contain uncertainties. The examples discussed here show how uncertainties in genealogical data, while they surely affect estimates of specific coefficients of relatedness, may sometimes have a less marked effect on the structure of relatedness at the level of a group.

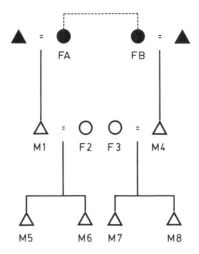

FIGURE 4.5. Descendants of two classificatory "sisters." (Data from Lawrence, 1984.)

First, consider an example from Lawrence (1984) of "genealogical amnesia." In Figure 4.5 are shown two groups of individuals linked through two deceased ancestresses (FA and FB) who were described by informants by means of a classificatory kinship term which Lawrence translates as "sisters." Lawrence emphasizes that the exact genealogical link between FA and FB had been forgotten. Table 4.2 shows PC1 and PC2 of **R** for the living individuals on three assumptions: (1) that FA and FB were full sisters ($r = 0.5$); (2) that FA and FB were half-sisters ($r = 0.25$); and (3) that FA and FB were first cousins ($r = 0.125$). Differences in the relatedness between FA and FB do not have a marked effect on these PCs. PC2 contrasts two subgroups which are identically constituted in

TABLE 4.2. PC1 and PC2 of **R** for the Group Illustrated in Figure 4.5, Showing the Effect of Different Values of the Coefficient of Relatedness r between FA and FB

	$r = 0.5$		$r = 0.25$		$r = 0.125$	
Individual	PC1	PC2	PC1	PC2	PC1	PC2
M1	0.342	0.268	0.326	0.289	0.317	0.298
F2	0.277	0.340	0.292	0.324	0.300	0.316
F3	0.277	−0.340	0.292	−0.324	0.300	−0.316
M4	0.342	−0.268	0.326	−0.289	0.317	−0.298
M5	0.391	0.395	0.393	0.395	0.393	0.395
M6	0.391	0.395	0.393	0.395	0.393	0.395
M7	0.391	−0.395	0.393	−0.395	0.393	−0.395
M8	0.391	−0.395	0.393	−0.395	0.393	−0.395
λ	2.41	2.16	2.34	2.20	2.31	2.25
Percent trace	30.1	27.0	29.3	27.8	28.9	28.1

each case. In all cases, PC1 shows that relatedness is concentrated on the off-spring M5, M6, M7, and M8. The major change caused by decreasing the relatedness between FA and FB is a decrease in the percentage of the variance in **R** accounted for by PC1 and an increase in the percentage of the variance in **R** accounted for by PC2. In other words, as the relationship between FA and FB is decreased, the relative importance of the contrast between the two subgroups is increased.

A more extreme case of genealogical amnesia is illustrated in Figure 4.6; the data are from Gulliver's (1955) study of the Jie of East Africa. Figure 4.6B illustrates the version of the genealogical connections among seven Jie men given by

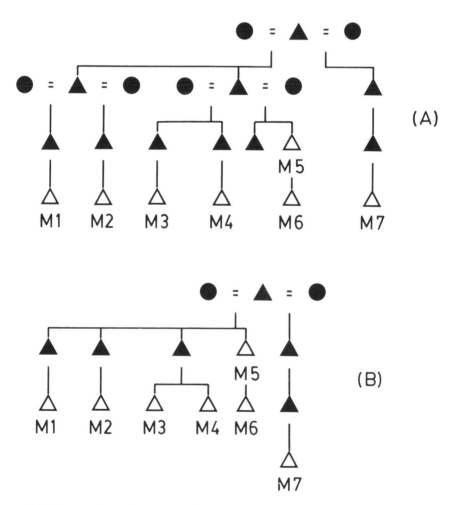

FIGURE 4.6. Two versions of the genealogical relationships among seven Jie men. (A) version given by M5; (B) version given by M6. (Data from Gulliver, 1955.)

one of them, M6. Figure 4.6A illustrates the presumably more accurate version of connections among the same individuals as given by M5, who is M6's father. M5 is aware of polygynous marriages in his parents' generation, leading him to recognize the parents of M3 and M4 as his half-siblings and the parents of M1 and M2 as half-siblings. M6 counts these individuals as full siblings. M6 also considers M3 and M4 to be full siblings, whereas his father's account shows them to be parallel cousins. Presumably when M5 dies, his more accurate version will be lost, at least among M6's direct descendants; thus we may be able to witness in progress a process of genealogical simplication.

Table 4.3 shows PC1 and PC2 of **R** for the versions of Figure 4.6A and 4.6B. The differences here are, not surprisingly, more marked than in Table 4.2. In both cases, PC1 shows that relatedness is concentrated on M5, and that M7 has little overall relatedness to other group members. The two versions differ in other aspects of PC1. In version A, PC2 contrasts M5 and M6 with other group members, especially M3 and M4. In version B, PC2 contrasts M3 and M4 with other group members, primarily M5 and M6. The difference is that in version B the subsidiary characters in the contrast are grouped with M5 and M6 rather than M3 and M4. Structurally, PC2 reflects much the same thing in both versions; namely, that the ties between M5 and M6 ($r = 0.5$) and between M3 and M4 ($r = 0.125$ in version A, $r = 0.5$ in version B) are the two closest ties of relatedness in the group. At one level, the two sets of PCs in Table 4.3 are quite dissimilar, but there are certain broad similarities. Whether the differences or the similarities are more important depends on what sort of hypothesis the data are being used to test.

In this example, it is possible that version B of the genealogy represents not so much a case of "genealogical amnesia" as a case of conscious or unconscious redefinition of relationships by M6 for reasons of his own. If so, an analysis like that of Table 4.3 helps to show the structural effects of such a redefinition. Of course, one can only compare redefined relationships with the actual genealog-

TABLE 4.3. PC1 and PC2 of **R** for the Two Versions (A and B) of Genealogical Connections among the Individuals in Figure 4.6

Individual	Version A		Version B	
	PC2	PC2	PC1	PC2
M1	0.149	0.326	0.300	0.177
M2	0.149	0.326	0.300	0.177
M3	0.271	0.507	0.433	−0.550
M4	0.183	0.610	0.433	−0.550
M5	0.666	−0.209	0.523	0.330
M6	0.636	−0.329	0.407	0.468
M7	0.037	0.080	0.083	0.075
λ	1.57	1.10	2.10	1.16
Percent trace	22.5	15.7	30.0	16.6

ical facts when one has, as in this example, a more accurate version with which to make comparisons. As time passes, on the other hand, the exact relatedness of the individuals in Figure 4.6 will be of decreasing structural importance for their descendants. As in the example of Figure 4.5, whether (for example) M3 and M4 were brothers or first cousins will have only minor effects on the structure of relatedness among their descendants.

Finally, I consider an example that shows how a descent group can be defined on the basis of its structural position relative to other descent groups, even when all traces of genealogical connections among its members are forgotten. The Navajo of the southwestern United States have a matrilineal clan system. The members of a clan that live in a given locality are called a "local clan element" (LCE) by Aberle (1961). Frequently LCEs of different clans in a given locality intermarry. The example of Figure 4.7, taken from the extensive Navajo genealogies collected by Reichard (1928), shows members of LCEs of Red Streak, Salt, and Zuñi clans. The Red Streak and Zuñi LCEs each constitute lineages descended from known common ancestors, but the Salt individuals in Figure 4.7 have no known genealogical connections. I estimated **R** on the assumption that r between any two Salt individuals is zero and that pater and genitor are the same. The latter is probably in general a reasonable assumption for Navajo; see the discussion in Hughes (1986a) as well as comments in Witherspoon (1975). I then applied canonical discriminant analysis to the first five PCs of **R**. Two highly significant discriminant functions correctly classified all members of the Red Streak, Salt, and Zuñi clans in Figure 4.7 into the correct

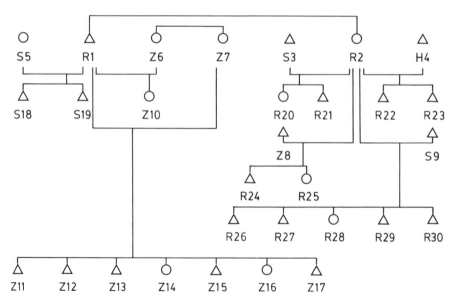

FIGURE 4.7. Navajo genealogy showing members of three matrilineal clans: Salt (S), Zuñi (Z), and Red Streak (R). (Data from Reichard, 1928.)

clan (Figure 4.8). In this example, the Salt clan members are all grouped together because of the structural position they occupy relative to the other two clans, even on the assumption that all Salt individuals are unrelated to each other. Salt individuals provide spouses to Red Streak individuals, and they can be grouped together on the basis of this structural role. This example shows that, even when ties of relatedness among clan members have been forgotten, their position relative to other clans provides a biological basis for their being grouped together.

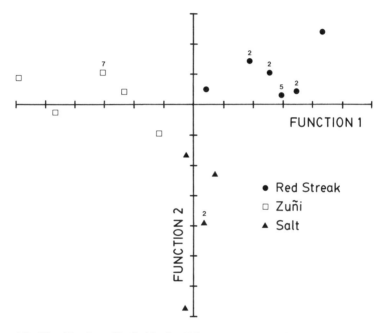

FIGURE 4.8. Classification of individuals of Figure 4.7 by canonical discriminant analysis, showing scores on the two discriminant functions of members of the three clans. (Redrawn from Hughes, 1986a.)

5

Kin Group Subdivision
and Conflict

And Lot also, which went with Abram, had flocks, and herds, and tents. And the land was not able to bear them, that they might dwell together: for their substance was great, so that they could not dwell together. And there was a strife between the herdmen of Abram's cattle and the herdmen of Lot's cattle: and the Canaanite and the Perizzite dwelled then in the land. And Abram said unto Lot, Let there be no strife, I pray thee, between me and thee, and between my herdmen and thy herdmen: for we be brethren. Is not the whole land before thee? separate thyself, I pray thee, from me: if thou wilt take the left hand, then I will go to the right; or if thou depart to the right hand, then I will go to the left.

Genesis 13: 5–9

5.1 Kin Group Membership

In this chapter some of the techniques presented in Chapter 4 are applied to empirical examples of three separate but conceptually related phenomena: (1) the fissioning of a residence group (household, village, etc.) into two or more daughter groups; (2) the subdivision of a kin group into two or more linguistically or behaviorally distinct subgroups; (3) conflict among kin. The theoretical basis of the discussion is kin selection theory (Chapters 2 and 3). Chagnon (1975), in his pioneering studies of village fissioning among the Yanomamö of South America, was the first to consider such questions in the light of kin selection theory. He found that when a Yanomamö village fissions, the average relatedness within the two daughter villages is greater than the average relatedness within the original village. Since cooperative and altruistic interactions are far more likely to occur within villages than between villages, Chagnon interpreted this result as consistent with kin selection theory. Hurd (1983) applied the same method to fissioning of Amish communities in the United States with similar results.

My purpose here is to develop a biological theory of kin group subdivision. Such a theory must go beyond the a posteriori observation that members of daughter subgroups are more closely related to one another, on the average, than are members of the parent group. It must seek predictive models of kin group subdivision which can be applied, at least in theory, prior to group division. I will consider how such models might be constructed and illustrate their application both to residence group fissioning and to other types of kin group subdivision.

Study by social anthropologists of group subdivision has been dominated by the model of segmentary lineage structure. When a descent group is defined by unilineal descent (descent in one line only, whether male or female), the descent group frequently divides in a "segmentary" fashion. For example, the matrilineal group in Figure 4.4 is subdivided in classic segmentary fashion. Both the simplicity of the segmentary model and the fact that numerous examples have been found have doubtless accounted for its popularity in social anthropology. However, even in an example as simple as that in Figure 4.4, one inadequacy of the model is apparent. Actual residence groups include individuals who are not members of the unilineal descent group. The unilineal structure simply provides a "skeleton" around which the actual household is organized. In any society with a unilineal organization, actual membership in residence groups is based on additional criteria besides unilineal descent.

This fact about unilineal social structure is most strikingly illustrated in the case of the Nuer (Evans-Pritchard, 1951). The Nuer are a patrilineal people of East Africa who provide the textbook example of a segmentary lineage structure. Yet if one actually looks at the structure of Nuer communities, one sees that they are not organized on strictly patrilineal lines. Typically there is a leading male who may be accompanied by one or more brothers or close patrilineal kin. However, most of the men in the community are not members of the leader's patrilineage but rather are linked to him in a number of other ways; they may be husbands of his sisters of daughters, brothers of his wives, and so on. In the Nuer, then, at the local level, the unilineal skeleton of society is richly fleshed out with a variety of other kin and affines. Anthropologists have found this aspect of Nuer society paradoxical; there have been frequent references in the literature to the "Nuer paradox" (cf. Geertz and Geertz, 1975; Kelley, 1974). The Nuer case is discussed further in Section 6.2, but I bring it up here as an indication of the problems posed for social anthropologists by their fascination with segmentary lineage structure. The emphasis on unilineal organization, in fact, blinded social anthropologists for some time to giving full attention to other types of social organization. Lawrence (1984) documents the hostile reception initially accorded to his description of a flexible cognatic social organization in New Guinea (a cognatic organization being one in which descent is traced in both male and female lines). Until Barnes (1962) demonstrated the inapplicability of the Nuer model to New Guinea, Lawrence's accounts were met with some skepticism.

As a frame of reference for this discussion, consider a very simple example of a fissioning process. The unit of consideration is not an entire village but a single household; nonetheless, the lessons to be learned apply to any group of interrelated individuals. The society in question, from the Polynesian island of Rapa, has a cognatic kinship system; thus the segmentary lineage model is inapplicable. Figure 5.1 shows a Rapan household which split, with some acri-

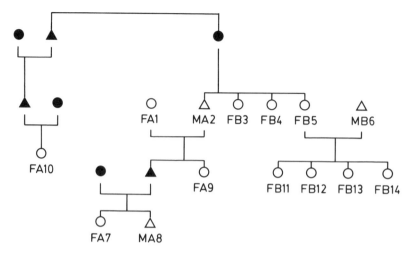

FIGURE 5.1. Genealogy of a Rapan (Polynesian) household which fissioned to form two daughter households, A and B. (Data from Hanson, 1970.)

mony, into two daughter households, A and B (data from Hanson, 1970). In this case, one cannot assign individuals to daughter households simply on the basis of average relatedness (Table 5.1). There is one individual, FA10, who is much less closely related on the average to members of the daughter household which she joined (A) than to members of the daughter household which she did not join (B). Further, FA10's average relatedness to B household members $\bar{r}_B$ exceeds her average relatedness to A household members $\bar{r}_A$ by a greater amount

TABLE 5.1.   Average Relatedness of Each Individual to Members of the Two Household Groups (A and B) in Figure 5.1 ($\bar{r}_A$ and $\bar{r}_B$), with Weights for PC1–PC3 of **R′R**

Individual	$\bar{r}_A$	$\bar{r}_B$	PC1	PC2	PC3
FA1	0.2000	0.0000	0.0536	−0.3139	0.4644
MA2	0.2125	0.3125	0.3132	−0.2835	−0.2250
FB3	0.1771	0.2857	0.2901	−0.1733	−0.3452
FB4	0.1771	0.2857	0.2901	−0.1733	−0.3452
FB5	0.1771	0.4286	0.3825	−0.0366	−0.2456
MB6	0.0000	0.2857	0.2139	0.3898	0.3849
FA7	0.2531	0.0781	0.1310	−0.3508	0.3209
MA8	0.2531	0.0781	0.1310	−0.3508	0.3209
FA9	0.3063	0.1563	0.2084	−0.3877	0.1774
FA10	0.0250	0.3138	0.0419	−0.0306	−0.0821
FB11	0.0885	0.4286	0.3388	0.2293	0.1033
FB12	0.0885	0.4286	0.3388	0.2293	0.1033
FB13	0.0085	0.4286	0.3388	0.2293	0.1033
FB14	0.0885	0.4286	0.3388	0.2293	0.1033
Percent trace			29.8	15.5	11.0

than $\bar{r}_B$ exceeds $\bar{r}_A$ for several B household members (FB3, FB4, MB6). Thus it is impossible to derive a discriminant function that will separate the two households on the basis of $\bar{r}_A$ and $\bar{r}_B$ alone.

One might conclude, as many anthropologists and even many biologists would no doubt do, that daughter household membership in this case is not based entirely on kinship. And yet it is possible to discriminate perfectly between daughter households A and B on the basis of a canonical discriminant function applied to PC1, PC2, and PC3 of **R** (Tables 5.1 and 5.2). The discriminant analysis suggests that some aspect of kinship does form the basis of daughter household membership. But this analysis does not test an a priori hypothesis for discriminating among daughter households.

Here I consider such an a priori hypothesis: the aspect of relatedness on which household membership is based is relatedness to terminal descendants (see Section 4.3). There are two principal sets of terminal descendants in Figure 5.1: (1) the sibship containing FA7 and MA8; (2) the sibship containing FB11, FB12, FB13, and FB14. I denote these sibships x and y respectively. Let r_x denote the maximum relatedness to each individual of members of the former sibship, and let r_y denote maximum relatedness to each individual of members of the latter sibship. The two daughter households can in fact be perfectly discriminated on the basis of the difference between r_y and r_x. If $r_y - r_x \leq 0$, then the individual will be a member of the daughter household A (Table 5.3). Individuals are not assigned to a daughter household simply on the basis of which of r_x and r_y are larger. On this basis, FA10 would be assigned to household B, and MA2 would have no assignment. Nor can household membership be assigned simply on the basis of r_y, for on that basis MA2 would join household B. Rather, an individual joins household B if closely related to children in that family (i.e., r_y is high) and if *not* very closely related to the children in household A (i.e., r_x is low).

This very detailed treatment of a simple example reveals a principle of group membership which has generally been ignored by anthropologists (and by sociobiologists) but has widespread application. This is the principle of relatedness to sets of focal offspring. I believe that this principle is the basis of residential group formation in all human societies. It can apply not only to households but to

TABLE 5.2.   Group Means for PC1–PC3 of **R′R** for the Household Groups in Figure 5.1, with Standardized Discriminant Function Coefficients

		Mean Score	
Household	*PC1*	*PC2*	*PC3*
A	0.1465	−0.2863	0.1530
B	0.3165	0.1155	−0.0172
Standardized discriminant function coefficients:			
	0.5935	0.9877	−0.4826

TABLE 5.3.   Maximum Relatedness to Individuals from
Figure 5.1 of Two Sets of Offspring, x and y; x Includes
FA7 and MA8, and y Includes FB11, FB12, FB13, and
FB14

Individual	r_x	r_y	$r_y - r_x$
FA1	0.25	0	−0.25
MA2	0.25	0.25	0
FB3	0.125	0.25	0.125
FB4	0.125	0.25	0.125
FB5	0.125	0.5	0.375
MB6	0	0.5	0.5
FA7	1	0.0625	−0.9375
MA8	1	0.0625	−0.9375
FA9	0.25	0.125	−0.125
FA10	0.015625	0.03125	0.015625
FB11	0.0625	1	0.9375
FB12	0.0625	1	0.9375
FB13	0.0625	1	0.9375
FB14	0.0625	1	0.9375

hamlets and villages as well. Focal offspring are offspring on which relatedness
is concentrated (see Section 3.6). In our Western society, the residential group
is the nuclear family household centered around a set of full or half-siblings. This
is a rather trivial case of relatedness to a set of focal offspring. In the case of
hamlets or villages, the set of focal offspring may include a number of different
siblings related to each other in various ways, on whom relatedness is concentrated. Adult group members may be unrelated to each other but share relatedness to focal offspring.

Residential groups are reproductive groups (with a few exceptions like military barracks and monasteries). Reproduction and the rearing of children are
the primary focus of their activities. In precapitalist (extractive, pastoral, peasant) economies, productive labor takes place within the local community itself;
those who are involved in productive labor, along with their children, share benefits derived from their activities. Insofar as these benefits are correlated with
fitness, as modeled in Chapter 3, it would make sense for individuals to cluster
on the basis of proximity of relatedness to dependent offspring, who will be the
primary recipients of these benefits. Children and adolescents are not themselves
highly productive community members, but their survival and eventual reproductive success are crucial to the inclusive fitness of their parents and of other
close kin of the parental and grandparental generations. Also, in general, offspring that are approaching reproductive age are the individuals of highest
reproductive potential in the population. The theory (see Section 3.3) predicts
that resources will be shared disproportionately with individuals of high reproductive potential and high relatedness to those doing the sharing. Thus it makes
sense for those who have both the ability to benefit dependent offspring through
their labor and a motive for doing so in terms of their own inclusive fitness to
base residence decisions on the presence or absence of such dependents.

One might ask why a group of related individuals—whether a household or a village—should ever reach the point of fissioning at all. One explanation, derived from behavioral ecology of nonhuman animals, is that conflict between less closely related subsections of the group will begin to occur when resources available to the group are insufficient to support all group members. In the case of a household, the resource in question may simply be space (as it evidently was in the Rapan example of Figure 5.1). For a hamlet or village, agricultural land, pastoral land, or hunting territory may be the limiting resource. In any case, the prediction of Wrangham (1982) and of the models developed in Chapter 3 is that when such a resource crunch comes, individuals will prefer that benefits accrue to their own offspring or other closely related individuals rather than distant kin or non-kin. Assuming that adequate resources are available elsewhere, it is better from the point of view of the inclusive fitness of all concerned for one subgroup to leave in search of a separate resource base, whether currently unexploited or exploited by an unrelated group. Thus, rather than competing with each other, the two interrelated subgroups will compete with unrelated individuals.

Interestingly, the author of Genesis in the passage quoted at the start of this chapter seems to have been aware of both of these aspects of the sociobiology of kin group fissioning, that is, both its origin in competition for resources and the desirability of competing with non-kin rather than kin. Two nomadic herdsmen, Lot and Abram, being kinsmen, decide to separate in order to avoid competition. Each is evidently head of a large household, perhaps including not only offspring but other kin and affines on the Nuer pattern (see Section 6.2). By separating, each will compete with unrelated individuals—the Canaanites and the Perizzites. At a casual reading, the mention of the latter tribes at this point may seem irrelevant, but in fact it is a telling detail in light of sociobiological theory. One is forced to concede that, although the authors of Genesis may have held quaint notions of human evolutionary history, they had a good intuitive grasp of the consequences that history has had for human nature.

Because daughter villages formed after a village fissions are focused on dependent offspring, they are often composed of affines. Thus lineally related kin split off from each other to go with those sharing kinship with their children. This process is nicely illustrated for the Yanomamö by Chagnon (1975). The repetition over time of this sort of process doubtless explains the widely observed phenomenon of dispersed clans and lineages. In societies with unilineal clan systems, a local community (settlement, village, etc.) will contain members of several different clans, which are connected by ties of marriage. Reichard (1928) provides numerous examples of this for the Navajo; a small portion of one of her genealogies is reproduced in Figure 4.7. Representatives of each clan will also be found in other settlements, so that the clan is broken up by the pattern of residence. On the hypothesis developed here, this residence pattern results because individuals have a closer common genetic interest with their close affines than with their distant clan brothers or sisters. It provides additional benefits in many cases; an individual traveling to a strange village may be able to expect hospitality from fellow clansmen (as is true for the Navajo; see Aberle, 1961).

Anthropologists have distinguished affinal links ("relationship by marriage") from consanguineal links (relationships of coancestry) but have often been unclear regarding the biological relevance of the former. From a biological point of view, an affinal link is important only when the linking marriage produces offspring. A fruitful linking marriage creates a genetic common interest between two groups that were previously unrelated or distantly related—the common interest in the offspring of the marriage. One would predict that an unfruitful marriage, since it creates no link of genetic common interest, should create no lasting alliance between groups of affines. Indeed, in many societies, a marriage is not considered to be consummated until a child is born, and childlessness is grounds for dissolution of the marriage. This attitude is attested in many non-Western societies (e.g., Evans-Pritchard, 1951) and in traditional enclaves within Western society (e.g. Fél and Hofer, 1969). Thus in cases of kin group fissioning, if two officially connected subgroups form a daughter group together and break away from their consanguineal kin, the theory predicts that they do so because of a close common interest in dependent offspring.

In many cases field anthropologists have no data on the actual process of kin group fissioning. Instead, they find a group of interrelated individuals which has been divided at some point in the past into two or more subgroups which occupy different areas, are distinguished by name, or play different roles in social or ritual contexts. As the example considered in the next section shows, the ideas presented here can be of use in describing the basis of such groupings as well.

5.2 The Basis of Kin Group Membership: An Example

In this section, I consider in detail an example in which individuals are grouped on the basis of relatedness to focal offspring. The data are from Bryant's (1981) outstanding study of an East Tennessee mountain neighborhood. Although much of Bryant's study is devoted to cultural issues, she does not study culture in the abstract but integrates the study of culture with that of social organization. Figure 5.2 reproduces a genealogy given by Bryant showing major connections among all individuals in the neighborhood. (Bryant mentions that some minor ties have been omitted, but it seems unlikely that any such omissions will have a substantial effect on estimates of relatedness.) Although in several cases members of this group are related in more than one way (e.g., there are some double first-cousins), few are inbred.

Bryant poses a problem with regard to the kinship system of these people. Residents of the area divide themselves into four more or less discrete, territorially distinct "families." There are only a few households whose "family" assignment is ambiguous in that some informants assign the household to one "family" and some to another. These families are known as the Bradleys, the Campbells, the Johnsons of Rocky Gap, and the Johnsons of Mine Flats. Thus the families are described in an idiom ordinarily used in English-speaking cultures to indicate descent, being denominated by surnames. Residents believe the community to have been founded by three men named Robert Johnson, Isaiah

Campbell, and Abraham Bradley, who arrived in the area around the middle of the last century. These three men, plus Hiram Johnson, who was one of Robert Johnson's sons, are viewed as the founders of the four family groups, Hiram Johnson being seen as the founder of the Johnsons of Mine Flats and Robert Johnson of the Johnsons of Rocky Gap. It is interesting, in view of the fact that the Johnsons of Mine Flats are considered to be a distinct group and not a subset of the Johnsons of Rocky Gap, that Hiram's exact relationship to Robert is not widely known and is frequently said to have been distant. Actually, there is good evidence (Bryant, 1981, pp. 30–32) that other families occupied the vicinity prior to the arrival of the three "founding" pioneers, and these other families provided spouses for some of the founders' descendants. Nonetheless, these other early families are largely forgotten.

In spite of the fact that the names of the four founders have provided labels for the family groups recognized today, the overlapping ancestries of living individuals (Figure 5.2) suggest that the current families are not descent groups in any straightforward sense. Bryant briefly considers and rejects the hypothesis that the families are patrilineally defined descent groups. That they are not unilineal descent groups is immediately obvious from the fact that, for example, not all the "Bradleys" are descended from Abraham Bradley in the male line and thus not all bear the surname Bradley. The same can be said for each other family group. Bryant does not consider the alternative hypothesis that the families represent cognatic descent groups on the Celtic pattern (see Fox, 1978), in which membership is assigned by descent in either line from an eponymous ancestor. This is perhaps a more appealing hypothesis than that of patrilineal descent, but it also fails to discriminate clearly among the families. Many individuals (as can readily be seen from Figure 5.2) are descended from two or more of the founding ancestors. For example, certain individuals are descended from both Robert Johnson and Isaiah Campbell and classified as Johnsons of Rocky Gap. And some individuals are descended from Hiram Johnson (and thus Robert Johnson) and from Abraham Bradley (the latter in a direct male line) and are classified with the Johnsons of Mine Flats.

Unfortunately, in her analysis of these data, Bryant has been misled both by the prevalence of unilineal models in anthropological thinking and by the antibiological views of certain cultural anthropologists. Her reaction, when faced with the fact that a unilineal model will not fit the data, is to lapse into skepticism. Citing Schneider (1972), Bryant argues that the families recognized by this East Tennessee community are not based on kinship at all. She writes (1981, p. 47):

> An appropriate "rule" explaining the allocation of individuals to family groups, constituted on the basis of observed regularities, would be: All descendants and affines of the descendants of the founder of a family are members of that family except those who are members of other families.

She then retreats into the idealist relativism so characteristic of American cultural anthropology (pp. 47–48):

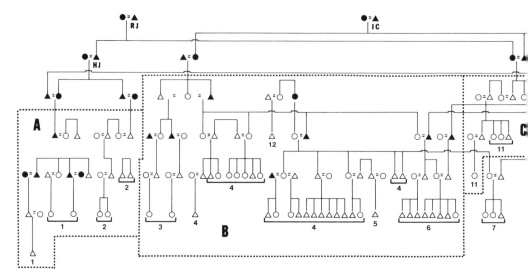

FIGURE 5.2. Genealogy of East Tennessee community. The four founding ancestors of the community are indicated by initials: RJ = Robert Johnson; HJ = Hiram Johnson; IC = Isaiah Campbell; AB = Abraham Bradley. Numbers identify the 12 focal offspring sets. The four "families" are indicated by letters: A = Johnsons of Mine Flats; B = Johnsons of Rocky Gap; C = Campbells; D = Bradleys. (Data from Bryant, 1981.)

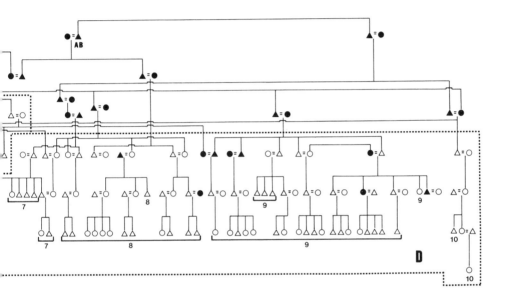

While it is possible to compose "rules" . . . that adequately "explain" these family groups insofar as they restate their composition and character in terms of general principles, these principles cannot be said truly to underlie and inform their creation unless they somehow accord with the indigenous understanding that both derives from and shapes these families.

On the contrary, I should argue that we cannot fully understand the culture or ideology of any kinship system unless we are able to examine how ideology corresponds to practice. There is a vast and largely unexploited potential for anthropological studies that relate poeple's concepts of kinship (the level of "culture" or ideology) to the actual biological facts of relatedness, insofar as we are able to ascertain them (the level of practice). I will illustrate here how such an approach might be applied to Bryant's data.

I tested the hypothesis that, rather than being based on descent, the families of Bryant's East Tennessee neighborhood are in fact based on relatedness to sets of focal offspring. To construct a minimal number of such sets, I first identified in the genealogy (Figure 5.2) all individuals that appeared to be of reproductive age or younger and were unmarried. These were unmarried individuals belonging to the youngest or first ascending generation; that is, unmarried individuals whose siblings were either unmarried or were parents (but not grandparents). I then divided these individuals ($N = 92$) into 12 sets (see Figure 5.2) on the basis of the following criteria:

1. Each member of a set is related to all other members of a set.
2. For any individual i of set m, there is no individual j who is not of set m such that $r_{ij} > r_{ik}$ for any individual k who is a member of set m. Thus no member of any other set is more closely related to i than any member of i's own set.

The resulting 12 focal offspring sets are the only ones possible which meet these criteria.

I used maximum relatedness of members of these offspring sets to individuals in Figure 5.2 as a basis for family classification. For each offspring set, I defined a variable ($R1-R12$) which takes the value of the highest r of any member of the set to a given individual. I computed values of these variables for all individuals from Figure 5.2 ($N = 94$) who are not themselves members of the focal offspring sets and who have values greater than zero for at least one of $R1$–$R12$. (The latter criterion excludes two childless inmarrying spouses.) I then applied canonical discriminant analysis to the variables $R1-R12$, to test their validity as predictors of group membership. The analysis yielded three highly significant canonical discriminant functions, which perfectly discriminated among the four family groups (Tables 5.4 and 5.5). The canonical coefficients set up complex contrasts among the variables $R1-R12$, reducing these 12 dimensions to three dimensions within which the four families are maximally separated.

The results certainly lead us to reject the extreme Schneiderian hypothesis that relatedness has nothing to do with family group membership in this East

TABLE 5.4. Raw Canonical Coefficients for the Focal Offspring Variables R1–R12 for Families in Figure 5.2, with Canonical Correlations and Probability Values for the Three Canonical Variables

Focal Offspring Variable	Canonical Variable 1	Canonical Variable 2	Canonical Variable 3
R1	5.67	19.49	9.14
R2	3.49	15.51	8.40
R3	8.82	−7.78	5.99
R4	6.47	−6.20	4.58
R5	6.17	−5.13	4.95
R6	7.47	−6.57	4.78
R7	−8.44	−1.97	3.75
R8	−7.52	−3.87	5.01
R9	−7.77	−4.14	5.22
R10	−9.47	−4.61	6.42
R11	0.24	−0.44	−6.32
R12	7.71	−6.62	6.03
Canonical correlation	0.958	0.940	0.770
P	<0.0001	<0.0001	<0.001

TABLE 5.5. Group Means of Canonical Discriminant Variables for East Tennessee Families from Figure 5.2

Family	Canonical Variable 1	Canonical Variable 2	Canonical Variable 3
A. Johnsons of Mine Flats	1.96	7.39	0.89
B. Johnsons of Rocky Gap	4.20	−2.03	0.42
C. Campbells	0.57	0.93	−3.21
D. Bradleys	−3.19	−0.61	0.33

Tennessee community. They further suggest that families are constituted on the basis of relatedness to focal offspring, rather than on the basis of descent. We are now in a position to pose some interesting questions about these people's ideology of kinship and their practice. They appear to use a metaphor of descent to describe groups that are in actuality based on relatedness to focal offspring. Why they should do so is a question worthy of serious investigation.

One possibility is that the descent metaphor has greater permanence over time than would group identity based on naming actual focal offspring sets. As long as the four "founding ancestors" are remembered by name, groups that contain at least some of their descendants can use their names as convenient labels even if group membership is in fact based on a principle other than descent. If the actual focus of family groups is dependent offspring, the offspring themselves will grow up and may move out of the area or even join other families. The composition of the local group will thus change considerably over time, but the ancestors provide an unchanging point of reference which can serve as a unifying symbol. It is interesting that each family has a graveyard at which "homecomings"—rituals of group solidarity—are periodically held (Bryant, 1981, pp. 93–94). It is hoped that the analysis presented here sheds additional light on these and other rituals of kin solidarity so vividly described by Bryant. The analysis furthermore raises the general question of whether there are other societies in which one finds groupings purportedly based on descent but in fact based on another principle of kinship.

5.3 Conflict within Kin Groups

In some cases where we have data on conflict within a kin group, the kin group, or some portion of it, can be divided into two warring factions. One might then be interested in explaining why individuals join one faction or another. In this case we may want to test the hypothesis that some aspect of biological related-ness is the basis for faction membership. Thus the problem is analogous to the problem of predicting daughter group membership in a case of fissioning. Con-flict between factions is, in fact, likely to precede village fissioning in the Yan-omamö (Chagnon, 1975). In many cases we have data on a conflict that initially involves a small number of individuals, perhaps just two combatants. Other individuals in the group may take sides with one combatant or the other; or they will remain neutral. In this section I apply kin selection theory to conflicts between two individuals within a group of kin and formation of factions in the support of combatants.

Suppose in a group of n individuals, two engage in a serious conflict over a resource correlated with fitness. How can we predict which side a given individ-ual will take? At first it might seem plausible to predict that an individual will support the combatant whose coefficient of relatedness to himself is higher. That is, individual i will side with individual j over k when $r_{ij} > r_{ik}$. However, this is not in fact what the theory predicts in a realistic situation. For human societies it is realistic to assume that in a serious conflict other individuals besides the two combatants have a stake in its outcome because the conflict will affect nepo-tistic sharing by the combatants in the future. The two combatants may actually be fighting over a resource which is likely to be shared nepotistically with kin. In many cases, however, there may be no obvious resource over which the com-batants fight. The ethnographic record is full of examples of conflicts among kin with apparently trivial causes. But even if the pretext of a fight is trivial, its outcome may be nontrivial. If either combatant is killed or driven from the group, any future acts of nepotism that he would have performed will be lost to his kin.

If conflicts impinge on future nepotistic sharing, we should predict that indi-vidual i will side with individual j rather than individual k when i's ultimate benefit in terms of inclusive fitness from j's activity is expected to exceed his ultimate benefit from k's activities. Since we are interested in nepotistic sharing, I assume (3.4) and (3.5) hold. Thus individual x's sharing with individual y will be proportional to r_{xy}. Individual i will side with individual j over individual k when

$$\sqrt{\frac{1}{\sum_{m=1}^{n} r_{jm}^2 v_m^2}} \; \mathbf{r}_i' \mathbf{V} \mathbf{r}_j > \sqrt{\frac{1}{\sum_{m=1}^{n} r_{km}^2 v_m^2}} \; \mathbf{r}_i' \mathbf{V} \mathbf{r}_k \qquad (5.1)$$

where $\mathbf{r}_i$ is the vector of coefficients of relatedness of all n individuals to i, and $\mathbf{r}_j$ and $\mathbf{r}_k$ are similarly defined. Thus i will side with j when j's kinship with other group members of high reproductive potential more closely matches i's than k's does.

In practice, it may be difficult to provide an estimate of $\mathbf{V}$ since exact ages are not known for nonliterate peoples. Unless one has made a very detailed census, one may not know all relevant persons who might benefit from nepotism of the protagonists in a conflict. Nonetheless, one can use less complete data to test the hypothesis that, when a conflict occurs between two individuals, others will side with the combatant with whom they have the greatest genetic common interest. One way to do this is to focus on individuals of high reproductive potential who are closely related to the combatants; in other words, sets of focal offspring, in the terminology used previously in this chapter. If an individual shares closely related focal offspring with one combatant and not with the other, we should predict that he will side with the former.

Consider an example from Lawrence (1984) of conflict within a New Guinea people known as the Garia. The principals were two adult men, M1 and P5 (Figure 5.3). Figure 5.3 includes all supporters of either combatant mentioned by

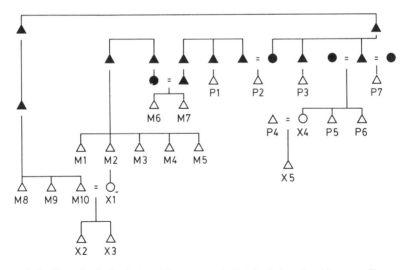

FIGURE 5.3. Genealogical relationships among individuals involved in a conflict among the Garia. The principals in the conflict are M1 and P5. For other individuals, M = supporter of M1; P = supporter of P5; X = other individual necessary to show links of genetic common interest but not involved in conflict. (Data from Lawrence, 1984.)

Lawrence for which he also provides information regarding a biologically significant connection with either combatant. By a biologically significant connection, I mean either a tie of common ancestry or a tie of affinity by a marriage which is known (from Lawrence's published data) to have produced offspring. This criterion in fact included all supporters of either combatant mentioned by Lawrence except one, who was linked affinally to one combatant but was excluded because no information was available concerning the fruitfulness of the linking marriage. Of course, only a fruitful linking marriage is of interest here, since only a fruitful marriage creates a genetic common interest. Women and children (X1–X5) are included in Figure 5.3 only where they are necessary for establishing ties of genetic common interest in offspring.

I estimated **R** for the 22 living individuals in Figure 5.3 and computed its principal components. A canonical discriminant analysis applied to PC1–PC3 of **R** correctly classifed the 17 adult males who took sides in the conflict, as regards the side favored (Table 5.6). PC1 indicates that relatedness in the entire

TABLE 5.6.   Principal Components of **R** for the Genealogy of Figure 5.3, with Scores for a Canonical Discriminant Function Applied to PC1–PC3 for All Adult Males ($N = 17$) Taking Sides in Conflict between M1 and P5 (Canonical Correlation = 0.882; $P <$ 0.005)

Individual	PC1	PC2	PC3	Discriminant Score
M1	0.353	−0.146	0.148	2.709
M2	0.404	−0.124	0.108	3.388
M3	0.353	−0.146	0.148	2.709
M4	0.353	−0.146	0.148	2.709
M5	0.353	−0.146	0.148	2.709
M6	0.066	−0.032	0.041	0.433
M7	0.066	−0.028	0.045	0.398
M8	0.111	0.281	−0.302	2.293
M9	0.111	0.281	−0.302	2.293
M10	0.159	0.326	−0.371	3.074
P1	0.004	0.009	0.012	−0.060
P2	0.015	0.140	0.099	−0.821
P3	0.010	0.137	0.102	−0.880
P4	0.007	0.094	0.091	−0.736
P5	0.022	0.341	0.306	−2.550
P6	0.022	0.341	0.306	−2.550
P7	0.017	0.226	0.186	−1.561
X1	0.334	−0.009	−0.042	—
X2	0.287	0.194	−0.263	—
X3	0.287	0.194	−0.263	—
X4	0.023	0.375	0.341	—
X5	0.018	0.295	0.267	—
λ	3.535	2.634	2.385	
Percent trace	16.1	12.0	10.8	
Discriminant coefficient	9.359	−2.374	−6.361	

group of Figure 5.3 is concentrated on M1 and his siblings, especially M2. The supporters of P5 are outsiders in the group as a whole, as indicated by their low weights on PC1. PC2 contrasts the group centered around P5 and P6 with those individuals not related to these men or any of their close relatives. Note that M8, M9, and M10, supporters of M1 in the conflict, are classified by PC2 with the supporters of P5, because M8–M10 are related to P5 but not to M1 and his kin. PC3 reflects the relationship between M8–M10 and X2 and X3. The discriminant function assigns M8–M10 to the group consisting of M1's supporters because of their relationship to X2 and X3 (as indicated by PC3). M8–M10 are not related to M1 himself and are distantly related to P5; but M8 and M9 are uncles to X2 and X3, M1's greatnephews, and M10 is the father of X2 and X3. Thus this tie of genetic common interest with M1 has led M8–M10 to side with M2 in spite of their relatedness to P5.

The importance of PC3 in correctly classifying M8–M10 suggests that, in this example, relatedness to focal offspring plays an important role in determining loyalties. This suggestion is further supported by the data in Table 5.7. These data show that relatedness to X2–X3 or X5 is a better predictor of side in the conflict than is relatedness to the protagonists M1 and P5. M1's supporters are more closely related to X2 and X3, and P5's to X5. The only exception is P1, who is unrelated to either X2 and X3 or X5. From Figure 5.3, we see that P1 is more closely related to P2 than to any of M1's supporters. Thus P1 may have been recruited to support P5 by P2, who is first cousin to both P1 and P5. With this exception, relatedness to the two focal sets of offspring explains the side taken by each individual.

TABLE 5.7. Relatedness to Adult Males from Figure 5.3 of the Two Combatants (M1 and P5) and of Focal Offspring X2, X3, and X5

Individual	r of M1	r of P5	r of X2, X3	r of X5
M1	1	0	0.125	0
M2	0.5	0	0.25	0
M3	0.5	0	0.125	0
M4	0.5	0	0.125	0
M5	0.5	0	0.125	0
M6	0.0625	0	0.015625	0
M7	0.0625	0	0.015625	0
M8	0	0.03125	0.25	0.015625
M9	0	0.03125	0.25	0.015625
M10	0	0.03125	0.5	0.015625
P1	0	0	0	0
P2	0	0.125	0	0.0625
P3	0	0.125	0	0.0625
P4	0	0	0	0.5
P5	0	1	0.015625	0.25
P6	0	0.5	0.015625	0.25
P7	0	0.25	0.015625	0.125

6

Kinship and Leadership

Quhen at the King and his folk ware
Arivit, as I tald yhow are,
At quhill in Carrik lendit he,
To see quha frend or fa wald be.
And nocht-for-thi the pepill wes
Inclynit to him in-to party;
Bot Inglis men sa angirly
Led thame wyth danger and wyth aw,
That thai na frendschip durst him schaw.
Bot a lady of that cuntre,
That wes till hym in neir degre
Of cosynage, wes wounder blith
Of his arivale, and als swith
Sped hir till hym, in full gret hy,
With fourty men in cumpany,
And betacht thame all to the King,
To help hym in his warraying.

JOHN BARBOUR, The Bruce (ca. 1375)

6.1 The Anthropological Study of Leadership

In this chapter I apply kin selection theory to the study of leadership and dominance in human local communities, including both stateless tribal societies and local kin-based communities that exist within the framework of a state. In the theoretical literature of social anthropology it has frequently been remarked that there is a relationship between kinship organization and leadership. For example, it has been remarked that individuals can make use of ties of kinship and affinity to achieve local leadership (e.g., Mair, 1962). Several ethnographic works have produced detailed evidence of this process in action. An excellent example is Thomas's (1982) study of leadership among the Pémon Indians. Thomas shows how leaders of various kinds in this society (both civil and religious) owe their positions, at least in part, to the number and strength of ties of kinship and affinity on which they can draw for support. Wilder's (1982) study of communication and social structure in rural Malaysia is another example; he documents the multiple ties of kinship and affinity linking the traditional elite of a Malaysian village.

In anthropological literature of this sort, it is generally taken for granted that one can make use of ties of kinship and affinity to achieve local political leadership. The authors apparently see no need of a theoretical framework to explain why it should be so. By implication, of course, they reject the extreme views of American cultural anthropologists, who hold that actual biological relatedness is irrelevant to social behavior. Instead, they adopt the theoretical framework of British social anthropology in the tradition of Radcliffe-Brown. This tradition accepted, largely without explanation, that solidarity among kin is a given of human social life.

Evolutionary biology, in particular the theory of kin selection, can provide an explanation for solidarity among kin, which was lacking in the earlier social anthropology. Chagnon (1982) was one of the first to explicitly link kin selection theory and the understanding of leadership in tribal societies. His argument, briefly, is that if natural selection has promoted the tendency to benefit and cooperate with kin, an individual who has abundant kin to provide support may be able to obtain a favored social position. The theory developed in Chapter 3 provides a method for making this argument more explicit. It yields the prediction that, in local communities of interrelated individuals, leaders will typically be individuals on whom, or on whose close kin, relatedness is concentrated (Hughes, 1986a).

For purposes of exposition, I will distinguish two types of leadership in human societies; in many actual cases, leadership involves elements of both pure types. I designate the two types of leaders Type I and Type II. A Type I leader receives a disproportionate share of some resource correlated with fitness. Well-known examples from the ethnographic literature include Yanomamö chieftains (Chagnon, 1982) and Melanesian "big men" (Sahlins, 1963). A Type II leader does not receive a disporportionate share of any resource but rather is chosen, because of his supposed impartiality, for a role involving the adjudication of disputes among others over resources correlated with fitness. Both types of leader are likely to be male. Type II leaders are often elderly, whereas Type I leaders are generally men in their prime.

In some human societies, access to food and shelter is essentially egalitarian. For example, in shifting agricultural economies like that of the Yanomamö, agricultural land is not in short supply and is not owned or defended. Yet, as Chagnon (1979) shows with his data on the Yanomamö, even in societies in which access to food and shelter is egalitarian, access to reproductive opportunity need not be egalitarian. Yanomamö chieftains obtain far greater than average reproductive success, obtaining multiple wives through the support of their close male kin. Reproductive opportunity itself is thus the resource of which these leaders obtain a disproportionate share. In more complex economies, material wealth is not equally distributed; in some of these, studies have shown a positive correlation between wealth and reproductive success. While studies of this sort are rare at present, it is of interest that such a correlation has been found in both polygynous (Betzig, 1986b; Borgerhoff Mulder, forthcoming; Irons, 1979) and monogamous societies (Hughes, 1986c).

Although there is evidence that the very wealthiest individuals in Western society have much greater than average reproductive success (Essock-Vitale, 1984), some studies in the developed countries of the Western world have found an inverse correlation between occupational status and reproductive success (e.g., Vining, 1986; Wrong, 1958). A partial explanation of this apparent contradiction may be that some occupations in Western society (including many of the so-called professions) have high status but relatively low average fitness. Mitchell and Pratto (1977) have found that certain "high-status" professional occupations involve a "career lifestyle" that deemphasizes the value of a family. In any event, the theory developed here depends on the assumption that there is a positive correlation between resources and fitness (Section 3.3). It is at least a plausible hypothesis that this relationship has held for most of human history and still holds in much of the developing world.

In the developed countries, an examination of all the data suggests that the relationship between "status" and reproductive success may resemble the curve in Figure 6.1. According to this hypothetical curve, for low-status classes, mean fitness increases with status. For low-status classes, it is assumed that income and status are closely correlated and that income predicts reproductive success. One reason for expecting this relationship is that infant mortality is high for the very poor even in developed countries (Stockwell and Wicks, 1984). Then, as one enters the "professional" classes, there is a leveling off or decline in reproductive success even as status increases. Finally, as Essock-Vitale's (1984) data suggest, the highest status and wealthiest individuals have greater than average reproductive success. The figure is hypothetical, but at least some data can be cited in support of each of its major features.

In stateless societies and probably in many local communities within states, an individual can obtain a disporportionate share of wives or resources only if he has the support of others. In general, those who lend such support are predicted to be individuals having a genetic common interest with the beneficiary. Any individual who does obtain a disproportionate share of any resource will be likely to use it to enhance his own fitness. If resources correlated with fitness are such that (3.4) and (3.16) hold, in a group of interrelated individuals a disproportionate share of resources will be given to individuals of high reproductive potential on whom relatedness is concentrated. Disproportionate resource shares should be given to individuals receiving the highest weights on PC1 of $(\mathbf{RV})'(\mathbf{RV})$. These individuals are predicted to include a Type I leader and/or his close dependent kin. When $\mathbf{V}$ is unknown, it is reasonable to predict that the leader and his close kin will receive high weights on PC1 of $\mathbf{R}$ or of $\mathbf{R}_w$.

A Type II leader should be chosen in such a way that, if he has any strong biases with regard to resource distribution, these accord well with the biases of a majority of group members. The leader himself will be biased in favor of his own close kin. This bias will be shared by other group members if relatedness is concentrated on the leader's close kin. Thus we should expect high weights on

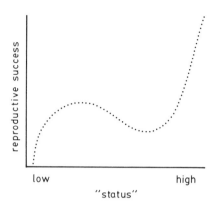

FIGURE 6.1. Hypothetical relationship between reproductive success and "status" in developed countries.

PC1 of $(\mathbf{RV})'(\mathbf{RV})$ for close kin of a Type II leader. However, a Type II leader will not himself receive a high weight on PC1 of $(\mathbf{RV})'(\mathbf{RV})$, since by definition a Type II leader does not himself receive a disproportionate share of resources correlated with fitness. There are two ways that a leader's close relatives receive high weights on PC1 of $(\mathbf{RV})'(\mathbf{RV})$ and yet the leader himself does not: (1) the leader may be an individual of low reproductive potential, such as a postreproductive individual; or (2) the leader may be an inmarrying spouse of a woman who has numerous ties of kinship within the group. The leader's children will thus be closely connected to group members even if the leader is not. For an apparent example of a leader of this sort, see Ross (1973) and Hughes (1986a).

In practice it will often be impossible to estimate $\mathbf{V}$. Also in real cases it may be difficult to assign a leader to either of these pure types since elements of both may be present. Nonetheless, the theory presented here yields a prediction that is both robust to variations in the mode of leadership and capable of being tested given the inevitable shortcomings in ethnographic data. For both types of leader, the theory predicts that the leader and/or his close dependent kin will receive high weights on PC1 of $\mathbf{R}$ or $\mathbf{R}_w$. Equivalently, if kinship relations are viewed as constituting a network, the leader will receive a high score for any measure of centrality or prestige within the network (see Section 4.1 above).

Anthropologists frequently speak metaphorically of kinship relationships as constituting a network (e.g., Thomas, 1982). The mathematics of network theory (Appendix B) and the concept of biological relatedness make the notion of a kinship network more than a mere metaphor. As mentioned previously, $\mathbf{R}$ itself defines a network. Even when the available data are such that we do not feel confident in estimating $\mathbf{R}$ itself, it may be possible to construct a network of kinship ties on the basis of minimal values of coefficients of relatedness (see, for example, Section 6.3 below). In subsequent sections of this chapter I test the foregoing prediction with data on leadership in some stateless societies. Next I examine how some of the same ideas can be used to understand the development of states and to understand aspects of kinship-based political interactions in states.

6.2 Nuer Headship and the "Nuer Paradox"

The Nuer are a cattle-herding people of East Africa. Evans-Pritchard (1951), in his classic study, describes their patrilineal segmentary kinship organization and also devotes some attention to the composition of local communities and leadership within them. A typical Nuer community is gathered around a headman, called the "bull" *(tut)* by the Nuer. In using this term, the Nuer make an explicit analogy between the leader of a local community and the dominant bull in a cattle herd. (Even an American cultural anthropologist should not object to the application of "sociobiological" models to Nuer society, since in this respect at least the Nuer themselves are "sociobiologists.") Evans-Pritchard's examples suggest that the bull is likely to be one of the wealthiest members of the community and is most likely to be polygynous. Wives in this society are obtained by paying a bride price in cattle, so there is a correlation between wealth and polygyny. Thus the Nuer bull, at least when in the prime of life, appears to approximate the ideal Type I leader as defined.

Nuer local communities include a variety of kin and affines of the bull. Evans-Pritchard's data suggest that the bull plays an active role in gathering such a community of supporters around him, and that the ability to gather a community of supporters determines which man becomes a bull. Evans-Pritchard writes (1951, pp. 27–28):

> It is the ambition of every man, of the dominant clan especially, to become a "bull" and the centre of a cluster of kin, and Nuer say it is for this reason among others that families often break up and cousins and brothers part, each to seek to gather his own community around him.

The "Nuer paradox" (Geertz and Geertz, 1975; Kelley, 1974) lies in the fact that, in spite of the emphasis the Nuer place on patrilineal descent, agnatic kin (male patrilineal kin) separate in this fashion, and actual Nuer communities contain a mixture of individuals related by patrilineal, matrilineal, and affinal ties.

The theory presented here predicts that if the bull himself gathers his own community, the community should be such that its members are predisposed by their own genetic self-interest to accept the bull's dominance. This will be so if relatedness within the group is concentrated on the bull and his offspring. The need to gather such a group would explain the fact that Nuer communities contain individuals linked to the bull in various ways, rather than necessarily including the bull's agnatic kin. Community members are likely to share relatives with the bull but are not necessarily related to each other. As a result, relatedness will concentrate on the bull or his children.

An example will clarify how this process works. Figure 6.2, from Evans-Pritchard (1951), shows the genealogy of a Nuer village. (Evans-Pritchard mentions

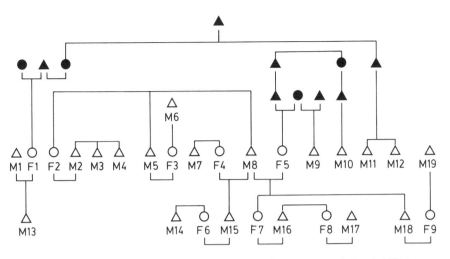

FIGURE 6.2. Genealogy of a Nuer village. (Data from Evans-Pritchard, 1951.)

that he was unable to include all village members because of censusing difficulties.) The bull is M8, the only polygynous male. The community includes, in addition to the bull and his wives and children, the following individuals: (1) the bull's brother M5, sister F2, and half-sister F1; (2) the bull's mother's brother's sons (M11 and M12), relatively close kin to the bull but not, of course, members of his patrilineage; (3) the bull's affines such as one wife's half-brother (M9) and her second cousin (M10) and the other wife's brother (M7); (4) his children's and siblings' affines. The pattern of concentration of relatedness is revealed by PC1 of **R** (Table 6.1). The bull M8 receives the highest weight, or "prestige score," in this kinship network. Other high weights are on the bull's daughter (F7), his son (M15), his brother (M5), and his sister (F2).

TABLE 6.1. Loadings on PC1 of **R** for the
Nuer Village in Figure 6.1

M1	0.036	M9	0.063
F1	0.229	M10	0.008
M13	0.157	M11	0.125
F2	0.356	M12	0.125
M2	0.000	M14	0.000
M3	0.000	F6	0.000
M4	0.000	M15	0.320
M5	0.356	F7	0.375
F3	0.000	M16	0.000
M6	0.000	F8	0.000
M7	0.056	M17	0.000
F4	0.086	M18	0.375
M8	0.455	F9	0.000
F5	0.178	M19	0.000

From a biological point of view, it makes good sense for a residential group to be clustered around individuals on whom relatedness is concentrated, especially when these individuals include dependent offspring (see Section 5.1). Intuitively, grouping individuals in this way makes more sense than grouping them on the basis of descent in one line only. What, then, are the functions of the Nuer patrilineal clans and lineages? One possibility, for which Evans-Pritchard's account provides some support, is that the emphasis on patrilineal descent serves to reinforce links among the bulls leading separate local communities. If one such local leader needs allies for some reason (such as a blood feud), ties with other local leaders could be invoked. A particular lineage can become "dominant" relative to others, as Evans-Pritchard terms it, if it includes a large number of such local leaders and thus has a wide power base.

6.3 Descent, Alliance, and Leadership

The emphasis of early social anthropologists on descent as a principle of social organization was countered in the 1950s and 1960s by an emphasis on "alliance" deriving from the work of Lévi-Strauss (1949), Dumont (1957), and Needham (1962), among others. The works of Lévi-Strauss have increasingly adopted an idealist perspective that has little in common with empirical science. Some others who have studied alliance shared this idealist perspective, while others such as Needham (1973) have focused on actual human behavior. The biological point of view adopted here shares an interest in alliance, while avoiding the idealist aspects of the "structuralism" of Lévi-Strauss. Relationships of alliance are affinal relationships among males. These relationships are indeed predicted to be significant, since a fruitful marriage alliance creates among two or more adult, potentially care-giving males a common genetic interest in dependent offspring (see Section 5.1).

However, as almost all anthropologists now realize, the controversy between "descent theorists" and "alliance theorists" was really unnecessary. The principles of descent and alliance are complementary in human social systems, and no system is likely to emphasize one at the expense of the other. From a biological point of view, this is exactly what one would predict. If the term "descent" is taken in a literal biological sense, when two individuals are grouped together on the basis of descent, such a grouping calls attention to the genes they are likely to share by virtue of descent from a common ancestor. Similarly, if a "marriage alliance" is understood in a biological sense, an alliance between two individuals or groups of individuals means that they share a common genetic interest in offspring which are relatives of each. The Nuer example shows how these principles complement each other in a society long taken as a paradigm of organization on the basis of descent. In spite of the patrilineal skeleton in Nuer society, affinal relations frequently determine local group membership.

Århem's (1981) data on the Makuna of Amazonia illustrate how ties of consanguinity and affinity interact in the achievement of leadership in a society superficially different from the Nuer. The Makuna live in small residence groups (averaging only 12.5 individuals) whose composition is variable over time. Most frequently, a residence group contains the nuclear families of two males who are close agnates, generally brothers, first cousins, father and son, and so forth. Such agnatically formed groups accounted for 56% of Århem's sample ($N = 18$ groups), while simple nuclear families accounted for 33%. Occasionally, affinally linked males may join a residence group (11% of Århem's sample). Århem argues that, in the Makuna, although local residence groups are based on patri-lineal ties, ties among groups are based on alliance. Thus in spite of the fact that both the Nuer and the Makuna have segmentary patrilineal descent systems, their social organizations are in a sense antithetical. In the Nuer local groups have an affinal basis and links between groups are by descent, whereas in the Makuna local groups tend to have an agnatic basis and links between them fre-quently are affinal. In both cases, however, ties of consanguinity and affinity are important for attaining leadership, since both are necessary for achieving a con-centration of relatedness on the leader and his close kin.

Århem provides genealogical data for Makuna inhabiting a specific area, the Komeña region, with a total population of just over 200. At the time of Århem's fieldwork, one individual ("Antonio") in this region had achieved a position of leadership extending beyond his own residence group. His leadership was acknowledged by nine residence groups in the region, including a little over half the population. Members of the 10 other residence groups in the region acknowl-edged no leader beyond the individual residence group. The genealogical infor-mation provided by the Makuna, as in the case of many other Amazonian peo-ples, is rather shallow, including four generations at most and often only three. In many cases exact relationships between males of the same patrilineal "sib" are not known or they are reported only as "classificatory brothers." For such reasons, some coefficients of relatedness are difficult to estimate, but the data are sufficient to test the hypothesis that a leader should occupy a central role in a kinship network. Indeed, the very form in which the Makuna keep track of kin-ship suggests an appropriate test, which illustrates the complementary roles of consanguinity and affinity.

The basic Makuna kinship group is a patrilineage, called a "sib" by Århem. There were six major sibs in the Komeña region at the time of Århem's field-work. These sibs are relatively small and vary considerably in number of adult male members (Table 6.2). I assume that, except perhaps in the smallest, nearly extinct Umua sib, each male has close agnatic kin of the same sib on whose support he can count. Within a sib, relatedness is relatively even (i.e., r^* not much greater than $\bar{r}$). Relatedness will be concentrated slightly on larger nuclear families as opposed to smaller nuclear families, but concentration of relatedness within a sib will be small relative to concentration of relatedness in a larger grouping containing two or more sibs linked by fruitful marriages. Thus if a male is to have relatedness concentrated on himself and his close kin, he should have strong ties to sibs besides his own.

For achievement of leadership, an adult male needs ties with other adult males who can be potential allies. Potential allies will be individuals with whom the prospective leader has genetic common interests; the strength of the tie will

TABLE 6.2.　Mean *T* Score and Number of Offspring for 62 Adult Male
Makuna, Compared with Leader Antonio

Sib	N	T	±S.D.	Number of Offspring	±S.D
Roe	16	0.673	0.126	2.06	1.98
Saina	26	0.724	0.116	2.15	2.30
Hemoa	7	0.679	0.163	3.43	2.88
Yiba	6	0.624	0.073	2.50	1.38
Rokhana	5	0.688	0.076	2.80	2.17
Umua	2	0.320	0.072	2.50	2.12
Antonio		0.895		8	

be proportional to the strength of the genetic common interest. A measure of a
male's common interest with males of all sibs can be constructed as follows. For
each adult male i, determine for each sib m the individual j who is the individual
most closely related to i who is also related to some adult male k of lineage m.
The product $r_{ij}r_{kj}$ is a measure of the strength of the genetic common interest in
j of i and k. Note that when i and j are consanguines, individual j is identical
with individual i and $r_{ij}r_{kj} = r_{ki}$. If there are n sibs in the society, a score of the
strength of individual i's genetic common interest with males of all lineages is
given by

$$T = \sum_{m=1}^{n} r_{ij}r_{kj} \qquad (6.1)$$

where j and k are as defined above.

I computed T values for adult males from Århem's genealogies. Means for
the six sibs are shown in Table 6.2 and compared with the value for the leader
Antonio. Males included in Table 6.2 are only those for whom Århem provided
data on age class; there were 15 other males, also assumed to be adult, for whom
T scores were computed. Antonio's T score was the highest of any adult male in
the genealogies, including those in Table 6.2 (mean = 0.676) and others
assumed to be adult (mean = 0.486). Antonio was a member of the most numerous lineage, the Saina. His leadership may thus have resulted both from the
numerical strength of his sib and from his close ties to other sibs as reflected by
the T score. Mean T score for the Saina sib was somewhat higher than that for
other sibs, but the difference is not significant (Table 6.2).

Antonio's ties with other sibs are illustrated in Figure 6.3. One of his wives
(K3) belongs to the Rokhana sib, but this fact does not create a known tie with
any Rokhana male because the exact relatedness of K3 to any other Rokhana
individual is not recorded. Thus T for Antonio may be underestimated. Such
flaws in the data affect T estimates for most males, but there is no evidence that
such flaws are more numerous in the case of any particular male or sib. It may
indeed be that individuals like K3 lack close relatives in their own sibs and thus
cannot be important for any close tie of alliance.

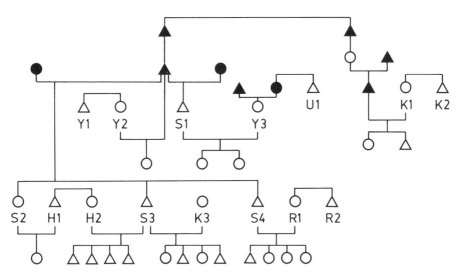

FIGURE 6.3. Genealogy illustrating the closest ties of Makuna leader Antonio (S3) of the Saina sib with adult males of other sibs. The sibs are indicated as follows: H = Hemoa; K = Rokhana; R = Roe; S = Saina; U = Umua; Y = Yiba. (Data from Århem, 1981.)

It is worthwhile to consider alternatives to the hypothesis developed here. It might be supposed, for example, that Makuna leadership is not a result of strength of kin ties but rather a result of some unique behavioral trait of the leader; or a result of accumulated monetary wealth (actually most unlikely in this subsistence economy); or a result of some source of power neglected by the ethnographer. A proponent of one of these hypotheses might argue that Antonio's T score is high because people are more likely to report (or perhaps even invent) kin ties with a leader so that they might benefit from his power. Now there is little doubt that, in societies (such as our own) where status derives from sources other than the kin group, people are more likely to keep track of distant relations with wealthy or powerful individuals than with poor or powerless ones (e.g., Firth, Hubert, and Forge, 1969). However, T as defined here is little affected by distant ties and so should not be greatly biased by differential gene-alogical memory. The fact that no data are available on close lineal relatives of K3 (Figure 6.3), for example, suggests that no one is likely to invent a close tie in order to appear close to the leader.

Århem himself (1981, p. 85) says the following about the sources of Anto-nio's leadership:

> He is headman of one of the largest residence groups in the territory, and he belongs to a senior segment of the Saina sib, by far the most numerous of the Komeña Makuna sibs. He also holds two ritual statuses—chanter and lead dan-cer. To these ascribed and achieved statuses, Antonio adds economic indepen-dence (he has two wives, many children and large gardens), physical ability (he is a good hunter and fisherman) and political skill and ambition. Finally, and

most importantly, Antonio controls the supreme political resource among the
Makuna—the only set of ceremonial feather head-dresses extant in the territory.
The fact that there is only one set of ceremonial feather head-dresses among the
Komeña Makuna and that it is kept in the long house of Antonio is the ultimate
source of his authority and political influence. By controlling the ritual ornaments of the territorial group, Antonio controls the ritual life of the whole river.
To the Makuna, the proper performance of communal rituals is considered necessary for the well-being of people in general, and communal rituals cannot be
held without the ritual ornaments. In the context of Makuna culture, then, control over the ritual life and property of the group means political power.

This passage calls for several comments. First, the hypothesis I have presented
here in no way implies that such traits as physical strength, intelligence, and
political skill are not important assets in a leader. It only states that a position
of centrality in the kinship network is a prerequisite for leadership; other aptitudes may make it possible for a particular indivdual to take advantage of the
position he has and to improve his position by wise marriage alliances. Surely
an incompetent person (invalid, retarded, insane) in a position of centrality in
a kinship network could not take advantage of it to achieve leadership. Antonio's possession of two wives and a large progeny cannot in itself be a major
factor in his achievement of leadership, since there are several polygynous males
in the genealogies and several males have as many children as does Antonio,
eight, and one has nine. As regards the importance of Antonio's possession of
ritual regalia, I do not dispute that this is an important symbol of leadership for
the Makuna and thus a *proximate* cause of Antonio's ability to be a leader; but
there are good reasons for doubting that it is the ultimate cause of his position.
First, ritual headdresses could easily be stolen or even destroyed. That the Makuna would probably never dream of doing such a thing, that they would consider
it the gravest sacrilege, is beside the point. The point is that Antonio possesses
the headdresses only because he has the sufferance of the community to do so.
I would argue that this sufferance is granted to Antonio not because of some
accident of inheritance (as might be true of an article of value in Western society) but because of his position in the kinship network. Since the value of the
headdresses is entirely symbolic, if so disposed the Makuna could cease to
accord their possession any importance—as they surely would if the headdresses
fell into the possession of some individual who had no "right" to them.

Århem here falls into the idealist trap of cultural anthropology. He sees a
mere symbol of leadership as a cause of leadership; he sees the level of the symbolic as causative on the realm of behavior. Further, like many anthropologists
(and many "sociobiologists"!), Århem shows a curious sort of Western ethno-
centricity in his attitude toward the possession of property. In a society without
police, law courts, or bank vaults, possession of any goods of real value (i.e.,
resources correlated with fitness) or of symbolic value is simply not the same as
in Western society. Any individual who possesses anything not shared by those
among whom he lives can have that possession only because those among whom
he lives *permit* him to have it. A single individual, no matter how personally
strong, intelligent, or domineering, is always at the mercy of a coalition of

aggressors. If one individual obtains, by whatever means, a disproportionate share of any resource and if his fellows do not immediately unite to strip him of his newfound wealth, they are in effect uniting to permit him to retain his disproportionate share. The theory developed in Sections 3.4 and 3.5 predicts that if a resource is correlated with fitness, an individual permitted to retain a disproportionate share will be one with high reproductive potential on whom relatedness is concentrated.

As it happens, centrality in the Makuna kinship network, as measured by T, is a predictor not only of the sort of wide-ranging leadership enjoyed by Antonio but also of a male's reproductive success. Århem classified individuals in 10 age categories, all of 5 years' breadth, except the last, which contains individuals 50 years or older. The 62 adult males in the sample of Table 6.2 are those over 15 years old, since the 15–19 year class is the first containing some individuals with offspring. For these 62 males, there is, as might be expected, a strong positive correlation between age class and number of children ($r = 0.780$, $P < 0.001$). There is no significant correlation between T and number of children ($r = -0.030$). But when one controls for the effect of age class, there was a highly significant positive partial correlation between T and number of children ($r = 0.679$, $P < 0.001$). This correlation does not prove that a high T score is a factor contributing to a high reproductive success, but it does support the hypothesis. Certainly it seems unlikely that a large number of children can cause a high T score. By his own admission, Århem's data do not include all children living at the time of his ethnography, but it also seems unlikely that a high T score would cause better reportage of numbers of children. Of course, a polygynous male, if he marries two women of different sibs, will create ties to both sibs that may increase his T score; and polygynous males may often have larger than average numbers of children. But some polygynous males have only average numbers of children; and polygyny does not always increase T, for example, when the woman has no close male kin within her sib (like K3 in Figure 6.3). In fact, there was no significant difference in mean T score between monogamous and polygynous males (on the basis of within-sib comparisons for the three sibs containing polygynous males.

The example discussed in this section gives some indication of how descent and alliance interact in a male's achievement of leadership and of reproductive success. It is important to be a member of a numerically strong lineage, but the creation of common genetic interest with other lineages may be even more important. This statement is supported by the fact that members of the Saina sib, in spite of its numerical superiority, have no greater mean numbers of children than males of other sibs. But ties with other lineages created by marriage may enable males to obtain greater than average reproductive success because they result in support and cooperation that would otherwise be lacking.

For the 62 adult male Makuna from Table 6.2, the regression of number of children on age class (starting with 15–19 as age class 1) is given by

$$\hat{Y} = -0.095 + 0.711X \tag{6.2}$$

Antonio, with eight children, has more than the predicted value for his age class

(4.17). Thus Antonio fits the definition of a Type I leader. Although not all men can be leaders to the extent that Antonio is, others can achieve a favorable position in terms of support from kin and affines, leading to above-average reproductive success. The positive relationship between T and number of children, controlling for the effect of age, suggests that ties of alliance create advantages for others beside the "leader." What those who would be leaders strive for is what all men strive for—reproductive success.

6.4 Marriage Preferences and Traditional Leadership among the Toda

In this section I consider a further example of leadership in a traditional society, which sheds additional light on the role of marriage in creating the ties that contribute to leadership. The society in question, the Toda of the Nilgiri Hills of South India, is of particular interest since it was the subject of a landmark study in the history of social anthropology (Rivers, 1906). Rivers provided data on traditional leadership within this society, of which neither he nor subsequent commentators have made much use. Because of the extensive genealogical material Rivers provided, his data can be used to test the hypothesis that leaders should be individuals occupying a central position in the kinship network. Certain peculiarities of the Toda marriage system, particularly the high incidence of fraternal polyandry, make exact estimates of **R** impossible. However, concepts of network theory make possible a test of this hypothesis even in the absence of precise data on coefficients of relatedness. Finally, the data on preferential marriage among the Toda illustrate the role of marriage in achieving local leadership.

The Toda, whose economy was based on water buffalo dairying, consisted of two endogamous divisions, called Tartharol and Teivaliol. The former division was superior in wealth and numbers. Within each division there were exogamous, localized patrilineal clans *(mad)*, each of which consisted of one or more lineages *(pòlm)*. Rivers identifies leaders for most of the pòlm (51 for Tartharol, 22 for Teivaliol). At the level of the entire Toda tribe, traditional leadership was vested in a council called the *naim,* which functioned to settle disputes. Rivers reports that the naim had a traditional clan composition; three Tarthar clans and one Teivali clan were represented. Rivers gives the membership of the traditionally constituted naim which had held office just prior to his fieldwork in 1902. By 1902, there was a new naim, lacking the traditional composition and having representatives of two clans from each division. This innovation was brought about by Kuriolv, a Teivali man of the largest clan (Kuudr), who was the dominant individual among the Toda at the time of Rivers's study. All traditional naim members were apparently pòlm leaders, but the new naim contained some members who were not pòlm leaders. Naim membership appears to have been a mixture of Type I and Type II leadership. The naim resolved disputes, but a member could use his position to advance his own interests, those of his close kin, or those of "friends" (Rivers, 1906, p. 553).

Two generations before Rivers's fieldwork, the British colonial government had instituted a new office among the Toda, called *monegar,* who was responsible for collecting the assessment paid by the tribe to the government (Prince Peter, 1955; Rivers, 1906). Apparently not realizing its potential as a source of power, the Tartharol considered this task beneath their dignity; thus it had been taken by members of the Kuudr clan of Teivaliol. In 1902 it was held by Ivievan, father's brother's son of Kuriolv. Prince Peter (1955) reports the existence of an office not noted by previous ethnographers of the Toda, the "purse-holder." This individual was a religious chief and repository of genealogical knowledge. But he also is said to have granted divorces and mediated disputes over compensation for stolen wives. Prince Peter names the holders of this office from the time of his fieldwork (1949) to the time of Rivers's fieldwork; all were members of Kars, one of the largest Tarthar clans.

The Toda practiced two types of polyandry: simultaneous, almost always fraternal polyandry; and sequential polyandry, caused by the custom called *teresthi* by which a married man could sell his wife to another for a number of buffaloes. Rivers's genealogies show that males who simultaneously shared one or more wives were almost always full or half-brothers, very rarely more distant agnates. Teresthi, on the other hand, generally involved males of different clans. Both Rivers (1906) and Emeneau (1941) accuse Toda women of "immorality" (by Western standards) and suggest that paternity confidence was low among the Toda. For example, Rivers (1906, p. 471) says that the Toda "among themselves attach little importance to paternity." However, this bold assertion is contradicted by other data reported by Rivers. A male acknowledged paternity of a particular child by a special ceremony in which he gave a bow and arrow to the mother. Even in a polyandrous household, each child was assigned to one of the co-husbands by this ceremony.

Rivers and Emeneau, in common with some other anthropologists discussing polyandrous systems, fail to distinguish two types of uncertainty about paternity which are in fact very different biologically. If we say that the paternity of a given child born to a polyandrous woman is uncertain, we may mean one of two rather different things: (1) it might be that the identity of the child's father is entirely unknown; or (2) it might be that there is little doubt that *one* of the mother's co-husbands is the father, although it is uncertain *which* co-husband is the father. In the latter case, since co-husbands were almost always brothers, even if a man were not the father of one of his wife's children, he would be closely related to the child. Rather than contributing to promiscuity, as Rivers and Emeneau supposed, polyandry can serve as a mechanism to ensure that a man's wives' offspring are related to him (Hughes, 1982, forthcoming).

There is some evidence that when paternity was uncertain among the Toda, polyandrous co-husbands at least had confidence that one of them was the father. First, the Toda traced the pedigree of their buffaloes in the female line only. They told Rivers (1906, p. 471) that they did not keep track of relatedness in the male line because it was impossible to assign paternities in the case of buffaloes, which were kept in mixed-sex herds. The Toda thus had a concept of paternity uncertainty and yet did assign paternity among themselves and trace descent in the male line. Rivers, applying a surprisingly modern "sociobiological" technique, tried to check Toda paternities by a genetic marker. He had obtained data on color-blindness among the Toda, which he compared with the genealogical record. Although the inheritance of sex-linked traits like color-blindness was not fully understood at this time, Rivers did apparently find that the trait ran in families, satisfying him that fathers were often related to their putative children. See Hughes (in press) for further discussion.

To examine leadership among the Toda, I constructed a network of kinship ties among pòlm leaders (and others who were members of the new naim) as follows. A kinship tie was defined to exist between two males if there existed at least one individual related to each of them by a minimum value of r equal to at least 0.125. The minimum value of r was based on the assumption that, in the case of a polyandrous male, his wife's offspring were actually his nephews or nieces ($r = 0.25$) rather than his own children ($r = 0.5$). From the network of such ties (Figures 6.4 and 6.5) I computed measures of centrality of an individ-

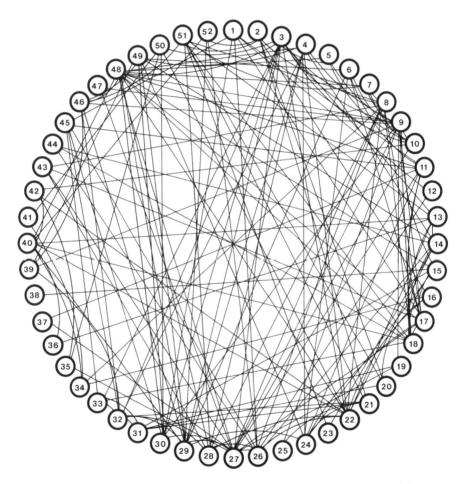

FIGURE 6.4. Network of kinship ties among 52 leading males of the Toda division Tartharol; an additional leading male is not included because he lacked any kinship ties. A kinship tie is defined to occur between two males if there exists some individual related by at least 0.125 to each.

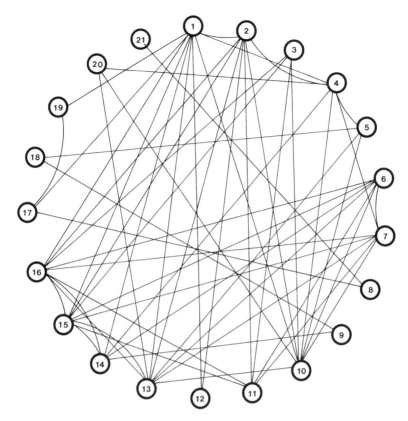

FIGURE 6.5. Network of kinship ties among 21 leading males of the Toda division Teivaliol; three additional leading males are not included because they lacked kinship ties. A kinship tie is defined as in Figure 6.4.

ual in his kin network: the number of other males reachable in one step in the network, the number reachable in two steps, and an eigenvector centrality score (4.2). Traditional and new naim members differed significantly from other leading males in both the Tartharol (Table 6.3) and Teivaliol (Table 6.4). The dominant individual in the tribe, Kuriolv, and the purse-holder, Parkurs, both scored especially high on these measures of centrality.

There is evidence that centrality in the kinship network is correlated with reproductive success. I obtained a conservative estimate of reproductive success as follows. For each male I counted the number of offspring, attributed to him and/or his co-husbands by Rivers, which either (1) were living at the time of Rivers's survey, or (2) had died at the time of Rivers's survey but had lived long enough to produce offspring of their own, who were living at the time of Rivers's survey. For polyandrous males, reproductive success was estimated as the number of offspring divided by the number of co-husbands. This measure of reproductive success was positively correlated with the number of other males reachable in one step ($r_s = 0.423$, $P < 0.01$ for Tartharol; $r_s = 0.682$, $P < 0.01$ for Teivaliol) and with centrality score ($r_s = 0.344$, $P < 0.05$ for Tartharol; $r_s =$

TABLE 6.3.   Members of the Tartharol on the Traditional Naim and New Naim
Compared with Other Leading Members with Respect to Number of Individuals
Reachable in One or Two Steps in the Kinship Network and Centrality Score, with
Probability Levels of Kruskal–Wallis Tests

Individual	Clan	One Step	Two Steps or Fewer	Centrality Score
Traditional Naim				
Kudòdrsvan (3)[a]	Nòdrs (3)[b]	13	46	0.260
Parkurs (9)	Kars (8)	17	47	0.292
Piutolvan (11)	Kars (10)	9	34	0.173
Ircheidi (22)	Taradr (20)	11	42	0.193
Mean		12.5	42.3	0.230
New Naim				
Pidrvan (6)	Kars (9)	6	35	0.125
Parkeidi (27)	Taradr (21)	15	43	0.274
Siriar (28)	Taradr (20)	8	41	0.163
Paners (29)	Taradr (23)	11	43	0.217
Mean		10.0	40.5	0.195
All others ($N = 45$)				
Mean		5.6	29.0	0.097
(Range)		(0–15)	(0–47)	(0–0.325)
P		<0.005	<0.025	<0.001

Source: Hughes (forthcoming).

[a]Numbers in parentheses refer to Figure 6.3.
[b]Numbers in parentheses refer to Rivers's (1906) genealogies.

0.639, $P < 0.01$ for Teivaliol). The higher correlations among the Teivaliol may
reflect greater scarcity of potential wives in this division (see below) and, accord-
ingly, a greater payoff to those able to manipulate kinship ties in order to obtain
wives of high quality. It should be noted that the relationship between centrality
in the kinship network and reproductive success is a complex one. It is hypothesized that a central position in a kinship network can actually enhance reproductive success, since the support of kin may enable a man to obtain more wives
or wives of better quality in terms of age and health, and may even increase
survival of offspring. On the other hand, a male may also increase his links to
other leading males by having children, as he would do if his wife's father or
brother were a leading male. But this effect cannot be a major factor in increasing
a male's centrality, since at most one such new link would be obtained per fertile
wife.

Like many other South Indian peoples (Trautmann, 1981), the Toda are
reported to have a system of preferential cross-cousin marriage, but neither Rivers (1906) nor Emeneau (1941) clarifies the entire set of referents of the term
matchuni, the preferred marriage category. The primary meaning of the term is
cross-cousin; it seems likely that for a male ego any woman of his generation of
the appropriate clan (i.e., his mother's clan or his father's sister's husband's clan)
would be his matchuni. I classified marriages as being of three types: (1) A man

marries his actual cross-cousin (father's sister's daughter or mother's brother's daughter), his matchuni in the strict sense. (2) The marriage is with the appropriate clan; thus a man marries a woman of his mother's clan or a woman whose mother belongs to his own clan. (3) The marriage is not according to the preferential rule in either of these senses.

There were 362 marriages in Rivers's genealogies for which sufficient information (clan membership of both spouses' parents) was available (Table 6.5). Inappropriate marriages are rare among the Teivaliol (9.7%) but common among the Tartharol (59.8%). But there is a different relationship between status and marriage type in the two divisions, if pòlm leaders and other naim members are classified as being of "high status" in comparison with other males. Among the Tartharol, high-status males were less likely to contract marriages of the "preferred" type. Among the Teivaliol, this trend was reversed; high-status Teivali males were more likely to contract marriages of the "preferred" type.

A man's own marriage and the marriages of his close kin can be used to create ties of genetic common interest where none existed or where only distant ties existed before. Thus marriage alliances can be used to achieve or enhance a position of dominance. It is in the context of striving for a position of dominance within the society that a preferential marriage "rule" needs to be examined. Marriage with a cross-cousin perpetuates an existing tie, but it does not create a new tie. From the point of view of building a base for leadership, the "preferred" marriage acutally seems inadvisable. Thus the very existence of the preference is paradoxical. The differences between the two Toda divisions in adherence to the rule (Table 6.5) also require explanation.

Here I discuss one hypothesis (Hughes, forthcoming) that might account for

TABLE 6.4. Members of the Teivaliol on the Traditional Naim and New Naim Compared with Other Leading Members with Respect to Number of Individuals Reachable in One or Two Steps in the Kinship Network and Centrality Score, with Probability Levels of Kruskal–Wallis Tests

Individual	Clan	One Step	Two Steps or Fewer	Centrality Score
Traditional Naim				
Kuriolv (1)[a]	Kuudr (52)[b]	10	19	0.309
New Naim				
Ivievan (2)	Kuudr (52)	8	17	0.300
Perner (15)	Keadr (68)	9	17	0.341
Tebner (16)	Keadr (68)	9	17	0.341
Mean		8.7	17.0	0.327
All others ($N = 20$)				
Mean		3.8	10.1	0.126
(Range)		(0–9)	(0–18)	(0–0.331)
P		<0.025	<0.05	<0.025

Source: Hughes (forthcoming).

[a]Numbers in parentheses refer to Figure 6.4.
[b]Numbers in parentheses refer to Rivers's (1906) genealogies.

TABLE 6.5.   Adherence to Preferential Marriage Rule by Toda with Log-Linear Model Analysis of Effects of Division (Tartharol vs. Teivaliol), Status, and Division by Status Interaction on Adherence to the Rule

Husband's Division and Status	Actual Kin	Appropriate Clan	Not According to Rule	Total
Tartharol				
Low status	22	56	115	193
High status	4	22	40	66
Teivaliol				
Low status	12	58	7	77
High status	5	18	3	26

Log-linear model ANOVA

Source of variation	Degrees of Freedom	χ^2	P
Intercept	2	46.08	0.0001
Division	2	43.38	0.0001
Status	2	2.28	n.s.
Division × status	2	11.11	0.004

Source: Hughes (forthcoming).

these data; this hypothesis also has implications for the understanding of marriage rules in general. If potential wives are truly in short supply, as they must be in a small endogamous community, the existence of a preferential rule may provide an advantage for a young marriageable male. The male will have a claim on any woman standing in the preferred category; this will give him an advantage over any competitors lacking anyone with the appropriate relationship. Marrying a woman in the preferred category can thus enhance both a male's status and his reproductive success, since individuals so unfortunate as to lack a potential spouse in the preferred category may have to remain unmarried or marry a woman who, with respect to age or health, is a less than ideal mate. Since the Teivali population was small, wives may have been in short supply. There was a higher incidence of sequential polyandry (teresthi) among the Teivaliol. Of 103 Teivali marriages in the sample, 61 (59.2%) involved sequentially polyandrous females. Of the 259 Tarthar marriages, 86 (33.2%) involved sequentially polyandrous females. The difference between divisions in proportion of teresthi marriages is significant ($\chi^2 = 20.69$; 1 d.f.; $P < 0.0001$). The high incidence of teresthi suggests scarcity of spouses. Patrilateral marriages were also more common among the Teivaliol (Table 6.6). Of 101 Tarthar marriages that could be classified as either matrilateral or patrilateral, 58 (57.4%) were matrilateral. On the other hand, of 66 unilateral Teivali marriages, only 19 (28%) were matrilateral. This difference also is significant ($\chi^2 = 13.17$; 1 d.f.; $P < 0.001$). Since patrilateral marriages involve delayed exchange (in alternating generations) of females by groups of agnatic kin, this difference may also reflect scarcity of women among the Teivaliol.

On the other hand, in a somewhat larger population, availability of potential wives may no longer be as much of a problem. In this case, it may be a better strategy for a male to avoid the preferred category. Instead, he can use marriage to establish a tie of genetic common interest with a group of males to whom he had no previous ties. The preferential rule would then become a default rather than a true preference. It may be to the male's advantage to keep the myth of a preference alive so that he will retain a claim on women in the preferred category. Thus he will have a default option in case he is unable to obtain a better marriage. The data on the Tartharol are consistent with this hypothesis. The Tarthar population was more than twice that of the Teivaliol, and the incidence of marriage in the "preferred" category was correspondingly reduced.

Anthropologists who have sought to measure the degree of compliance with preferential marriage rules have reported widely divergent results. Consider a few examples from the Dravidian speakers of South India and Sri Lanka. Grigson (1938) and Sivertson (1963) record compliance of over 50% among the Hill Maria and in Tanjore, respectively. At the other extreme, among the Kandy of Sri Lanka, Yalman (1967) records compliance of only 13% and Robinson (1968), only 6%. The hypothesis advanced here might account for such divergences; one way of testing it would be to test for a correlation between adherence to the rule and availability of spouses. Availability of spouses is a function of the size of the endogamous community. In a tribal society, the endogamous community may be equivalent to the tribe. In complex caste societies, such as many in South India, the size of the endogamous community depends on geographical mobility of potential spouses.

It is a logical consequence of the foregoing hypothesis that when the option of a "preferred marriage" is no longer needed even as a default, consanguineous marriages may actually be prohibited. When there is no scarcity of potential spouses and the formation of alliances with a number of different groups is a prerequisite to dominance or leadership, it may be in parents' interest to forbid consanguineous marriages by their children.

The occurrence of such prohibitions is widespread. They have been found in

TABLE 6.6. Toda Marriages which Follow Preferential Rule, Classified as Matrilateral or Patrilateral or Both

	Tartharol			Teivaliol		
	Low Status	High Status	Total	Low Status	High Status	Total
Wife = cross-cousin						
FaZDa	13	1	14	8[a]	3	11
MoBrDa	9	3	12	3[b]	2[b]	5
Both	0	0	0	1	0	1
Wife of appropriate clan						
H clan = WMo clan	22	7	29	29	11	40
HMo clan = W clan	31	15	46	13	4	17
Both	3	0	3	16	1	17

Source: Hughes (forthcoming).
Key: Br = brother; Da = daughter; Fa = father; H = husband; Mo = mother; W = wife; Z = sister.

[a]Includes three cases where HFaZDa clan = HMo clan.
[b]Includes one case where HMoBrDaMo clan = H clan.

societies which, although considerably larger than either Toda moiety, are still quite small. An example is the Omaha, who numbered just over a thousand in 1883 (when, however, they had probably been much reduced by disease; Barnes, 1984). Prohibitions against consanguineous marriages are often found in much larger societies, such as the Bantu tribes of East Africa (e.g., Wagner, 1970). Anthropologists have noted that such prohibitions lead to "dispersed alliance" (McKinley, 1971); but they have generally seen the advantage of dispersed alliance in terms of the cohesion of the society as a whole (e.g., Wagner, 1970). See Alexander (1979) and Chapter 1 above for a discussion of objections to functional explanations which see a function at the level of the society as a whole. The quest for a position of dominance provides an advantage to dispersed alliance operating at the level of the individual, or of a small group of closely related individuals, rather than the society as a whole.

There are, of course, individual-level advantages to dispersed alliance which have been suggested by ethnographers. Many of these suggestions are based on the hypothetical advantage of using marital ties to make potential allies of what otherwise might be enemies, as first suggested by Tylor (1888). The hypothesis presented here is in harmony with such explanations but emphasizes the positive advantages of gaining allies rather than mere appeasement of potential enemies.

6.5 Kin Politics and the Development of the State

In this section I speculate briefly on the role of processes discussed earlier in this chapter in the development of small-scale states. Mair (1962, 1977) discusses the development of states in East Africa, using available historical evidence and ethnographic data. Similar processes of development have occurred elsewhere in the world, for instance, in the development of feudal lordships among the tribes of early Medieval Europe. I next consider how some of the scenarios discussed by Mair can be modified to incorporate an explicit role for biological relatedness.

One process of state formation begins with a Type I leader: a "big man" on whom relatedness within a group is concentrated, a leader whose position depends on his numerous ties of consanguinity and affinity. The next stage of development occurs when such a chieftain is able to gather around himself a band of young warriors in order to enforce his wishes. Some of these young warriors may be close kin to the chief, but others will not be. The chief's ability to gather such a band apparently depends on several factors. First, the economy must be prosperous enough that young men can be spared for the chief's retinue. Second, the chief must be able to recompense retainers who are not his close kin. The theory predicts that if the chief's military activities serve to enhance his own fitness (e.g., by capturing livestock or women), the chief's close kinsmen will want little or no recompense beyond the increase in their own inclusive fitness deriving from the increase in their leader's personal fitness, presuming this increase is large enough to offset any risk or cost to themselves. But the case will be different with supporters that lack close genetic common interest with the chief. To obtain the support of such retainers, it is important that the chief and his band be able to engage in mutually profitable plundering, yielding sufficient spoils so that all band members can have a share. Thus for this sort of chieftainship to develop, mobile portable wealth must be available.

Chieftainships of this sort seem to have recurred repeatedly in human history. Mair (1962) gives examples from East Africa. Tacitus describes a virtually identical situation among the ancient Teutonic tribes (*Germania* 13–14). The chieftains and petty "kings" of early Medieval Wales held a similar plunder-based rule (Davies, 1982). A Welsh chieftain was called *bonheddig,* a "man of stock," meaning a man with a large kin group (Davies, 1982). This term serves as a reminder that no chieftain could reach the point of gathering a band of retainers without the support of a large kinship network.

A further stage in the development of the state occurs when, often under the leadership of a warlike chieftain of the sort just described, one tribe or people is able to conquer an unrelated people (Mair, 1962). This sort of conquest creates a stratified society, the conquered becoming a peasant class who are forced to pay a tribute or tax of their produce to support their new ruling class. After such stratification is established, new leaders can arise within the ruling class by a process similar to that occurring in a stateless society; that is, one individual can achieve leadership within the ruling class by achieving a position of centrality in its kinship network.

The ruling classes created by the Norman conquest of England and Scotland seem to have fit this pattern. An excellent example of how an individual could make use of ties within such a ruling class to achieve leadership is provided by the career of Robert Bruce (1274–1329), who became King Robert I of Scotland. As documented by Barrow (1976), Bruce had multiple ties of kinship and affinity with other powerful Norman–Scottish nobles. When the throne was unoccupied in a period of attempted annexation by England, Bruce was able to call on these ties to achieve support for his claim to the throne. In the long period when Bruce was an outlaw, support from his kin and affines enabled him to escape his English pursuers. The cost borne by his supporters was not trivial, since the penalty for sheltering Bruce was death. I do not wish to deny the importance of traits of character and skillful use of political propaganda, which clearly contributed to Bruce's success (Barrow, 1976). It is doubtful, however, that even these traits would have been enough to ensure his eventual triumph were it not for his central position in the kinship network of the Scottish ruling class. Of course, Bruce did not himself have vastly greater than average reproductive success; but he did seem to use his throne, when he had finally secured it, to enhance his inclusive fitness—most notably by rewarding his relatives with estates confiscated from his opponents (Barrow, 1976).

Betzig (1986b) examines historical examples of "despotism" in which despotic rulers have had far greater than average reproductive success by possessing numerous wives. It is unclear how much insight such despotic rulers can give us regarding the origin of the state in general, since the data suggest that extreme despotism has been rare in human history. For example, some of the African kingdoms which provide the most spectacular examples of despotism were based on a unique situation: rulers and their armies possessed firearms, and subject peoples lacked them (Mair, 1977). In fact, it is difficult to come up with an objective definition of "despotism." In any event, it is doubtful how relevant extreme despotisms are for a general theory of the origin of the state. A general theory of state origins must take into account not only extreme despotisms but also kingdoms like those of feudal Europe, in which rulers lacked both the vast harems of some oriental and African potentates and much of such potentates' absolute power.

Many Medieval rulers (including Robert Bruce) had mistresses in addition to their legal wives and thus were perhaps able to achieve slightly greater than average reproductive success; but there is a vast difference in reproductive success between the feudal ruler and the polygynous despot. It is no explanation at all to attempt to attribute this difference to the imposition of monogamy by the Church, since this leaves unexplained why Medieval rulers (or other Medieval Europeans) chose to accept the Church's authority in this matter. One explanation is that the role of the monarch in a feudal kingdom may have been different from that of a "despot." The Medieval European monarch may have been more of a Type II leader than a Type I leader. At least within the nobility itself, the monarch may have had no greater than average reproductive success, although the nobility may well have had greater average reproductive success than the lower classes.

The relationship between feudal upper and lower classes was no doubt exploitative in many respects, although it is worth mentioning that the armed nobility did provide protection for the unarmed peasantry, in return for the resources they extracted (e.g., Davies, 1982). The nobles themselves, although often in conflict with one another, were capable of joining in a mutualistic relationship, and the monarch was the focus and orchestrator of this mutualism. The primary cooperative activity of the nobles was, of course, warfare, the aim of which was to gain resources (land, ransoms from defeated enemies, and so forth). If successful, the ruler distributed the resources gained among his supporters. Robert Bruce's distribution of confiscated lands after his victory at Bannockburn (Barrow, 1976) certainly fits this model. Indeed, the primary function of a Medieval ruler seems to have been the acquisition of plunder, which was then distributed among supporters (Davies, 1982; Tuck, 1985). The same sort of activity characterized several African monarchies as well (Mair, 1977); thus, despite their polygynous tendencies, many African rulers may have been nearer to the feudal model than to the model of "despotism" Betzig (1986b) envisages.

The maintenance of a dynasty in a kingdom whose ruling class is united by ties of kinship and affinity involves reforming and strengthening of alliances by marriage at each generation. Thus, rather than simply inheriting his position without a struggle, the ruler of such a kingdom has continually to reaffirm it by gaining support through ties of genetic common interest with currently powerful nobility. There is evidence of this process in African kingdoms (Mair, 1977) as well as Medieval England (Tuck, 1985) and Wales (Stephenson, 1984).

When, as in Medieval Europe, there are continuous shifts in the relative power of various groups of nobility, then royal families may have to readjust their alliances at each generation. Under more stable circumstances, certain noble families may maintain power for generations. In this case, a royal lineage may pursue a different sort of marital strategy. One function of royal incest (marriage between a king and his sister), as practiced at various times in history, may be that it maintains a high relatedness of the king's progeny to individuals related to him. Thus it seems to slow the weakening of ties to the throne over time (Figure 6.6). Also, brother–sister incest within a royal family does not favor any group of their kin, as marriage with a cousin would do. Royal incest can serve to maintain unchanged a set of alliances with groups whose power remains stable.

Finally, it is possible that when a kingdom has existed for some time, the monarch, rather than being an actual ruler, becomes himself only a symbol of rule—rather like the Makuna ceremonial headdresses mentioned earlier. In this case, the "power behind the throne" may be an individual occupying a central position in a kinship network of the nobility, who possesses the monarch as a symbol of his authority and rules through him.

6.6 Patronage: Kin Politics in Advanced Societies

Once a complex, stratified society has developed, new social relations come increasingly into being in which kinship is not involved. Advanced industrial economies require cooperative, productive labor involving individuals who are neither kin nor affines; close cooperation among individuals lacking any genetic common interest has no doubt been a great rarity for most of human history. Frequent mobility and urban living patterns cause people to live among non-kin—again surely an unprecedented situation for most of human history. Under these circumstances, it is not surprising that interactions among kin have diminished importance in political life, in comparison with simpler societies. Yet there remain a few areas in which kinship interactions retain political and economic importance in advanced societies. Interestingly, English speakers tend to group these types of interactions under a single heading—patronage—even though

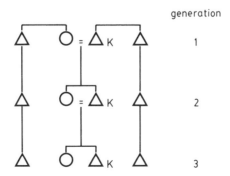

FIGURE 6.6. Hypothetical genealogy showing how royal incest maintains symmetrical relatedness of two kin groups to the king, K, and his offspring.

they really have little in common other than that they involve kinship and that they are considered vaguely unethical in democratic political systems.

Separate senses in which the term patronage is commonly used include the following:

1. A system in which those holding political office give positions to their relatives, irrespective of their abilities, is often called a patronage system.

2. Also called patronage is a system in which employers, while paying relatively low wages, recompense their employees by taking a "paternal" interest in their lives; this paternal interest includes preferential hiring of the relatives of trusted employees (e.g., Shifflett, 1982).

3. In many societies there is a ruling class or caste whose members lack virtually any ties of kinship with the subject class or caste. However, the subject class lives in communities within which there are numerous ties of relatedness. (Actually, of course, there may be more than two such classes, arranged in hierarchical fashion, but it is simplest to consider the interaction of only two classes.) Members of the ruling class require support from the subject class in order to maintain their position. In an electoral political system this support may take the form of votes. In an authoritarian system it is simply the tacit consent of the governed and the absence of rebellions. Members of the ruling class have some limited patronage—employment or other favors—at their disposal. They dispense patronage in such a way as to maximize support for themselves on the part of the subject class.

The first two types of patronage are easily related to inclusive fitness theory. In the first case, a nepotistic official may enhance his inclusive fitness by helping his relatives—especially when the latter are unable to help themselves. In the second case, the employer is paying his employees partly in units of inclusive fitness rather than in cash, doubtless a profitable arrangement from his point of view and one in which the workers may be willing to acquiesce *faute de mieux*. Hughes (1986a) suggests a way in which the third type of "patronage" can be related to inclusive fitness theory and predicts an optimal strategy of patronage in this case. The ruling class can patronize only one or a small number of individuals, because the resources available for patronage are limited. If the resources given are correlated with fitness, then the individuals patronized will have enhanced personal fitness, while their close kin will have enhanced inclusive fitness. The ruling class should use the limited patronage available to maximize the number of individuals who benefit in terms of inclusive fitness. Thus the beneficiaries of patronage should be individuals of high reproductive potential on whom relatedness in the subject community is concentrated. If **RV** is computed for the subject community, the optimal strategy is to patronize individuals receiving high weights on PC_1 of $(\mathbf{RV})'(\mathbf{RV})$. Obviously, for this type of patronage to operate, the subject populations must have low mobility so that communities consist of large numbers of interrelated individuals.

There are at least qualitative data supporting the prediction that ruling classes pursue this strategy of patronage. Campbell (1964) describes how, in rural Greece, members of the nomadic shepherd community (Sarakatsani) may be patronized by prosperous and politically powerful village dwellers. Although they are nomadic, shepherds may vote in elections, in a village near which they spend part of the year, for such officials as the village president.

> It is by no means certain that a President will accept any Sarakatsanos as his political client. . . . The chief service the shepherd is able to pledge in return is his vote and those of his family and associated kinsmen. But to accept a man as a client commits the patron to protection instead of exploitation, and to that extent it is a restriction on the free expression of his power. A President generally prefers to assume these obligations only to Sarakatsani with some influence. (Campbell, 1964, p. 231)

A similar situation is described by Caudill (1962), who relates in picturesque terms the tactics employed by elected school board trustees in the Cumberland Plateau region of eastern Kentucky in the early decades of the twentieth century:

> The political school trustees discovered that many teaching positions were occupied by men and women from other states. Their qualifications might be excellent; an illiterate trustee was unlikely to know what the qualifications were. But he could appreciate that these "fotched-on" [i.e., "fetched in" or imported from outside] instructors were without local relatives who could vote for him, the superintendent and his other allies, while there were other applicants for the job who could point to dozens of first and second cousins and a small army of uncles and aunts. The politicians could not resist the temptation to profit from this situation. One by one the competent teachers from outside the plateau were dropped from the rosters and the sons and daughters of local citizens assumed their duties. (Caudill, 1962, pp. 135–136)

In many cases the same sort of "patronage" may be involved in "indirect rule" by colonial governments over subject peoples or of state governments in the developing world over "primitive" tribes within their borders. If a native leader is an individual with a central role in the local kinship network and if the outside government patronizes the native leader, the government is in effect pursuing the optimal strategy of patronage. In the selection of the Toda monegar, the British colonial government appears to have pursued this strategy, at least with respect to the Teivaliol, because those who hold this office often seem to have occupied central positions in the Teivali kinship network (Section 6.4).

In some cases rulers may have reasons for not wanting to follow this simple strategy of patronage. Wilder (1982) describes how local headmen in Malaysian villages are chosen because of their central position in the kinship network. Recently, several state legislatures have suggested that village headmen should be appointed instead on the basis of their ability to "administer official business." The rationale was that "this step would bring villages into closer contact with the administration" (Wilder, 1982, p. 173). The traditional headmen are apparently sometimes deficient in the skills a modern bureaucracy requires. But however convenient the proposed change might be for the government, the theory presented here predicts that it cannot be adopted without causing serious social disruptions and widespread resentment.

Sometimes, when a ruling class has newly established dominance over a subject people, the rulers have an interest in crushing the preconquest leadership of the subject people. The rulers may have reason to expect resistance to their rule from the old leadership. If members of the old leadership occupy central positions in local kinship networks, the new rulers may seek instead to patronize individuals who lack numerous local kinship ties. Yet such clients may themselves have to reach some accomodation with those having powerful kinship connections if they are effectively to exercise indirect rule on behalf of the conquerors.

Humphrey (1983) provides an interesting example from Soviet Buryatia. The Buryats, a Mongolian people, were nomadic pastoralists before the Russian Revolution. The Tsarist government pursued a policy of indirect rule, with little impact on the traditional Buryat way of life, which appears to have accorded wealth and leadership to those occupying central positions in the kinship network. During the Soviet collectivization of agriculture in the 1930s, the Buryats were forced onto collective farms. The traditional Buryat leadership, because of their relative wealth in livestock, were classified as "kulaks" and were politically suspect. When the Soviets sought to form a new native leadership, they looked for individuals whose class background was considered more reliable; in other words, those who came from a relatively poor prerevolutionary background. As Humphrey shows, although the selection of a collective farm director appears undemocratic by Western standards, the director is in effect dependent on the cooperation of collective farm members for remaining in office. This is because the director will be removed from office if he is unable to meet the production goals set by the state; his ability to do so depends in turn on the cooperation of farm workers. Workers can secure the removal of an unwanted director by slacking off in such a way that he is unable to meet his goals. In Buryatia, collective farm members are likely to be interrelated in numerous ways. A collective farm director, even though he is likely to occupy a peripheral position in the kinship network, relies on the support of those with more central positions. One way he can obtain this support is by using his influence with state officials and the greater material wealth accompanying his position to do favors for those with powerful positions in the kinship network.

Figure 6.7 illustrates an example from Humphrey (1983). Individual Z was the long-time director of a Buryat collective farm. He was thus apparently successful in gaining support from farm members. Humphrey mentions that the lineage branch (on the right in Figure 6.7) to which Z belonged was a subordinate branch relative to the other two. The latter two branches were numerically superior. They may also have been better connected with other lineages, although Humphrey does not provide data to this effect. In any event, it appears that members of the dominant branches of the lineage were politically unacceptable under Soviet rule. Individual X had died young; he may have been killed as a kulak. Interestingly, Z adopted and reared within his own family not only his own younger sister and sister's daughter, but also X's three youngest children. Presumably, the superior income of a farm director made it possible for Z to do this. X's children were only distantly related to Z but in rearing them Z benefited Y and X's eldest son in units of inclusive fitness. Y's descendants, being either

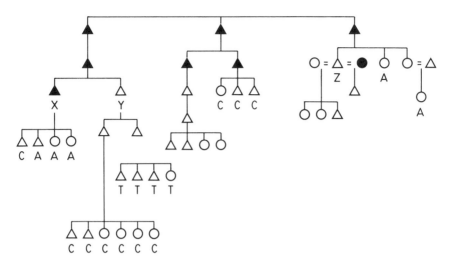

FIGURE 6.7. Genealogy showing relationships of Buryat collective farm leader, Z, to other members of his patrilineage. A = individual adopted by Z; C = resident of collective farm; T = resident of nearby town. (Data from Humphrey, 1983.)

residents of the collective farm (C in Figure 6.7) or in the nearby town (T in Figure 6.7) would thus presumably reciprocate by providing support for Z. Since Y or one of his sons would be leaders of the dominant lineage branch (left branch in the figure), Z appears to have advanced his career by currying favor with them. Though Z may not have had greater than average reproductive success, he appears to have used his position to enhance the quality if not the quantity of his offspring; one of his children was in a medical institute and the other was in a forestry institute. Admission to such a technical institute in the Soviet Union is a privilege not open to many and one of the rewards of office (Humphrey, 1983).

These examples suggest that kinship-based politics may play a wider role than we often suppose even in "advanced" societies. I could have cited other studies, illustrating how kin ties can play a role in phenomena as diverse as the formation of agrarian aristocracies (Ramírez, 1986), selection of public officials in the Roman Republic (Bush, 1982), and the inner workings of organized crime (Ianni and Reuss-Ianni, 1972). Consideration of a wide variety of such processes in the light of kin selection theory will, I suspect, throw into even sharper light the pervasiveness and power of kin ties.

7

The Structure
of Kinship Terminologies

La Nature est un temple où de vivants piliers
Laissent parfois sortir de confuses paroles;
L'homme y passe à travers des forêts de symboles
Qui l'observent avec des regards familiers.

Baudelaire, Correspondances (1857)

When we analyze kinship terms, we are talking about what words mean. We are in the realm of semantics; and the study of semantics is, to borrow McCawley's phrase, a "hairy mess."

Keesing (1972)

7.1 The Analysis of Kinship Terminologies

Since Lewis Henry Morgan's monumental *Systems of Consanguinity and Affinity of the Human Family* was published in 1870, the study of kinship terminologies has been a major subject of anthropological research. Morgan was not only the first to describe and categorize the great majority of non-European kinship terminologies, he was also the first to suggest that there can be an association between kinship terminology and social behavior involving kin. Since Morgan's time, there has been continued controversy regarding the relationship between kinship terminology and kinship behavior. Radcliffe-Brown and other British social anthropologists favored the view that kinship terminologies and social systems are correlated, although most seem to have realized that there is no simple one-to-one correspondence between a given type of kinship terminology and a given system of behavior. Kroeber (1909) was one of the first to question the association between kinship terminology and social behavior; his views have had adherents, primarily in the Unites States, ever since.

One aspect of Morgan's approach to kinship terminology has received virtually universal rejection by twentieth–century anthropologists. In keeping with the goals of the "evolutionary" school of anthropology (see Section 1.4), Morgan's primary interest was in reconstructing a hypothetical "evolutionary" history of human behavior. Morgan believed that kinship terminologies would provide evidence regarding past social behavior and thus aid in elucidating the evolutionary sequence. When the evolutionary paradigm was rejected (Radcliffe-Brown, 1941), doubt was also cast on the idea that present kinship terminologies can provide any usable information about past events.

Interestingly, Trautmann (1981) has more recently shown that present kinship terminologies can provide information about past terminologies and sometimes even about aspects of past behavior. The information they can provide is much more limited than what Morgan envisaged and has nothing to do with anything so grandiose as the evolutionary history of the species. Trautmann shows that the methods of historical linguistics can be used to reconstruct the ancestral kinship terminology of the languages belonging to one language family. He makes the important distinction between the lexicon (the actual words) and the semantics (their meaning) in a kinship terminology. Comparative analysis of the lexicon and semantics of a kinship terminology can provide evidence of historical changes. For example, the two major language groupings in India are Indo-Aryan and Dravidian. Each of these is associated with a particular lexicon of kin terms and a particular semantic pattern. There exist, however, some kinship terminologies that are lexically Indo-Aryan but semantically Dravidian, and vice versa (Trautmann, 1981). The implication of such findings is that a people speaking a language of one family may adopt the form of kinship semantics used by another language family, presumably in response to their adopting the type of social behavior associated with the latter semantics. Dravidian kinship semantics is associated with preferential cross-cousin marriage, which is widely practiced among Dravidian-speaking peoples of south India and generally forbidden among the Indo-Aryan speakers of north India. Indo-Aryan speakers who have adopted a Dravidian kinship semantics have evidently done so along with their adoption of cross-cousin marriage (Trautmann, 1981). In addition, it is possible to find terminologies whose semantics can plausibly be considered as occupying a transitional state between one type and the other (Trautmann, 1981).

Anthropologists since Morgan have been aware of the need for some sort of categorization of kinship terminologies; for an introduction to the systems of classification that have been used, see Pasternak (1976). Any attempt to categorize kinship terminologies can be criticized as "typological" in that it must inevitably ignore unique facets of individual terminologies in the quest for a limited number of broad categories into which all the world's kinship systems can be placed. Perhaps the best solution to such philosophical problems is to recognize that a system of classification is a useful prelude to discussion but that each individual case must be considered in its own society and historical setting. Even though classification into broad categories (including the "types" illustrated in Figures 7.3–7.6) is inevitably an oversimplification, it is certainly a remarkable fact that all of the world's kinship terminologies, belonging to a great variety of unrelated language families, show recurring similarities which allow them to be grouped into about six categories. There is, of course, no chance that the occurrence of these types of kinship terminology around the globe represents diffusion of cultural traditions from a few sources (as Morgan held; thus his argument that the similarity between Dravidian and Iroquois terminologies was evidence for the Asiatic origin of the American Indian). To a biologist, the recurrence of a limited number of patterns in human kinship terminology suggests that adaptive systems of kin-naming are drawn from a relatively limited set of possibilities and that the set of viable possibilities must be in some way constrained by our genetic heritage. It also suggests that there must often be a causal relationship between the system of kinship terminology and the social system. That this relationship is not a simple one-to-one correspondence may be due to two factors. First, social systems are at least as resistant to categorization by "type" as are kin terminologies. While certain elements of social behavior (e.g., pattern of marriage or descent) may predispose a social group toward one or another type of kin terminology, these elements need not be combined in the same way in every case. Second, at times there may be features of kin terminology that lack any reflection in social behavior as a result of historical factors such as those which Trautmann (1981) has documented for south India. Change in kinship terminologies may lag behind change in social structure. Here I have been interested in testing the hypothesis that major aspects of human social behavior are adaptive in the biological sense (see Section 1.1). Kin-naming behavior may be one potentially adaptive aspect of human behavior. It may be that the way an individual categorizes his kin can affect his behavior toward them and thus his inclusive fitness. But it is possible that the way one categorizes one's kin actually has a relatively minor effect on inclusive fitness. If so, kin-naming behavior would be under less pressure to change in response to the environment than would other aspects of social behavior.

The hypothesis that there is a relationship between kinship terminology and social behavior deserves serious testing. However, problems have arisen regarding the appropriate test. One possible approach is the worldwide comparative approach adopted by Murdock (1949) and others. Murdock categorized numerous societies according to both kinship terminology and aspects of social behavior and then looked for statistically significant associations. Perhaps for the reasons mentioned above, these associations are far from perfect even when they are statistically significant. Thus such associations have failed to convince many anthropologists.

An alternative approach is to focus on one particular society and to examine in a single case correspondences between kinship terminology and social behavior. This in general was the approach of Radcliffe-Brown and his school. For some classic examples, see Eggan (1937) and Radcliffe-Brown and Forde (1950). However, such studies have generally been entirely qualitative. What is needed is a mathematical formalization of the structure of a kinship terminology. This formalization can then be compared to formalizations of aspects of social behavior, such as networks of cooperation or exchange (e.g., Hage and Harary, 1983). Furthermore, an analogous approach can be used to test the hypothesis that systems of kinship terminology actually reflect the realities of biological relatedness (e.g., Fox, 1979). The structure of a kinship terminology can be compared to the structure of relatedness (see Chapter 4) within the social group that uses the terminology.

7.2 An Extensional Model of Kin Terms

In the past few decades several mathematical approaches have been taken to kinship terminologies (Balanoff, 1974). The approach taken here differs from other models in that they have attempted to examine the semantics of kinship terminologies, whereas this model looks at the set of concrete referents of a kinship term; that is, the actual individuals to whom it is applied. This model can thus be called an extensional model in the philosophical sense of the term. There are philosophical reasons for expecting that the search for meanings in the abstract, apart from the set of objects on which the term is predicated, is a task beset with difficulties (Quine, 1960). These difficulties are nicely illustrated in the case of kinship terminologies. For example, the English kinship term "father" is defined to imply a particular biological relationship. Yet in an actual case the term may be used when the biological relationship is not in fact present. Thus we have the dilemma of deciding whether the term means the actual relationship is present or only that it is believed to be present. If the latter, we are faced with a further dilemma. We cannot tell whether anyone is using the term correctly (and thus cannnot judge truth or falsity of statements using the term) because the user's beliefs are not accessible to our empirical examination.

The model I present here is not concerned with analyzing the structure of a kinship terminology as an abstract system. Rather, it provides a method applicable to the set of kinship terms used by real people in a real social group referring to one another, addressing one another, or both. I envisage this set of real-life kinship terms as a system, having a structure that involves repeated grouping of certain individuals together under certain common headings ("kinship terms"). The problem I pose is how to identify major patterns in the way individuals are grouped. For a given social group using a given kinship terminology, I seek a means of answering the following questions: (1) Which individuals are referred to most frequently by kinship terms? (2) Which individuals are grouped together most frequently by kinship terms? In other words, I ask how the kinship terminology as a whole concentrates attention on certain groupings within the community.

A kinship term can be represented by a digraph (Appendix B). For example, Figure 7.1A shows genealogical relationships among six individuals. Let us suppose that these individuals speak English and use the English vocabulary of kin terms of reference in the standard way. In Figure 7.1B the term "brother" is represented as a digraph whose vertices correspond to the six individuals. An arrow in the digraph connecting point X to point Y indicates that individual X refers to individual Y by the term "brother."

A digraph like that in Figure 7.1B can be represented by a matrix as well as by a figure. In general, the adjacency matrix for the diagraph D of n vertices is an $n \times n$ matrix whose elements a_{ij} are defined as follows. If there is an arc from

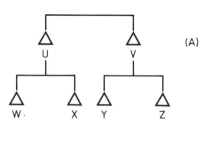

FIGURE 7.1. (A) Hypothetical genealogical relationships among six individuals. (B) The application by individuals from (A) of the English kinship term "brother," expressed as a digraph: an arrow is drawn from one point to another if the individual corresponding to the former refers to the individual corresponding to the latter as "brother."

v_i to v_j in D, then $a_{ij} = 1$; if there is no arc from v_i to v_j in D, then $a_{ij} = 0$. A set of m kin terms (whether of address or reference) thus can be represented by a set of digraphs $D_1 \cdots D_m$. The element in the ith row and jth column of $\mathbf{A}_k$, the adjacency matrix of $\mathbf{D}_k$, can be denoted by a_{ijk}. Define

$$\mathbf{X} = \sum_{k=1}^{m} \mathbf{A}_m \qquad (7.1)$$

Let $\mathbf{x}$ be the vector ($n \times 1$) of diagonal elements of $\mathbf{X}$.

The matrix $\mathbf{X}$ can be viewed as an uncorrected matrix of sums and cross-products for p observations of a random vector variable $\mathbf{y}$ of dimension n. The number of observations of this vector variable, p, is such that $p \leq mn$. For a given $\mathbf{A}_k$, let r_k be the number of rows which contain at least one nonzero element. Then

$$p = \sum_{k=1}^{m} r_k \qquad (7.2)$$

The mean of $\mathbf{y}$ is estimated by

$$\mathbf{y} = \frac{1}{p} \mathbf{x} \qquad (7.3)$$

Then let

$$\mathbf{S}_k = \frac{1}{p-1}\left(\mathbf{X} - \frac{1}{p}\,\overline{\mathbf{y}}\,\overline{\mathbf{y}}'\right) \qquad (7.4)$$

$\mathbf{S}_k$ is a variance–covariance matrix for $\mathbf{y}$. The principal components of $\mathbf{S}_k$ can be computed readily. The principal components of $\mathbf{S}_k$ are defined to constitute the structure of the kinship terminology.

Ideally, one would obtain data on the actual use of kinship terms by a set of living members of a social group. Most published anthropological data are not of this sort. Typically, anthropologists abstract rules for the use of kin terms rather than showing how they are used by all social group members. This approach has the advantage of ease of presentation, but there is the disadvantage that it cannot take into account individual differences in the use of kinship terms. In the next section I discuss some examples. The first are simulated examples which are useful for illustrating the method. The second is an example from the ethnographic literature.

7.3 Some Examples

The first examples I discuss, in order to illustrate the application of the model, are examples of a peculiar sort. Although the purpose of the model is to analyze kinship terminologies in use by real social groups, I apply it first to simulated terminologies in simulated groups because I believe that doing so constitutes a useful academic exercise.

The simulated terminologies I examine correspond to some of the ideal "types" into which kinship terminologies have been classified. I do not, however, intend my examples to represent ideal types in any sense; rather they are *simulations* of real terminologies. In each case I assume that the group in question is a group of 21 individuals whose social (though not necessarily biological) relationships are as illustrated in Figure 7.2. I examine four simulated terminologies, which I call "Eskimo," "Hawaiian," "Crow," and "Omaha." These

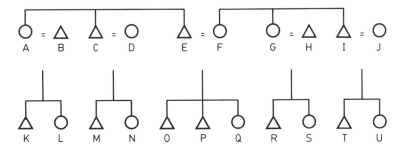

FIGURE 7.2. Social genealogical relationships of a hypothetical group of individuals.

correspond in their basic structure to the ideal types given these names by clas-
sifiers (Figures 7.3–7.6). In actual systems, there is often a separate term for elder
brother, younger brother, and so forth. These age distinctions are often ignored
by compilers of ideal types, and I assume that such distinctions are lacking in
my simulated terminologies. Ideal typological classifications generally exclude
any consideration of terms for affines. In a real system, it would be desirable to
include terms for affines in the analysis. The distinction between "affines" and
"consanguines" is one that one should not impose a priori on a terminology,
since it is a distinction extrinsic to the terminology.

When I say that this distinction is extrinsic to the terminology, I do not
imply that it is useless or meaningless. A cultural anthropologist would, of
course, be likely to argue that we should not impose this distinction when it is
not part of the native's culture; that is, when they do not make the same distinction themselves. However, I do not deny the validity of making such a distinction when it is useful, whether or not it is made by the people studied. I only
feel that, in general, it is inappropriate to influence the application of this model
of kinship terminology by making such distinctions a priori. Of course it is often
true also that affines and consanguines are the same individuals when consanguineous marriage is practiced; in such cases, if individuals are distinguished it
must be on some other basis (e.g., wife-givers vs. wife-takers). This point would

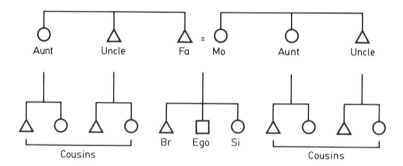

FIGURE 7.3. Structure of the Eskimo kinship terminology.

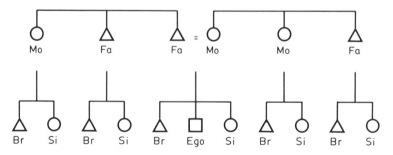

FIGURE 7.4. Structure of the Hawaiian kinship terminology.

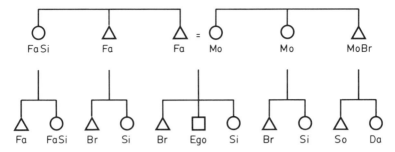

FIGURE 7.5. Structure of the Crow kinship terminology.

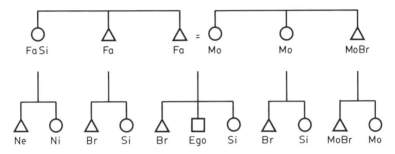

FIGURE 7.6. Structure of the Omaha kinship terminology.

not be worth belaboring were it not that such a greal deal of nonsense has been written about this issue by cultural anthropologists.

In Figures 7.7–7.10 I graph the first two principal components of S_k for the four simulated terminologies. These graphs show that the principal components of S_k call attention to features of the kinship terminologies that anthropologists have often held to be characteristic of the "types" to which they belong. For instance, Eskimo kinship terminologies (a class that includes the English terminology) are said to contrast lineal with collateral kin. PC1 and PC2 of S_k for the Eskimo group (Figure 7.7) set apart the sibship O, P, and Q from their relatives on both sides and also contrast those of the parental generation (parents, aunts, and uncles) with those of the same generation as O, P, and Q (their cousins). The Hawaiian group (Figure 7.8) shows a somewhat different pattern in PC1 and PC2 of S_k. Here the contrast between generations is also present; but now, within the offspring generation, attention is drawn to a contrast between the two sexes.

Crow and Omaha terminologies are associated with matrilineal and patrilineal descent systems, respectively. Crow and Omaha systems thus often are said to be mirror images of each other (see Figures 7.4 and 7.5). Even in the relatively simple simulated examples considered here, the Crow and Omaha systems appear as mirror images. The Crow example isolates K, C, and E from other group members on PC2 (Figure 7.9). These three males would all be members

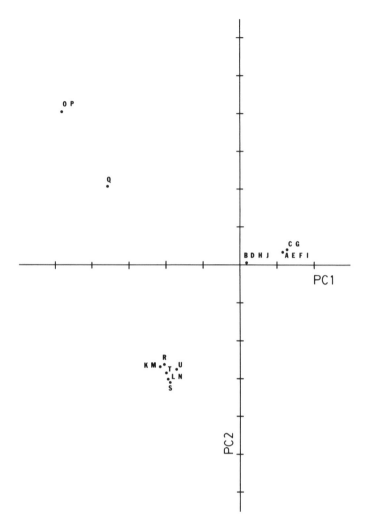

FIGURE 7.7. Plot of PC1 and PC2 of S_k for the Eskimo kinship terminology applied to the simulated group from Figure 7.2.

of the same matrilineal clan. On the other hand, the Omaha example (on PC1) isolates U, F, and G from other group members (Figure 7.10). These three females would be members of the same patrilineal clan. Both Crow and Omaha show the classificatory feature of grouping O, P, M, and R together and N, Q, and S together.

The association of Crow terminologies with matrilineal descent raises an interesting question in light of Alexander's (1974, 1979) hypothesis about matrilineal descent systems. Alexander was concerned with a biological explanation of matrilineal systems, particularly of the extreme form of matriliny known as the avunculate, in which the mother's brother takes a primary role in the care of children, especially male children. Alexander pointed out that if confidence of paternity is low, it would make good genetic sense for a male to invest in his sister's offspring rather than his wife's offspring, since he would be certain that his sister's offspring would bear some of his genes. Low paternity confidence probably does not account for all occurrences of matrilineal descent in human societies (Flinn, 1981; Hughes, 1986a); but it remains a viable general hypothesis (in the sense of Section 1.3) that low confidence of paternity can be a factor contributing to the development of matrilineal organization.

Thus it is of interest to examine how the simple Crow example of Figure 7.9 relates to the idea of low paternity confidence. Given the social genealogical rela-

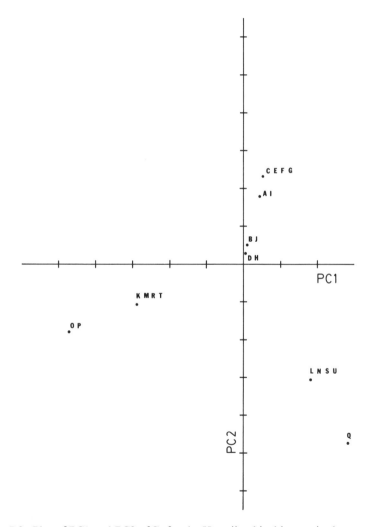

FIGURE 7.8. Plot of PC1 and PC2 of S_k for the Hawaiian kinship terminology applied to the simulated group from Figure 7.2.

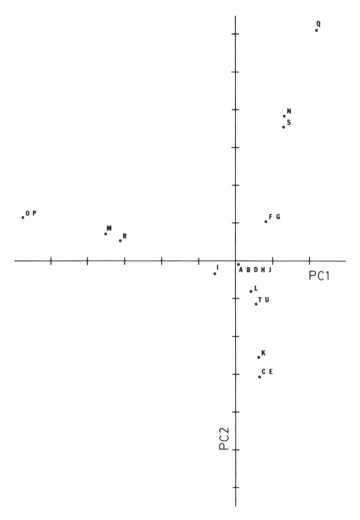

FIGURE 7.9. Plot of PC1 and PC2 of $\mathbf{S}_k$ for the Crow kinship terminology applied to the simulated group from Figure 7.2.

tionships as in Figure 7.2, I computed matrices of coefficients of relatedness for two possible sets of biological relationships: (1) $\mathbf{R}_c$ represents the matrix of coefficients of relatedness on the assumption that paternity confidence is 100%; that is, social and biological paternity are everywhere the same for individuals in Figure 7.2; (2) $\mathbf{R}_n$ represents the matrix of coefficients of relatedness on the assumption that paternity confidence is 0%; that is, in every case the putative father is not the biological father and all putative siblings are in fact half-siblings. The PCs of $\mathbf{R}_c$ and $\mathbf{R}_n$ represent the structure of relatedness under these two extreme assumptions. One way of testing how well the kinship terminology reflects biological relatedness structure under the two assumptions is to estimate the canonical correlation between a set of PCs of $\mathbf{R}_c$ or $\mathbf{R}_n$ and a set of PCs of $\mathbf{S}_k$. Canonical correlation measures the strength of the linear relationship between two sets of variables just as simple correlation measures the strength of the linear relationship between two variables. I computed canonical correlations between PC1 and PC2 of $\mathbf{S}_k$ for the Crow example and PC1 and PC2 of $\mathbf{R}_c$ and $\mathbf{R}_n$, respectively. For $\mathbf{R}_c$, the higher of the two possible canonical correlations was 0.360 (not significant with $N = 21$), while for $\mathbf{R}_n$ the higher canonical correlation was 0.682 ($P = 0.027$). Thus at least in this simple simulation, the structure of the Crow kinship terminology shows a much better fit with the facts of biological relatedness when paternity confidence is low.

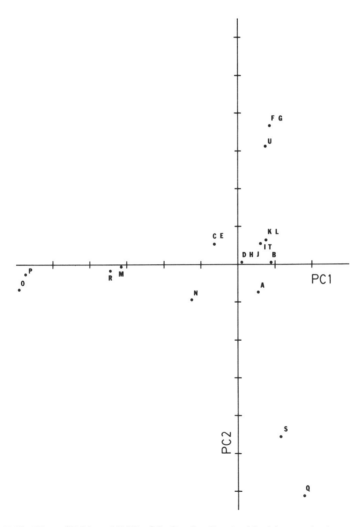

FIGURE 7.10. Plot of PC1 and PC2 of $\mathbf{S}_k$ for the Omaha kinship terminology applied to the simulated group from Figure 7.2.

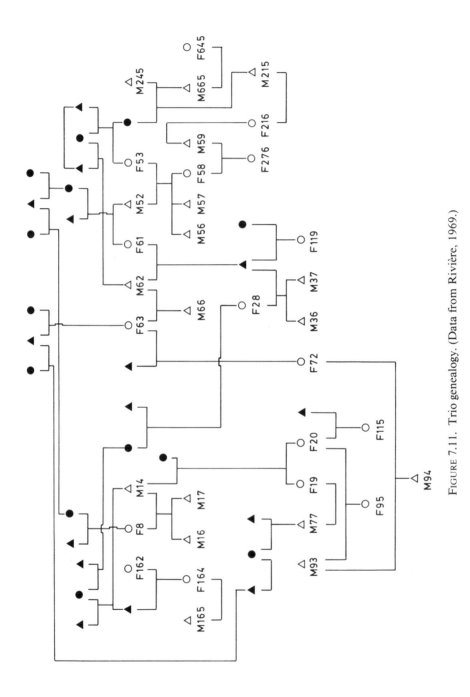

FIGURE 7.11. Trio genealogy. (Data from Rivière, 1969.)

128

These simple examples ignored complexities of real terminologies, in particular the inclusion of terms for affines. In fact, the distinctive features of some terminologies—notably those of the Dravidian/Iroquois type first studied in detail by Morgan—cannot be understood fully without consideration of the terms for affines. These are best considered in a real example. Figure 7.11 shows the genealogy of a Trio (South American Indian) village, collected by Rivière (1969). Table 7.1 shows PC1–PC4 of **R'R** for this village, on the assumption that the putative father is the biological father in all cases. The ethnographic data provide no strong evidence that this is not likely to be true. In light of the discussion in Chapter 6, it is of interest that M52, whose children receive the highest weights on PC1 of **R'R** is reported to be the village leader. PC2 (accounting for 17.6% of the variance in **R'R**) indicates that there is an important division in the village. PC2 separates the village into two subgroups, one centered on M14 and his offspring (M16, M17, F19, F20) and the other centered on the offspring of the leader M52 and F53 (M56, M57, F58). Together PC1 and PC2 suggest that the village is divided into a dominant subgroup centered around M52 and his kin and affines and a subordinate group centered around M14 and his offspring.

The Trio kinship terminology is of the Iroquois–Dravidian type, although with unusual features. Using the rules provided by Rivière (1969), I constructed $\mathbf{S}_k$ for the kin terms of reference which are expected to be used by all individuals in Figure 7.11. Table 7.2 shows PC1 and PC2 of $\mathbf{S}_k$. PC1 draws attention to four males, M56, M57, M665, and M215. These males include the sons of the leader M52, who receive high weights on PC1 of **R'R**, and their closest same-generation male kin, their first cousins. PC2 of $\mathbf{S}_k$ draws attention to a group of females, particularly F61 and F63, who are the wives of M62. These are contrasted with males M16 and M17, who belong to the other subdivision of the community (as indicated by PC2 of **R'R**). Together, PC1 and PC2 of $\mathbf{S}_k$ thus draw attention to aspects of community structure also reflected by PC1 and PC2 of **R'R**. There is a single significant canonical correlation between the two, which equals 0.538 ($P < 0.02$). If we compute a canonical correlation between PC1–PC4 of **R'R** and PC1–PC4 of $\mathbf{S}_k$, the correlation is still higher (0.726, $P < 0.005$).

This result suggests that kinship terminologies group individuals in ways that are biologically important and concentrate attention on biologically significant individuals. Further research on the relationship between kinship terminology and biology might extend this approach to larger social groups. Another area worthy of attention is the cognitive psychology of kinship terminologies, which might be studied by the methods advocated by Lumsden and Wilson (1981, 1985). For example, one might predict that children will learn more easily kinship terminologies that correspond to biologically and socially significant groupings (the role of which the child would also perceive). In the "blended" families now widespread in Western societies with high divorce rates, parents often teach children to use the same kin term for full sibs, half-sibs, and step-sibs. If kin terminology corresponds to biological groupings, one would predict a lowered readiness to learn the use of a sibling term for half-sibs and step-sibs, if behavioral circumstances make the distinction between these and full sibs apparent (e.g., visitation with a nonresident natural parent).

TABLE 7.1   Loadings on the First Four Principal Components of **R′R**
for the Trio Community Illustrated in Figure 7.11

Individual	PC1	PC2	PC3	PC4
F162	0.010	−0.044	−0.018	−0.005
F8	0.074	−0.145	−0.091	0.004
M14	0.112	−0.437[a]	−0.092	0.023
M64	0.002	−0.012	−0.005	0.002
F164	0.044	−0.171	−0.044	−0.014
M16	0.106	−0.334[a]	−0.113	0.019
M17	0.106	−0.334[a]	−0.113	0.019
F19	0.082	−0.343[a]	−0.055	0.052
M77	0.007	−0.030	0.120	0.059
F20	0.093	−0.394[a]	−0.033	0.084
M93	0.024	−0.087	0.330[a]	0.132
F95	0.068	−0.286[a]	0.189	0.141
F115	0.059	−0.258[a]	−0.024	0.065
M94	0.028	−0.068	0.473[a]	0.122
M245	0.059	0.027	0.031	0.164
M215	0.150	0.058	0.043	0.183
F216	0.028	0.012	−0.013	0.042
M665	0.150	0.058	0.043	0.183
F645	0.000	0.000	0.000	0.000
F53	0.308[a]	0.112	0.006	0.164
M52	0.321[a]	0.090	0.091	−0.002
F61	0.241[a]	0.050	0.050	−0.162
M62	0.179	0.038	0.159	0.182
F63	0.032	−0.028	0.430[a]	0.033
M56	0.359[a]	0.120	−0.068	0.129
M57	0.359[a]	0.120	−0.068	0.129
F58	0.380[a]	0.129	−0.075	0.150
M59	0.051	0.020	−0.022	0.065
F276	0.255[a]	0.088	−0.055	0.129
F119	0.155	0.026	0.055	−0.243[a]
F28	0.093	−0.094	0.027	−0.401[a]
M36	0.197	−0.032	0.065	−0.467[a]
M37	0.197	−0.032	0.065	−0.467[a]
M66	0.121	0.055	0.374[a]	−0.100
F72	0.024	−0.028	0.415[a]	0.056
percent trace	22.0	17.6	9.9	7.9

[a]Weights ≥ 0.200 in absolute value.

Some cultural anthropologists have taken the radical position that human social kinship can be studied without any reference to biological kinship (Schneider, 1972). Elsewhere I have criticized this position by means of an analogy (Hughes, 1986a). I compare the facts of biological relatedness within a society—and they are facts, whether or not they are knowable to us in any given case—to an *objective* map with which the *subjective* maps of the people's kinship systems can be compared. My argument was that cultural anthropologists have thrown away their objective maps. They have produced sensitive and illuminating studies of subjective kinship maps, but the theoretical framework of cultural anthropology has prevented any comparison of subjective with objective maps.

For one thing, such comparison is necessary for a test of the extreme claim that people's subjective kinship maps have *nothing* to do with biological relatedness (e.g., Sahlins, 1976). Data such as those presented in this section call this extreme claim into question. Evidence of a statistical association between social and biological kinship argues against the two being completely unconnected. But merely to falsify the extreme antibiological position is relatively uninteresting, since it can be falsified without any consideration of the form taken by the association between social and biological kinship. Indeed, even a demonstration that social kinship is *negatively* correlated with biological kinship would falsify the claim that the two are independent.

What are needed are comparative studies, from many different societies, of the form of the relationship between social kinship and actual biological relatedness. Only if we can compare each of many subjective kinship maps with the facts of biological relatedness in the particular social group for which the map was formed, can we gain some general insight into the rules by which our subjective kinship maps are made. That we may discover any general rules for the formation of subjective kinship maps is at present no more than a hope, but it is a hope in keeping with the best traditions of social anthropology.

TABLE 7.2   Loadings on the First Two Principal Components of S_k for the Trio Community Illustrated in Figure 7.11

Individual	PC1	PC2	Individual	PC1	PC2
F162	0.038	0.040	M645	0.015	−0.011
F8	0.022	−0.018	F53	0.073	0.237[a]
M14	−0.116	0.015	M52	−0.008	−0.043
M64	0.003	−0.001	F61	0.119	0.601[a]
F164	0.031	−0.084	M62	0.016	−0.023
M16	0.070	−0.256[a]	F63	0.095	0.493[a]
M17	0.072	−0.281[a]	M56	−0.525[a]	0.030
F19	0.049	−0.144	M57	−0.507[a]	0.023
M77	0.039	−0.049	F58	0.035	0.099
F20	0.040	−0.081	M59	−0.023	−0.053
M93	0.042	−0.061	F276	−0.030	−0.154
F95	0.019	−0.011	F119	−0.030	−0.168
F115	0.016	−0.009	F28	0.012	−0.001
M94	0.015	−0.007	M36	0.038	−0.177
M245	−0.071	0.007	M37	0.037	−0.191
M215	−0.465[a]	0.089	M66	0.021	−0.013
M216	0.026	0.029	F72	0.010	−0.011
M665	−0.420[a]	0.085			
percent trace				14.9	8.5

[a]Weights ≥ 0.200 absolute value.

8

Prospects for a
Biologically Based Social Science

Original sin standeth not in the following of Adam, (as the Pelagians do
vainly talk;) but it is the fault and corruption of the Nature of every man,
that naturally is engendered of the offspring of Adam; whereby man is very
far gone from original righteousness, and is of his own nature inclined to evil,
so that the flesh lusteth always contrary to the Spirit. . . .

Thirty-Nine Articles of Religion (1562)

Ethik und Aesthetik sind Eins.

Wittgenstein (1922)

8.1 Fact, Value, and Social Sciences

In this concluding chapter I should like to discuss, at times rather speculatively
and tentatively, ways in which the science of human sociobiology might be
applied. Following Radcliffe-Brown (1957), my aim is to create a "theoretical
science of society," that is, a branch of "pure" science which develops and tests
its theories independently of their potential applications. But I feel that all
"pure" theoretical sciences do from time to time yield results of interest to those
working in applied areas. This is true of physics, chemistry, and molecular biology; I do not see why it should not be true of evolutionary biology, including
the branch of evolutionary biology that constitutes the evolutionary study of
human social behavior. However, before discussing potential applications
of human sociobiology, I want to point out two related ways in which I think
human sociobiology cannot legitimately be applied. The first is in the construction of a political ideology. I do not think that scientific sociobiologists have ever
suggested that their research should be applied in this way, but many of their
critics have been convinced that it would be. The second is in the construction
of an "evolutionarily based ethics." Philosophers make a distinction between
"substantive" or "normative" ethics (the part of ethics that tells us what we
should or should not do) and metaethics, which dispassionately examines the
bases, origins, or internal logic of ethical statements made by substantive ethi-

cists (Ruse, 1986). I am here concerned only with the claim that there can be an evolutionarily based substantive ethics, leaving for the end of this section a discussion of metaethics.

Critics of sociobiology, particularly those identified with self-proclaimed "Marxism" or other "leftist" viewpoints, have complained that sociobiology paints a nasty picture of human nature. If our behavior, like that of other animals, springs from reproductive selfishness, if even altruism can be shown by the theory of kin selection to be ultimately selfish from the gene's point of view, must we not conclude that human beings are innately selfish? If so, will not all attempts at socialism, communism, and the like, fail through our inability to place the collective good above our personal good? And if one can draw this conclusion from sociobiology, then isn't sociobiology just another form of capitalist ideology?

In response to criticisms of this sort, a number of points can be made. First, I note that even if a pessimistic view of human nature is characteristic of sociobiology, it is certainly not original with sociobiology. As evidence that pessimistic views of human nature have long been current in Western culture, I adduce the quotation at the start of this chapter from the Thirty-Nine Articles, the doctrinal basis of Anglicanism. Controversies between "optimists" and "pessimists" with regard to human nature date at least as far back as the fifth-century monk Pelagius. Second, and more important, I take it as a cardinal principle of modern science that value judgments have no place in scientific discourse. Although scientists, being human, do make value judgments, these value judgments can be kept separate from their science because they utilize different forms of language from the language of science. The forms of language used to express value judgments are separable from the forms used to express scientific theory and observation by means of objective criteria relating to the logical structure of the statements used (Quine, 1960). Science as we know it depends on the "fact–value distinction" of the positivist philosophers. By and large practicing scientists have agreed that one cannot deduce an "ought" from an "is"; that is, one cannot logically deduce a statement about the way things ought to be from any set of statements purporting to describe the way things are. It is true that some popular or semipopular "sociobiological" writings have transgressed egregiously against the fact–value distinction; but the fact that sociobiologists have erred in this regard does not give critics of sociobiology the right to dispense with the fact–value distinction altogether.

The critical role of the fact–value distinction in the development of Western science in recent centuries should not be underestimated, nor should the dangers of any assault on this principle. It is not surprising that would-be tyrants attack this principle with particular vehemence. Thus Naziism denounced certain aspects of science as "Jewish" and therefore not to be trusted, while in the Soviet Union Lysenko and his supporters rejected genetics and evolutionary biology as "bourgeois." Not only did such intellectual bigotry result in persecution of innocent scientists; it has an extremely adverse effect on the development of science in the countries involved.

In recent years there have been signs within the scientific community of an inchoate disaffection with the fact–value distinction, a disaffection encouraged by a few irresponsible philosophers (e.g., Putnam, 1981). I think that this is a most unfortunate development and I am not sure why it has come about. I should think that scientists would realize that the fact–value distinction constitutes their bill of rights. Perhaps, because many scientists have rejected traditional ethical and religious value systems, they feel the lack of a value system and hope that science can somehow be made to fill the void. But trying to turn science into an ethical or quasi-religious system cannot be good for either science or ethics. I personally feel that it would be far better for scientists who feel such a need to adopt a traditional ethical or religious system. Of course, to do so, they will need to overcome the widespread impression that science somehow contradicts or disproves such systems. Religious fundamentalists have done nothing to counter this impression, but instead have mounted their own vigorous attack on the fact–value distinction, which is not really surprising given their totalitarian, inquisitorial mentality.

Perhaps an example will illustrate most clearly the futility of attempts to deduce values from facts. Wilson (1978) constructs an "adaptive" story for how homosexuality might have been a viable strategy for some human males in the evolutionary history of our species, if homosexuals invested in kin instead of reproducing themselves. Wilson then argues that we should show more tolerance toward homosexuals because homosexuality may have a "genetic basis." I am not concerned here with the plausibility of Wilson's evolutionary scenario, but only with pointing out the non sequitur in his argument for the moral position of tolerance for homosexuality from the possibility of a genetic basis. For an opponent might just as plausibly construct an adaptive story for the rise of a genetic predisposition toward homophobia—the fear and hatred of homosexuals. After all, an adaptive value to homophobia is fairly easy to imagine (avoidance of decreased reproduction, reduced risk of venereal disease, etc.). The same sort of non sequitur could then be used to bolster a moral position exactly the opposite of that favored by Wilson. Finally, what if it were to turn out that homosexuality and homophobia were *both* adaptive strategies for certain individuals under certain circumstances? What ethical conclusions could we draw then?

One gets the impression that when serious sociobiologists have violated the fact–value distinction, they have done so in a misguided attempt to soften the leftist criticism that sociobiology is "right-wing." I suspect that the example from Wilson just discussed arose from motivation of this sort. Sociobiologists may have felt that, if they could find support in sociobiology for a few liberal-sounding ethical positions, their attackers might leave them alone. In this they were mistaken. Indeed, some of the most hysterical recent attacks on sociobiology have come from "moral philosophers," who themselves routinely violate the fact–value distinction but find ventures by sociobiologists into the field of ethics unforgivable (e.g., Kaye, 1986; Scruton, 1986).

Returning to the issue of sociobiology's view of human nature, in seeking the biological roots of human behavior, sociobiology (at its best, at any rate) makes no value judgments regarding good or evil. If sociobiological theory predicts that human behaviors, like those of other animals, are likely to be largely reproductively "selfish," it makes no value judgment as to whether this is a "good" or a "bad" thing. Science is concerned with observation, explanation, and prediction of the material world and not with passing judgment on it. The authors of Medieval bestiaries passed judgment on the alleged moral qualities of the animal species they described. We find such an idea ridiculous today, and an ecologist seeking to understand predation does not need to reassure his readers that he is not concerned with condemning or praising the behavior of predators. One day, it is to be hoped, we will have a fully mature science of human society, and its practitioners will likewise feel no need of explaining that they are unconcerned with praise or blame. When that day comes, the "ethical" criticisms of sociobiology will seem as quaint and ludicrous as the Medieval bestiaries.

Some critics have argued that whatever the intention of sociobiologists, their writings are bound to give the impression that humans are a nasty lot, and this impression is bound to encourage further nastiness. It may be true that too pessimistic a view of human nature, whatever its source, can have unfortunate behavioral consequences. But it is also true that too optimistic a view of human nature can have unfortunate consequences. Proponents of the French, Russian, and Cambodian revolutions (to name but a few) confidently predicted that once liberated from the chains of oppression, human beings would show a cooperative spirit missing in previous ages. Needless to say, these predictions proved to be overoptimistic.

When a theoretical prediction is not supported by data, scientists say that the theory has been falsified. Insofar as optimistic predictions about human behavior have been based on theories of human nature, it would seem that history has falsified such theories.

If sociobiology (like orthodox Christian theology) sees a dark side to human nature, such a view may at least not lead us into a tragic overestimate of our own capacity for perfection. It is, of course, a value judgment on my part, but I do not think that a sense of human fallibility is necessarily a bad thing.

While expressing doubts similar to my own regarding an evolutionarily based substantive ethics, Ruse (1986) argues for the value of an evolutionarily based metaethics. Although I do not deny that such an enterprise might be of interest, I rather doubt that Ruse realizes what such an investigation would entail if it were to become a genuine scientific program of research. If a truly scientific metaethics were to be attempted, it would have to be based on the study of ethical beliefs of human beings of a large number of different societies. The data would ideally come from representative samples of the populations studied rather than a small number of "informants." In collecting the data, one would of course need to employ methods which ensured that the study subjects expressed their beliefs sincerely, rather than merely repeating what they thought the investigator wanted to hear. Also, in preparing questionnaires and in collating the data, one would encounter formidable problems of translation of ethical terminology from one language to another. An alternative research strategy, much easier to pursue but with obvious pitfalls, would be to use as sources for a people's ethical beliefs their proverbs or (if they are literate) any ethical literature that has gained widespread acceptance among them. This research strategy would have the advantage that it would not require extensive fieldwork, but it would provide little information regarding intrasocietal variation in ethical beliefs.

In any event, whatever the source, one would need a fairly substantial body of cross-cultural data before one could begin to test generalizations about human ethical beliefs. Only with cross-cultural data, for example, could one test the claim that any particular form of ethical belief is universal or near-universal. Further, one could use such data to look for correlations between intersocietal differences in ethical belief and intersocietal differences in social structure, economy, and habitat. If one had good data on intrasocietal variation in ethical beliefs, one could attempt to correlate differences in ethical belief with intrasocietal differences in self-interest or class-interest.

No philosopher studying metaethics has adopted such an ambitious research program, nor to my knowledge has any "evolutionary ethicist" proposed it. Instead, metaethicists, whether evolutionary or not, continue to rely on the subjective methods moral philosophers have employed since ancient Greece: the ethical beliefs the ethicist studies are his own, derived from introspection; they are uncritically adopted from the author's own culture (and often assumed to be universal); or they are derived from the writings of some previous normative ethical philsopher. (Examples of all of these can be found in Ruse, 1986.) That such methods are totally unscientific and can tell us nothing about human ethical beliefs in general should be obvious to any empirical scientist. It is all very well to come up with hypotheses about the evolutionary basis of ethical beliefs; but unless we have reasonably objective data on actual human ethical beliefs, we can never test such generalizations.

8.2 Applications of Sociobiology

Although the aim of this book is to propose foundations for a "pure" science of human society, I believe that this science can have important applications. Rather than serving as ammunition for ethical or ideological positions, these applications will be exactly analogous to the applications of any other science. For example, an engineer makes use of the "pure" science of physics as a source of predictions. If the engineer is contemplating building a structure of a particular sort, the science of physics yields predictions regarding the consequences of his or her plan, in terms of its feasibility or factors bearing on its feasibility, such as stresses on the materials. In the same way, sociobiology can be a source of predictions for "social engineers," that is, for those who formulate social policies, especially when these policies impinge on human reproductive strategies or kinship interactions. Even those who take a dim view of the type of social experimentation typical of leftist regimes must admit that, in the complexities of the modern world, virtually every act of social or economic policy by any government has far-reaching consequences that justify the analogy between policy-making and engineering. Even in what is called in the United States the "private sector," decisions by large corporations can have equally far-reaching effects.

There are three areas in which I believe biological considerations are relevant to policy-makers: (1) international development, that is, interactions between developed and less developed countries, an area in which the role of social anthropology is already recognized (Mair, 1984); (2) family law and policy, relating to divorce, child support, and custody; and (3) urban and industrial policy in developed countries. I will make a few remarks about each of these in turn, briefly mentioning ways in which a biological perspective may aid policy formation.

The role an understanding of kinship networks can have in determining strategies of "indirect rule" was noted in Section 6.6. Indirect rule is, as Mair (1977, p. 36) remarks, "one of the oldest political devices in history, although it is now popularly believed to be a peculiarly wicked invention of the British." Of course, the end of colonialism did not mean the end of indirect rule. The new national governments of the developing world are frequently confronted with problems of exercising indirect rule over tribal populations within their borders. Also, a bureaucratic governmental administration, in dealing with any highly interrelated local population, must choose whether to patronize those with positions of traditional kinship-based leadership or to attempt to create a new local leadership. In decisions such as these, an understanding of local kinship patterns is predicted to be important (Section 6.6), and I should also predict difficulties for any scheme of bureaucratic rule that does not come to terms with local leadership patterns based on kinship. For example, problems often result from attempts to introduce Western-style "democratic" politics to traditional societies. Individuals likely to run for office in elections frequently are Western-educated individuals who occupy a peripheral position in the local kinship system.

As regards family law and policy, sociobiologists have gathered data showing that, as predicted on biological grounds, children are at greater risk of abuse from step-parents than from natural parents (Daly and Wilson, 1981a, 1981b, 1985). This information is potentially useful to policy-makers interested in decreasing levels of child abuse. To decrease the incidence of step-parentage by forbidding or limiting divorce is, of course, not a serious or desirable option in modern societies. However, the data suggest that there are more palatable options that would decrease child abuse. It is well known that in Western countries there is a very low rate of compliance by divorced fathers with court-ordered child-support payments (e.g., Cassety, 1978). One may predict that a stepfather should be much more likely to abuse a stepchild not receiving adequate support from the biological father, since such a stepchild will draw resources that might be used to support the stepfather's own either actual or potential biological children. Thus it is to be expected that any social policy which increases support-payment compliance will decrease child abuse.

In modern urban communities, people live among non-kin to an extent that is surely unprecedented in our whole evolutionary history. Modern industrial production has introduced a further novelty: people are involved in their major productive activities in cooperation with non-kin. Both of these factors may have contributed to the "anxiety" said to be characteristic of modern life (e.g., Fried, 1975; Goodwin, 1986; Ilfeld, 1979). It is instructive to contrast our current urban living patterns with those of our relatively recent ancestors. For example, traditional English rural laborer populations were interrelated in numerous ways, and those who ventured into an adjoining village without a good reason risked a ruckus (Strathern, 1981). If this was the case in a society with a strong state devoted to the suppression of acts of violence, one can easily imagine the situation in "primitive" societies. For much of our evolutionary history, to venture outside the network of kin and affines has meant almost certain death. While none can deny the importance of such factors as poverty, unemployment, drugs, and alcohol, and the ready availability of handguns and other weapons in contributing to the extraordinary levels of violence in modern cities, it is at least a hypothesis worthy of serious consideration that a further factor contributing to urban violence is the fact that all inhabitants are living among non-kin. In affluent suburbs, individuals also live largely among non-kin; but there, the fact that all are likely to lack for nothing as regards resources means that competition with non-kin can take the harmless ritualized form of a quest for status symbols (Packard, 1960; Sobel, 1983). In urban slums, where all feel a want of resources to some degree, hostility to non-kin appears often to find a more direct expression. It is well known that a great deal of urban violence is domestic; but here too the absence of kin networks may be a factor, since in many societies a wife's kin protect her from abuse by her husband (e.g., Lawrence, 1984).

Yet urban working-class life need not imply a community in which kin ties are few. In areas such as the East End of London, there were until recently neighborhoods occupied by the same families for several centuries (Young and Willmot, 1957). The recent great increase of mobility into urban areas has destroyed most kinship-based urban communities. Even if the current high population mobility were to cease, it would take a long time for interrelated communities to develop. Nonetheless, policy-makers might well consider the advisability of any policy that would lower the long-term mobility of urban populations. Doing so might decrease both "alienation" and urban violence. The boom-or-bust cycle of plant closings and "runaway" industries so characteristic of modern capitalist economies seems a particularly disruptive influence in this regard; and it might be found that policies decreasing this tendency would help foster urban communities stabilized by numerous ties of genetic common interest which would be less prone to violence.

As well as being an integrative force, kinship can be a disruptive force. On the theory developed here, I should predict a society in which feuding among kin groups will occur to be one in which (1) there are groups of individuals among whom interrelatedness is high and relatedness is concentrated; (2) wealth is controlled corporately by such groups and thus can be concentrated where relatedness is concentrated; and (3) there are abrupt discontinuities between such groups. This seems to be true in feuding societies (e.g., Brown, 1986). To minimize social violence, policy-makers should seek to avoid these conditions as well as avoiding the situation in which kin ties are absent altogether.

8.3 Toward a Science of Society

I wrote this book in the hope that a biological perspective will have an influence on future research in the study of human social behavior, particularly by anthropologists. I believe that the addition of a biological perspective makes it possible for social anthropology to develop into the mature science of society envisaged by Radcliffe-Brown (1957). Whether social anthropologists actually take advantage of this opportunity for development depends on their willingness to do so, which in turn reflects factors at work in their society and world.

In the first half of this century, social anthropology developed as a science in Britain to a far greater extent than any other country. It might be argued that a major cause of this development was that the British Empire needed a scientific social anthropology. The Empire came into contact with a vast diversity of societies, and it needed social scientists capable of understanding their dynamics and of making reasonably accurate predictions regarding how those societies would respond to political or economic changes. Since the forcible pacification of the North American Plains Indian tribes, anthropology in the United States lacked any such urgent applied mission. American anthropologists concentrated on detailed historical description of dying cultures, which usually lacked, by the time they were studied, any remnant of the economic and social basis that gave them meaning. The interest of American anthropologists was from the beginning encyclopedic and static, whereas that of British social anthropologists was dynamic and practical.

Since World War II the United States increasingly assumed a global role that, while lacking the political trappings of the old colonial empires, certainly involves some of the responsibilities and problems of imperialism. That the United States has on the whole made such a bad job of this role (in Vietnam, Iran, Nicaragua, and elsewhere) can be attributed to many factors; but the deficiencies of American anthropology as a serious science of society may be at least partly to blame for the seeming inability of United States policymakers to understand or predict accurately the effects their policies will have in any unfamiliar cultural setting. If policy-makers in the United States get their ideas of how societies function from undergraduate readings of Mead, Benedict, and Schneider, it is small wonder that they have difficulty in dealing with the rest of the world.

Indeed, at the present time, all developed countries are involved in wide-ranging economic interactions with less developed countries. I believe that, in this world situation, the availability of a reliable and robust science of society is a prerequisite for international peace and orderly development.

I also believe that academic anthropology, as it now exists, fails to provide such a science. At the present time, academic administrators frequently classify anthropology with the arts and humanities rather than with the sciences. This is, from my point of view, a lamentable situation; I am certain that W. H. R. Rivers, A. R. Radcliffe-Brown, and the other founders of twentieth-century social anthropology would view it as a repudiation of their life's work. It is a consequence of the influence of American cultural anthropology, with its rejection of scientific objectivity, and its use of methods more akin to those of literary criticism than to those of empirical science. Classification of anthropology with the humanities leads to acceptance in graduate programs of arts graduates who are totally unfamiliar with the methods of science—for instance, they are incapable of understanding or applying simple statistical tests—and further contribute to the development of an antiscientific climate in anthropology.

What is needed is for social anthropology to return to its roots; and it will find these roots in evolutionary biology. Just as evolutionary theory provides the only basis for uniting all the various subdisciplines of biology itself (from molecular biology to ecosystem ecology), evolutionary theory provides the only potential common ground for all the activities of anthropologists, including paleontology, population genetics, demography, and social anthropology (cf. Penniman, 1965). In saying this, I do not mean to imply that enlightened biologists can show benighted anthropologists the error of their ways. Sociobiologists have been perceived, perhaps with some justice, as taking such an arrogant stance; but I certainly do not wish to convey any such impression. Nor have other sociobiologists always expressed such views. For example, Wilson (1979) argued that the interaction between anthropologists and biologists must involve mutual influences and that anthropology has as much to contribute to the development of biology as biology has to contribute to the development of anthropology.

Historically, one can go even further and argue that, for much of this century, social anthropology in some respects had a more advanced theoretical perspective than the biological study of animal social behavior. If one reads studies of animal social organization from the 1930s to the 1960s, one finds that they are almost always organized around the description and analysis of dominance hierarchies. While this approach undoubtedly provided important insights into animal social behavior, it is interesting to note how rarely these studies make any reference to kinship relations in the social groups studied. One reason for this, no doubt, is that funding constraints rarely permitted long-term studies of the sort needed to establish kinship relations in animals. But also one feels that the researchers involved lacked anthropologists' understanding of the importance of kinship. The only major exception to this picture was the work in Japan on Japanese macaques. There long-term study was possible, and kinship data were gathered. But another important factor was that the researchers involved were strongly influenced by social anthropology.

When the theory of kin selection was developed, zoologists realized the importance of kinship data in the analysis of social behavior. But they found that estimates of relatedness were not readily available even for animal species whose social behavior was assumed to be relatively well known. One reason for my own interest in testing kin selection theory with data from human societies was that I discovered that, even today, the sort of data needed are not available for nonhuman animal societies (Hughes, 1983).

Indeed, it is my hope that researchers engaged in long-term studies of animal social behavior will be able to make use of some of the approaches presented here to further their studies. At the level of analysis considered in this book, there is little relevant difference between human and nonhuman societies. The general theory (Chapters 2, 3, and parts of 4) is applicable to any animal society. Group fissioning and conflict (Chapter 5) occur in nonhuman animals, and dominance in animal societies is closely analogous to types of human local leadership (Chapter 6). Only the symbolic subdivision of groups, the limits of genealogical memory, and kinship terminologies represent a distinctly human subject matter (Chapter 7). In a mature science of society, there will be general principles applicable to any animal society as well as specific principles applicable only to a given taxonomic group. The use of linguistic categories and symbolism is obviously a unique hominid trait, but I can find no evidence that the existence of this unique trait makes the rest of human social behavior any different in its essential principles from that of other animals.

Finally, I hope that the mathematical techniques adopted here provide a way of avoiding the simplistic reductionism of which sociobiologists have been accused, sometimes justifiably (Hendrichs, 1983). All science seeks to understand the multiplicity of observed phenomena in terms of a smaller number of general principles; in that sense all science is reductionistic. Only an antiscientific mystic would be wary of reductionalism in this sense. Yet in another sense there is always a danger in science that the explanations advanced by a theory will be too simplified to have much power or generality. Scientific laws are of little utility if they apply only under limited sets of conditions rarely met in nature. The science of society which I envisage will not seek to deny the rich complexity of animal and human social organization. Neither will it seek to ignore the effects of what phenomenologists call "intersubjectivity"—the interplay between different individuals' subjective perceptions of the social environment (Husserl, 1977). But it will provide a set of landmarks for us to use in explaining the social world, a level of social structure that lies deeper still than symbolic or behavioral structure: the genetic structure of the social group.

APPENDIX A

A matrix is an array of numbers, arranged in rows and columns. A matrix of dimensions $r \times c$ has r rows and c columns. A column vector is a matrix with only one column, thus of dimenstions $r \times 1$; a row vector is a matrix with only one row, thus of dimensions $1 \times c$. In this book the names of matrices and vectors are printed in boldface type, with an uppercase boldface letter denoting a matrix and a lowercase boldface letter denoting a vector. Let a_{ij} denote the element of matrix $\mathbf{A}$ which is found in the ith row and the jth column. A square matrix is one for which $r = c$. A symmetric matrix is one for which $a_{ij} = a_{ji}$ for all i and j. A diagonal matrix is a square matrix whose elements are all equal to zero except those on the diagonal.

Matrices may be added, subtracted, and multiplied; but the rules for performing these operations on matrices are different from the rules for analogous operations on ordinary scalar numbers. For addition or subtraction to be possible, the matrices must have the same number of both rows and columns. If

$$\mathbf{A} + \mathbf{B} = \mathbf{C}$$

then $c_{ij} = a_{ij} + b_{ij}$. And if

$$\mathbf{A} - \mathbf{B} = \mathbf{D}$$

then $d_{ij} = a_{ij} - b_{ij}$.

For two matrices to be multiplied, the order in which they are multiplied makes a difference. (Order of course makes no difference in multiplication of scalars.) To perform the multiplication

$$\mathbf{XY} = \mathbf{Z}$$

$\mathbf{Y}$ must have the same number of columns as $\mathbf{X}$ has rows. If $\mathbf{X}$ is $r \times c$,

$$y_{ij} = \sum_{k=1}^{c} x_{ik} y_{kj}$$

There is also an operation in matrix algebra which is analogous to division of scalars. This involves the inverse of a matrix. The inverse can be computed only for a square matrix. The inverse of $\mathbf{A}$ is written $\mathbf{A}^{-1}$ and is defined such that

$$\mathbf{AA}^{-1} = \mathbf{I}$$

where $\mathbf{I}$ is an identity matrix. The identity matrix is defined to be a diagonal matrix of appropriate size whose diagonal elements are all equal to 1. The identity matrix also has the property that for any square matrix $\mathbf{B}$, if it is multiplied by the identity matrix of appropriate size,

$$\mathbf{BI} = \mathbf{B}$$

Computing the inverse of any matrix larger than 2×2 is extremely tedious and is best left to computers. Fortunately, there are now readily available packaged programs that can be used to compute matrix inverses.

Computer programs are also needed and are readily available to solve an important problem in matrix algebra known as the eigenvalue problem. Suppose we have an equation in the form

$$(\mathbf{X} - \lambda\mathbf{I})\mathbf{b} = \mathbf{O}$$

where $\mathbf{X}$ is a square matrix ($n \times n$), λ is a scalar, $\mathbf{b}$ is a vector ($n \times 1$), and $\mathbf{O}$ is a vector ($n \times 1$) of zeros. Equations of this sort arise naturally in the attempt to solve simple maximization problems. There is, of course, a trivial solution in which $\lambda = 0$ and $\mathbf{b}$ is a vector of zeros. But ordinarily the trivial solution is of no interest. Assuming that the vector $\mathbf{b}$ is scaled to a unit length (i.e., $\mathbf{b}'\mathbf{b} = 1$), there are in general n nontrivial solutions. These solutions may be ranked on the basis of the value of λ. The solution $\mathbf{b}$ for which λ is highest is called the first eigenvector; this value of λ is called the first eigenvalue. Similarly all n eigenvectors and eigenvalues may be denoted. Eigenvectors may also be called characteristic vectors or principal components.

In statistics, it is often of interest to compute eigenvectors of a covariance matrix or of a correlation matrix. A covariance matrix is a symmetric, square matrix each of whose off-diagonal elements represents the covariance between two of a set of variables, while the diagonals represent the variance of the variables in question. A correlation matrix is similarly a matrix of correlation coefficients; alternatively, it is a covariance matrix when each of the variables is standardized to a unit variance. The sum of the eigenvalues equals the trace or sum of diagonal elements of the covariance matrix. The eigenvectors represent a set of new or derived variables which are weighted sums of the original variables. The new variables have the property of being orthogonal to one another. The eigenvalue corresponding to a given eigenvector, divided by the sum of all eigenvalues, represents the proportion of the variance of the original variables accounted for by that derived variable.

APPENDIX B

A digraph or directed graph is defined as the basis of a set of elements called "vertices" or "points" and a set of elements called "directed lines" or "arcs" or simply "lines." A directed line connects two points; that is, for each directed line x, there is one point that is the first point of x and another point that is the second point of x. In a digraph these two points must be distinct. There is no possibility of a "loop" (a line connecting a point to itself) in a digraph. A digraph can be represented by a figure (e.g., Figures 4.2, 4.3, and 7.1). It can also be represented by an adjacency matrix. This is a square matrix whose n rows and columns correspond to the n points $(v_1, v_2, \ldots, v_n)$ of the digraph. Each off-diagonal element a_{ij} of the adjacency matrix $\mathbf{A}$ takes the value of 0 or 1. If there is a line from v_i to v_j, $a_{ij} = 1$. By the definition of a diagraph, all diagonal values of $\mathbf{A}$ are equal to 0.

A network is a valued graph. In a network, directed lines have associated numbers or values. Also, loops are permitted. The network can be represented by a square matrix $\mathbf{K}$, each element of which (k_{ij}) represents the value of the line from k_i to k_j. If there is no line from i to j, $k_{ij} = 0$. Certain types of square matrices, such as matrices of relatedness, can be considered as networks.

For further information regarding graphs and networks and their potential applications in the social sciences, see Hage and Harary (1983); Harary et al. (1965); and Knoke and Kuklinski (1982).

BIBLIOGRAPHY

Aberle, D. F. 1961. Navajo. In D. M. Schneider and K. Gough (eds.), Matrilineal Kinship. Berkeley, University of California Press, pp. 96–201.

Abugov, R. and Michod, R. E. 1981. On the relation of family structured models and inclusive fitness models for kin selection. J. Theoret. Biol. 88: 743–754.

Alexander, R. D. 1974. The evolution of social behavior. Ann. Rev. Ecol. Syst. 5: 325–383.

Alexander, R. D. 1977. Natural selection and the analysis of human sociality. In C. E. Goulden (ed.), Changing Scenes in the Natural Sciences: 1776–1976. Philadelphia Academy of Natural Science Special Publication No. 12, pp. 283–337.

Alexander, R. D. 1979. Darwinism and Human Affairs. Seattle, University of Washington Press.

Alexander, R. D. 1981. Evolution, culture, and human behavior: Some general considerations. In R. D. Alexander and D. W. Tinkle (eds.), Natural Selection and Social Behavior. New York, Chiron Press, pp. 509–520.

Aoki, K. 1982. Additive polygenic formulation of Hamilton's model of kin selection. Heredity 49: 163–169.

Århem, K. 1981. Makuna Social Organization. Uppsala Studies in Cultural Anthropology 4. Stockholm, Almqvist and Wiksell.

Balanoff, P. A. (ed.). 1974. Genealogical Mathematics. Mouton, Publications of the Maison des Science de l'Homme.

Barnes, J. A. 1962. African models in the New Guinea Highlands. Man 62: 5–9.

Barnes, R. H. 1984. Two Crows Denies It: A History of Controversy in Omaha Sociology. Lincoln, University of Nebraska Press.

Barrow, G. W. S. 1976. Robert Bruce and the Community of the Realm of Scotland. Edinburgh, Edinburgh University Press.

Benedict, R. 1934. Patterns of Culture. Boston, Houghton Mifflin.

Betzig, L. 1986a. Vaulting, leaping, skipping, and trudging ambition. Q. Rev. Biol. 61: 517–521.

Betzig, L. L. 1986b. Despotism and Differential Reproduction: A Darwinian View of History. Hawthorne, NY, De Gruyter Aldine.

Black-Michaud, J. 1975. Cohesive Force: Feud in the Mediterranean and the Middle East. Oxford, Oxford University Press.

Borgerhoff Mulder, M. forthcoming. On cultural and reproductive success: Kipsigis evidence. Amer. Anthrop.

Borgerhoff Mulder, M. and Caro, J. M. 1985. The use of quantitative observational techniques in anthropology. Curr. Anthrop. 26: 323–335.

Brown, K. M. 1986. Bloodfeud in Scotland 1573–1625. Edinburgh, John Donald.

Bryant, F. C. 1981. We're All Kin: A Cultural Study of a Mountain Neighborhood. Knoxville, University of Tennessee Press.

Bush, A. C. 1982. Studies in Roman Social Structure. Washington, D.C., University Press of America.

Campbell, J. K. 1964. Honour, Family, and Patronage. New York, Oxford University Press.

Cannings, C. and Thompson, E. A. 1981. Genealogical and Genetic Structure. Cambridge, Cambridge University Press.

Cassety, J. 1978. Child Support and Public Policy. Lexington, MA, D. C. Heath.

Caudill, H. M. 1962. Night Comes to the Cumberlands: A Biography of a Depressed Area. Boston, Little, Brown.

Cavalli-Sforza, L. L. and Bodmer, W. F. 1971. The Genetics of Human Populations. San Francisco, Freeman.

Cavalli-Sforza, L. L. and Feldman, M. W. 1981. Cultural Transmission: A Quantitative Approach. Princeton, NJ, Princeton University Press.

Cebul, M. S. and Epple, G. 1984. Father–offspring relationships in laboratory families of saddle-back tamarins *(Saguinus fuscicollis)*. In D. M. Taub (ed.), Primate Paternalism. New York, Van Nostrand Reinhold, pp. 1–19.

Chagnon, N. A. 1975. Genealogy, solidarity, and relatedness: Limits to local group size and patterns of fissioning in an expanding population. Yearbook of Phys. Anthrop. 19: 95–110.

Chagnon, N. A. 1979. Is reproductive success equal in egalitarian societies? In N. A. Chagnon and W. Irons (eds.), Evolutionary Biology and Human Social Behavior: An Anthropological Perspective. North Scituate, MA, Duxbury Press, pp. 374–401.

Chagnon, N. A. 1982. Sociodemographic attributes of nepotism in tribal populations: Man the rule-breaker. In King's College Sociobiology Group (eds.), Current Problems in Sociobiology. Cambridge, Cambridge University Press, pp. 291–318.

Cheverud, J. M. 1985. A quantitative genetic model of altruistic selection. Behav. Ecol. Sociobiol. 16: 239–243.

Crow, J. F. and Kimura, M. 1970. An Introduction to Population Genetics Theory. New York, Harper and Row.

Daly, M. and Wilson, M. 1981a. Abuse and neglect of children in evolutionary perspective. In R. D. Alexander and D. W. Tinkle (eds.), Natural Selection and Social Behavior. New York, Chiron Press.

Daly, M. and Wilson, M. 1981b. Child maltreatment from a sociobiological perspective. New Direct. Child Develop. 11: 93–112.

Daly, M. and Wilson, M. 1985. Child abuse and other risks of not living with both parents. Ethol. Sociobiol. 6: 197–210.

Davies, W. 1982. Wales in the Early Middle Ages. Leicester, Leicester University Press.

Dickemann, M. 1981. Paternal confidence and dowry competition: A biocultural analysis of purdah. In R. D. Alexander and D. W. Tinkle (eds.), Natural Selection and Social Behavior. New York, Chiron Press, pp. 417–438.

Dumont, L. 1957. Hierarchy and Marriage Alliance in South Indian Kinship. Occasional Paper No. 12, Royal Anthropological Institute.

Eggan, F. (ed.). 1937. Social Anthropology of North American Tribes. Chicago, University of Chicago Press.

Einzig, P. 1966. Primitive Money, 2nd edition. New York, Pergamon Press.

Eisenberg, J. F. 1981. The Mammalian Radiations. London, Athlone.

Emeneau, M. B. 1941. Language and social forms: A study of Toda kinship and dual descent. In L. Spier, A. I. Hallowell, and S. S. Newman (eds.), Language, Culture, and Personality: Essays in Memory of Edward Sapir. Menasha, WI, Sapir Memorial Publication Fund.

Engels, W. R. 1983. Evolution of altruistic behavior by kin selection: An alternative approach. Proc. Natl. Acad. Sci. USA 80: 515–518.

Essock-Vitale, S. M. 1984. The reproductive success of wealthy Americans. Ethol. Sociobiol. 5: 45–49.

Evans, H. E. 1968. Life on a Little-Known Planet. New York, Batton Press.

Evans-Pritchard, E. E. 1950. Social anthropology: Past and present. Man 50: 118–124.

Evans-Pritchard, E. E. 1951. Kinship and Marriage among the Nuer. Oxford, Oxford University Press.

Falconer, D. S. 1981. Introduction to Quantitative Genetics, 2nd edition. New York, Longman Press.

Fél, E. and Hofer, T. 1969. Proper Peasants: Traditional Life in a Hungarian Village. Chicago, Aldine.

Firth, R., Hubert, J., and Forge, A. 1969. Families and Their Relatives: Kinship in a Middle-Class Sector of London. London, Routledge and Kegan Paul.

Fletcher, A. C. and LaFlesche, F. 1911. The Omaha Tribe. Annual Report of the Bureau of American Ethnology. Vol. 27. Washington, D.C., U.S. Government Printing Office.

Flinn, M. 1981. Uterine vs. agnatic kinship variability and associated cousin marriage preferences. In R. D. Alexander and D. W. Tinkle (eds.), Natural Selection and Social Behavior. New York, Chiron Press, pp. 439–489.

Forde, D. E. 1934. Habitat, Economy, and Society. London, Methuen.

Fortes, M. 1959. Descent, filiation, and affinity: A rejoinder to Dr. Leach. Man 59: 193–197, 206–212.

Fox, R. 1967a. Kinship and Marriage: An Anthropological Perspective. Harmondsworth, Penguin Books.

Fox, R. 1967b. The Keresan Bridge: A Problem in Pueblo Ethnology. London, Athlone.

Fox, R. 1967c. In the beginning: Aspects of hominid behavioural evolution. Man n.s. 2: 415–433.

Fox, R. 1975. Primate kin and human kinship. In R. Fox (ed.), Biosocial Anthropology. London, Malaby Press, pp. 9–35.

Fox, R. 1978. The Tory Islanders: A People of the Celtic Fringe. Cambridge, Cambridge University Press.

Fox, R. 1979. Kinship categories as natural categories. In N. A. Chagnon and W. Irons (eds.), Evolutionary Biology and Human Social Behavior: An Anthropological Perspective. North Scituate, MA, Duxbury Press, pp. 132–144.

Freeman, D. 1983. Margaret Mead and Samoa: The Making and Unmaking of an Anthropological Myth. Cambridge, MA, Harvard University Press.

Fried, M. 1975. Effects of social change on mental health. In M. F. Shore and F. V. Mannino (eds.), Mental Health and Social Change. New York, AMS Press, pp. 35–64.

Geertz, H. and Geertz, C. 1975. Kinship in Bali. Chicago, University of Chicago Press.

Gobineau, A. de. 1915. The Inequality of Human Races. London, William Heinemann.

Goodwin, D. W. 1986. Anxiety. New York, Oxford University Press.

Goody, E. N. 1962. Conjugal separation and divorce among the Gonja of Northern Ghana. In M. Fortes (ed.), Marriage in Tribal Societies. Cambridge, Cambridge University Press, pp. 14–54.

Goody, J. 1983. The Development of the Family and Marriage in Western Europe. Cambridge, Cambridge University Press.

Gould, S. J. and Lewontin, R. 1979. The spandrels of San Marco and the Panglossian paradigm: A critique of the adaptationist programme. Proc. R. Soc. Lond. B. Biol. Sci. 205: 581–598.

Grafen, A. 1982. How not to measure inclusive fitness. Nature 298: 425–426.

Grafen, A. 1984. Natural selection, kin selection, and group selection. In J. R. Krebs and N. B. Davies (eds.), Behavioural Ecology: An Evolutionary Approach, 2nd edition. Oxford, Basil Blackwell, pp. 62–84.

Grant, M. 1921. The Passing of the Great Race, 4th edition. London, G. Bell.

Grigson, W. 1938. The Maria Gonds of Bastar. Oxford, Oxford University Press.

Gulliver, P. H. 1955. The Family Herds: A Study of Two Pastoral Tribes in East Africa, the Jie and Turkana. London, Routledge and Kegan Paul.

Hage, P. and Harary, F. 1983. Structural Models in Anthropology. Cambridge, Cambridge University Press.

Hames, R. B. 1978. A behavioral account of the division of labor among the Ye'kwana Indians of Southern Venezuela. PhD thesis, University of California, Santa Barbara.

Hamilton, W. D. 1963. The evolution of altruistic behavior. Am. Nat. 97: 354–356.

Hamilton, W. D. 1964. The genetical evolution of social behaviour. I, II. J. Theoret. Biol. 7: 1–16, 17–52.

Hamilton, W. D. 1975. Innate social aptitudes of man: An approach from evolutionary genetics. In R. Fox (ed.), Biosocial Anthropology. London, Malaby Press, pp. 133–155.

Hamilton, W. D. 1987. Discriminating nepotism: Expectable, common, overlooked. In D. J. C. Fletcher and C. D. Michener (eds.), Kin Recognition in Animals. New York, Wiley, pp. 417–437.

Hanson, L. A. 1970. Rapan Lifeways: Society and History on a Polynesian Island. Boston, Little, Brown.

Harary, F., Norman, R. E., and Cartwright, D. 1965. Structural Models: An Introduction to the Theory of Directed Graphs. New York, Wiley.

Hasluck, M. 1954. The Unwritten Law in Albania. Cambridge, Cambridge University Press.

Hendrichs, H. 1983. On the evolution of social structure in mammals. In J. F. Eisenberg and D. G. Kleiman (eds.), Advances in the Study of Mammalian Behavior. American Society of Mammalogists Special Publication No. 7, pp. 738–750.

Herskovits, M. J. 1926. The cattle complex in East Africa. Amer. Anthrop. 28: 230–272, 361–388, 494–528, 633–664.

Hill, W. G. 1979. A note on effective population size with overlapping generations. Genetics 92: 317–322.

Holder, P. 1970. The Hoe and the Horse on the Plains. Lincoln, University of Nebraska Press.

Hughes, A. L. 1982. Confidence of paternity and wife-sharing in polygynous and polyandrous systems. Ethol. Sociobiol. 3: 125–129.

Hughes, A. L. 1983. Kin selection of complex behavioral strategies. Am. Nat. 122: 181–190.

Hughes, A. L. 1984. Some methods for analyzing the structure and behavior of human kin groups. Ethol. Sociobiol. 5: 179–192.

Hughes, A. L. 1985a. Seasonal trends in body size of adult male mosquitofish *Gambusia affinis* with evidence for their social control. Env. Biol. Fishes 14: 251–258.

Hughes, A. L. 1985b. Male size, mating success, and mating strategy in the mosquitofish *Gambusia affinis* (Poeciliidae). Behav. Ecol. Sociobiol. 17: 271–278.

Hughes, A. L. 1986a. Biological relatedness and social structure. J. Social Biol. Struct. 9: 151–168.

Hughes, A. L. 1986b. Kin coalitions and social dominance. J. Theoret. Biol. 123: 55–66.

Hughes, A. L. 1986c. Reproductive success and occupational class in eighteenth century Lancashire, England. Social Biol. 33: 109–115.

Hughes, A. L. forthcoming. Kin networks and political leadership in a stateless society, the Toda of South India. Ethol. Sociobiol.

Humphrey, C. 1983. Karl Marx Collective: Economy, Society, and Religion in a Siberian Collective Farm. Cambridge, Cambridge University Press.

Huntington, E. 1924. The Character of Races: As Influenced by Physical Environment, Natural Selection, and Historical Development. New York, Charles Scribner's Sons.

Hurd, J. P. 1983. Kin relatedness and church fissioning among the "Nebraska" Amish of Pennsylvania. Social Biol. 30: 59–66.

Husserl, E. 1977. Phenomenological Psychology. The Hague, Martinus Nijhoff.

Ianni, F. A. J. and Reuss-Ianni, E. 1972. A Family Business: Kinship and Social Control in Organized Crime. New York, Sage.

Ilfeld, F. W. 1979. Persons at risk for symptoms of anxiety. In B. S. Brown (ed.), Clinical Anxiety/Tension in Primary Medicine. Princeton, NJ, Excerpta Medica, pp. 24–38.

Irons, W. 1979. Cultural and biological success. In N. A. Chagnon and W. Irons (eds.), Evolutionary Biology and Human Social Behavior. North Scituate, MA, Duxbury Press, pp. 257–272.

Jacquard, A. 1974. The Genetic Structure of Populations. Berlin, Springer-Verlag.

Jeffreys, A. J., Brookfield, J. F. Y., and Semeonoff, R. 1985. Positive identification of an immigration test-case using human DNA fingerprints. Nature 317: 818–819.

Karp, I. 1978. Fields of Change Among the Iteso of Kenya. London, Routledge and Kegan Paul.

Kaye, H. L. 1986. The Social Meaning of Modern Biology. New Haven, Yale University Press.

Keesing, R. M. 1972. Simple models of complexity: The lure of kinship. In P. Reining (ed.), Kinship Studies in the Morgan Centennial Year. Washington, D.C., Anthropological Society of Washington, pp. 17–31.

Kelley, R. C. 1974. Etoro Social Structure. Ann Arbor, University of Michigan Press.

Keyfitz, N. 1968. Introduction to the Mathematics of Population. Reading, MA, Addison-Wesley.

Kitcher, P. 1985. Vaulting Ambition: Sociobiology and the Quest for Human Nature. Cambridge, MA, MIT Press.

Kleiman, D. G. 1977. Monogamy in mammals. Q. Rev. Biol. 52: 39–69.

Knoke, D. and Kuklinski, J. H. 1982. Network Analysis. Beverly Hills, CA, Sage Publications.

Kroeber, A. L. 1909. Classificatory systems of relationship. J. Royal Anthrop. Inst. 34: 77–84.

Kurland, J. A. 1977. Kin Selection in the Japanese Monkey. Contributions to Primatology, Vol. 12. Basel, S. Karger.

Kutty, A. R. 1972. Marriage and kinship in an Island society. University of Sangar Monographs in Anthropology and Sociology. Delhi, National Publications House.

Lawrence, P. 1984. The Garia: The Ethnography of a Traditional Cosmic System in Papua New Guinea. Manchester, Manchester University Press.

Leach, E. 1982. Social Anthropology. Oxford, Oxford University Press.

Lerner, J. M. 1950. Population Genetics and Animal Improvement. Cambridge, Cambridge University Press.

Levine, L. 1973. Biology of the Gene. St. Louis, Mosby.

Lévi-Strauss, C. 1949. *Les Structures Élémentaires de la Parenté.* Paris, Presses Universitaires de France.

Lévi-Strauss, C. 1963. Structural Anthropology. New York, Basic Books.

Luce, R. D. and Raiffa, H. 1957. Games and Decisions. New York, Wiley.

Lumsden, C. J. and Wilson, E. O. 1981. Genes, Mind, and Culture. Cambridge, MA, Harvard University Press.

Lumsden, D. J. and Wilson, E. O. 1985. The relation between biological and cultural evolution. J. Social Biol. Struct. 8: 343–359.

Lush, J. L. 1947. Family merit and individual merit as bases for selection. I, II. Am. Nat. 81: 241–261, 362–379.

McKinley, R. 1971. Why do Crow and Omaha kinship terminologies exist? A sociology of knowledge interpretation. Man n.s. 6: 408–426.

Mair, L. 1962. Primitive Government: A Study of Traditional Political Systems in Eastern Africa. Harmondsworth, Penguin Books.

Mair, L. 1977. African Kingdoms. Oxford, Clarendon Press.

Mair, L. 1984. Anthropology and Development. London, MacMillan.

Matessi, C. and Karlin, S. 1986. Altruistic behavior in sibling groups with unrelated intruders. In S. Karlin and E. Nevo (eds.), Evolutionary Processes and Theory. Orlando, FL, Academic Press.

Maynard Smith, J. 1964. Group selection and kin selection: A rejoinder. Nature 201: 1145–1147.

Maynard Smith, J. 1982. Evolution and the Theory of Games. Cambridge, Cambridge University Press.

Mayr, E. 1982. The Growth of Biological Thought: Diversity, Evolution, and Inheritance. Cambridge, MA, Harvard University Press.

Mayr, E. 1983. How to carry out the adaptationist program? Am. Nat. 121: 324–334.

Merz, J. T. 1896–1914. A History of European Thought in the Nineteenth Century. 4 vols. Edinburgh, W. Blackwood and Sons.

Michod, R. 1982. The theory of kin selection. Ann. Rev. Ecol. Syst. 13: 23–55.

Michod, R. E. and Anderson, W. W. 1979. Measures of genetic relatedness and the concept of inclusive fitness. Am. Nat. 114: 637–647.

Michod, R. E. and Hamilton, W. D. 1980. Coefficients of relatedness in sociobiology. Nature 288: 694–697.

Mitchell, D. F. and Pratto, D. J. 1977. Social class, familism, interest in children, and childbearing: A preliminary test of a "commitment" model of fertility. Social Biol. 24: 17–37.

Morgan, L. H. 1870. Systems of Consanguinity and Affinity of the Human Family. Smithsonian Contributions to Knowledge No. 218. Washington, D.C., Smithsonian Institution.

Morrison, D. F. 1976. Multivariate Statistical Methods, 2nd edition. New York, McGraw-Hill.

Murdock, G. P. 1949. Social Structure. New York, MacMillan.

Murdock, G. P. 1972. Anthropology's mythology. Proc. Royal Anthrop. Inst. Great Britain and Ireland for 1971, pp. 17–24.

Needham, R. 1962. Structure and Sentiment. Chicago, University of Chicago Press.

Needham, R. 1973. Prescription. Oceania 43: 166–181.

Packard, V. O. 1960. The Status Seekers. New York, McKay.

Pamilo, P. and Crozier, R. H. 1982. Measuring genetic relatedness in natural populations: Methodology. Theoret. Popn. Biol. 21: 171–193.

Pasternak, B. 1976. Introduction to Kinship and Social Organization. Englewood Cliffs, NJ, Prentice-Hall.

Penniman, T. K. 1965. A Hundred Years of Anthropology, 3rd edition. London, Duckworth.

Plotkin, H. C. and Odling-Smee, F. J. 1981. A multiple level model of evolution and its implications for sociobiology. Behav. Brain Sci. 4: 225–268.

Popper, K. R. 1934. *Logik der Forschung.* Vienna, Julius Springer.

Price, G. R. 1972. Extension of covariance selection mathematics. Ann. Human Genet., Lond. 35: 485–490.

Prince Peter of Greece and Denmark. 1955. The Todas: Some additions and corrections to W. H. R. Rivers' book, observed in the field. Man 65: 89–93.

Putnam, H. 1981. Reason, Truth, and History. Cambridge, Cambridge University Press.

Quine, W. V. 1960. Word and Object. Cambridge, MA, MIT Press.

Quine, W. V. 1969. Ontological Relativity and Other Essays. New York, Columbia University Press.

Radcliffe-Brown, A. R. 1935. On the concept of function in social science. Amer. Anthrop. 37: 394–402.

Radcliffe-Brown, A. R. 1940. On social structure. J. Royal Anthrop. Inst. 70: 1–12.

Radcliffe-Brown, A. R. 1941. The study of kinship systems. J. Royal Anthrop. Inst. 71: 1–18.

Radcliffe-Brown, A. R. 1957. A Natural Science of Society. Glencoe, IL, Free Press.

Radcliffe-Brown, A. R. and Forde, D. (eds.). 1950. African Systems of Kinship and Marriage. London, Oxford University Press.

Ramírez, S. E. 1986. Provincial Patriarchs: Land Tenure and the Economics of Power in Colonial Peru. Albuquerque, University of New Mexico Press.

Reichard, G. A. 1928. Social Life of the Navajo Indians. New York, Columbia University Press.

Rivers, W. H. R. 1900. A genealogical method of collecting social and vital statistics. J. Royal Anthrop. Inst. 3: 74–82.

Rivers, W. H. R. 1906. The Todas. London, MacMillan.

Rivière, P. 1969. Marriage among the Trio. Oxford, Clarendon Press.

Robinson, M. S. 1968. Some observations on the Kandyan Sinhalese kinship system. Man n.s. 3: 402–423.

Rood, J. P. 1978. Dwarf mongoose helpers at the den. Z. Ticrpsychol. 48: 277–287.

Ross, H. M. 1973. Baegu: Social and Ecological Organization in Malaita, Solomon Islands. Urbana, University of Illinois Press.

Ruse, M. 1986. Taking Darwin Seriously. Oxford, Basil Blackwell.

Sahlins, M. 1963. Poor man, rich man, big man, chief: Political types in Melanesia and Polynesia. Comp. Stud. in Soc. and Hist. 5: 285–303.

Sahlins, M. D. 1976. The Use and Abuse of Biology: An Anthropological Critique of Sociobiology. Ann Arbor, University of Michigan Press.

Schneider, D. M. 1965. Some muddles in the models: Or, how the system really works. In M. Banton (ed.), The Relevance of Models for Social Anthropology. London, Tavistock, pp. 25–85.

Schneider, D. M. 1968. American Kinship: A Cultural Account. Englewood Cliffs, NJ, Prentice-Hall.

Schneider, D. M. 1972. What is kinship all about? In P. Reining (ed.), Kinship Studies in the Morgan Centennial Year. Washington, D.C., Anthropological Society of Washington, pp. 32–63.

Schneider, H. K. 1979. Livestock and Equality in East Africa. Bloomington, Indiana University Press.

Scruton, R. 1986. Sexual Desire. London, Weidenfeld and Nicholson.

Shifflctt, C. A. 1982. Patronage and poverty in the tobacco South: Louisa County, Virginia, 1860–1900. Knoxville, University of Tennessee Press.

Sivertson, D. 1963. When Caste Barriers Fall: A Study of Social and Economic Change in a South Indian Village. Oslo, University Forlaget.

Smith, D. G. 1982. Use of genetic markers in the colony management of non-human primates: A review. Lab. Anim. Sci. 32: 540–546.

Smith, J. B. 1986. *Llewelyn ap Gruffudd: Tywysog Cymru.* Cardiff, University of Wales Press.

Sobel, M. G. 1983. Lifestyle differentiation and stratification in contemporary U.S. society. Research in Social Stratification and Mobility 2: 115–144.

Spiess, E. B. 1977. Genes in Populations. New York, Wiley.

Stephenson, D. 1984. The Governance of Gwynedd. Cardiff, University of Wales Press.

Stockwell, G. C. and Wicks, J. W. 1984. Patterns and variations in the relationship between infant mortality and socioeconomic status. Soc. Biol. 31: 28–39.

Strathern, M. 1981. Kinship at the Core: An Anthropology of Elmdon, a Village in North-West Essex in the Nineteen-Sixties. Cambridge, Cambridge University Press.

Thomas, D. J. 1982. Order Without Government: The Society of the Pémon Indians of Venezuela. Urbana, University of Illinois Press.

Trautmann, T. R. 1981. Dravidian Kinship. Cambridge, Cambridge University Press.

Trivers, R. L. 1971. The evolution of reciprocal altruism. Q. Rev. Biol. 46: 35–57.

Tuck, A. 1985. Crown and Nobility 1277–1461. London, Fontana.

Tylor, E. B. 1888. On a method of investigating the development of institutions applied to the laws of marriage and descent. J. Royal Anthrop. Inst. 18: 245–327.

Vining, D. R. 1986. Social versus reproductive success: The central theoretical problem of human sociobiology. Behav. Brain Sci. 9: 167–216.

Wade, M. J. 1978. Kin selection: A classical approach and a general solution. Proc. Natl. Acad. Sci. USA 75: 6154–6158.

Wade, M. J. 1985. Soft selection, hard selection, kin selection, and group selection. Am. Nat. 125: 61–73.

Wagner, G. 1970. The Bantu of Western Kenya. London, Oxford University Press.

Wallace, A. C. 1956. Revitalization movements. Amer. Anthrop. 58: 264–281.

Wilder, W. D. 1982. Communication, Social Structure and Development in Rural Malaysia. London, Athlone.

Williams, G. C. 1966. Adaptation and Natural Selection. Princeton, NJ, Princeton University Press.

Wilson, E. O. 1975. Sociobiology: The New Synthesis. Cambridge, MA, Harvard University Press.

Wilson, E. O. 1978. On Human Nature. Cambridge, MA, Harvard University Press.

Wilson, E. O. 1979. Biology and anthropology: a mutual transformation. In N. A. Chagnon and W. Irons (eds.), Evolutionary Biology and Human Social Behavior. North Scituate, MA, Duxbury Press, pp. 519–521.

Witherspoon, G. 1975. Navajo Kinship and Marriage. Chicago, University of Chicago Press.

Witherspoon, G. 1977. Language and Art in the Navajo Universe. Ann Arbor, University of Michigan Press.

Wittgenstein, L. 1922. *Tractatus Logico-Philosophicus.* London, Routledge and Kegan Paul.

Wrangham, R. W. 1982. Mutualism, kinship, and social evolution. In King's College Sociobiology Group (eds.), Current Problems in Sociobiology. Cambridge, Cambridge University Press, pp. 269–289.

Wright, S. 1922. Coefficients of inbreeding and relationship. Am. Nat. 56: 330–338.

Wright, S. 1969. Evolution and the Genetics of Populations. Vol. 2: The Theory of Gene Frequencies. Chicago, University of Chicago Press.

Wrong, D. 1958. Trends in class fertility in Western nations. Can. J. Econ. Polit. Sci. 24: 216–229.

Yalman, N. 1967. Under the Bo Tree: Studies in Caste, Kinship, and Marriage in the Interior of Ceylon. Berkeley, University of California Press.

Yokoyama, S. and Felsenstein, J. 1978. A model of kin selection for an altruistic trait considered as a quantitative character. Proc. Natl. Acad. Sci. USA 75: 420–422.

Young, M. and Wilmot, P. 1957. Family and Kinship in East London. London, Routledge and Kegan Paul.

Author Index

Subject Index